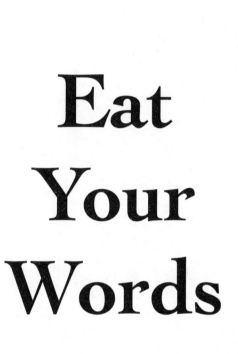

Eat Your Words

Eat Your Words

THE DEFINITIVE DICTIONARY FOR THE DISCERNING DINER

Paul Convery

Mango Publishing

Coral Gables

For permission requests, please contact the publisher at:

Mango Publishing Group
2850 Douglas Road, 2nd Floor
Coral Gables, FL 33134 USA
info@mango.bz

For special orders, quantity sales, course adoptions and corporate sales, please email the publisher at sales@mango.bz.
For trade and wholesale sales, please contact Ingram Publisher Services at
customer.service@ingramcontent.com or +1.800.509.4887.

Eat Your Words: The Definitive Dictionary for the
Discerning Diner

Library of Congress Cataloging
ISBN: (p) 978-1-64250-134-6 (e) 978-1-64250-135-3

BISAC: CKB071000 COOKING / Reference

LCCN: 2019948611

Printed in the United States of America

For eatymologists, bibliophagists, and
verbivores everywhere

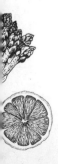

Table of Contents

What's Cooking?

Something to Digest

PART TWO

All the Trimmings

You Are What You Eat

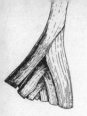

Whet Your Appetite

Catering for Every Taste

Come Dine with Me

Preface

Welcome to *Eat Your Words*—the most gloriously gluttonous glossary of all things grub and gastronomy.

An advanced alimentary vocabulary for *bon viveurs* and verbivores alike, *Eat Your Words* brings to the table a *cordon bleu* compilation of six thousand often unusual and unfamiliar terms across twenty-one fact-packed courses, offering the reader a unique feast of learning as well as a fun and flavour-filled dip into the fascinating language of food and eating.

Anyone with a hunger for weird and wonderful words, or simply consumed with curiosity about the wider world of cooking and cuisine, will assuredly find something to savour and devour on every page of this richly satisfying read and indispensable reference work.

This is the one dictionary you will always be glad you swallowed.

Spice up your lex life with a banquet of recondite and recherché words sure to make your mouth water—from *abligurition*, *abrosia* and *abyrtaca* to *zomotherapeutics*, *zoosaprophagy* and *zuuzuus & whamwhams*.

Do you know the difference between *macaroni* and *macaroon*, *macadamia* and *macedoine*, *madeleine* and *madrilène*? What about *mazagan*, *mazamorra* and *mazzard*? All are items of food, and more *manna* than *maw-wallop* to the *magirologist*. Mind and apply your *masticators* to the *manducation* of said fare, or you may get *maldigestion*. And always consume in moderation, lest you bloat with the girth of a *macrogaster*.

When would you use a *frixory* or a *furcifer*, and where would you find a *boar-frank* or a *broilerhouse*? What would

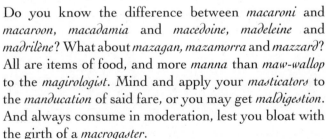
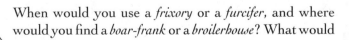

you buy from an *oporopolist* or an *opsonator*, and whom would you meet at a *parrillada* or a *poggle-khana*? Why would you *calver* or *caveach*, *concasse* or *consewe*? How does your fave plate taste: *saccharaceous*, *salsamentarious*, *subacidulous*?

Find out inside—and prepare to dazzle family, friends and all the foodies you know with your effortless eatymological erudition.

Eat Your Words is no standard, straight-through A to Z, however. It is, rather, the first work to showcase the terminology of food, cookery, and stomach-stuffing across a number of discrete subject areas, covering curious meals from far and wide and their many intriguing ingredients, the craft and artifice of the culinarian, food science and technology, diet and appetite, the catering trade, dining in and out, the pleasures of the palate, and so much more besides. The result is a specially themed and structured encyclofeedia no word buff, food lover or good writer will want to be without.

Here's what's on the menu.

Our starter section, Of Flora, Fauna, & Food, addresses the very substance and source of food itself. Chapter 1 treats of food groups and food in the general sense — classes and categories, qualities and quantities. Chapters 2 and 3 provide a modest inventory from the myriad basic stuffs and staples found across the plant and animal kingdoms, respectively, alongside some of the many primary food products humankind has derived therefrom. Finally, Chapter 4 deals with food production, processing, and provision—from primitive hunting and harvesting to early agriculture and animal husbandry to modern farms, fisheries and factories.

The following section, Dainty Dishes & Choice Cuisine, then presents a smorgasbord of the finest prepared fare anywhere for the reader's delectation. Chapter 5 offers a generous serving of old concoctions and odd confections from the good kitchens of the Anglosphere. This is complemented in Chapter 6 by a wide selection of delicacies honouring the culinary traditions and diverse cuisines of communities across all four corners of planet Earth.

Our next main section asks, What's Cooking? Chapter 7 answers by way of a comprehensive digest of cooks and chefs, domestic and professional alike, along with a treasury of tips, tricks, and techniques used in the kitchen. Chapter 8, meantime, considers the properties and particularities of foods both fair and foul, itemizing the different tastes, textures, and so forth of the multitudinous victuals and viands cooked and eaten by man.

By way of a side, Something to Digest shifts our lexical focus away from cookery and cuisine onto consumption and chemistry. Chapter 9 is devoted to matters pertaining not to what, but rather to how we eat and digest, cataloguing the full gamut of gastric processes—and problems—running from gob through gullet to gut. The themes of nourishment and human dietary health are developed further as Chapter 10 delves into the language of food science and safety.

You Are What You Eat examines our eating habits both good and bad, listing the wealth of dietary choices and lifestyles commonly available today (Chapter 11) and, contrariwise, those cravings best considered downright crazy or depraved (Chapter 12). As an accompaniment to the above, the feeding practices and preferences of assorted vores, trophs, and phages across the natural world are also classified (Chapter 13).

Our subsequent courses enjoin you, dear reader, to Whet Your Appetite. Moving swiftly from feast to fast to famine, Chapter 14 expresses the lexicon of gluttony and excess, Chapter 15 explores the idiom of aversion and disgust, while Chapter 16 outlines the language of hunger and want.

The penultimate section, Catering for Every Taste, looks at the vocabulary of provisioning and purveying — covering the retail and restaurant trades, merchants and markets, food stores and eating establishments (Chapter 17) — before kitting out the kitchen and setting the table, checklisting the profusion of utensils and utilities used internationally in the several acts of cooking, serving, and eating (Chapter 18).

We round our wordfest off with an invitation to Come Dine with Me. Here, we take an all-inclusive lexical tour of dinners, the fine dining experience, and finally diners themselves. Chapter 19 dishes up a gallimaufry of meals and mealtimes, light bites and courses, and occasions for feeding and feasting. Chapter 20 embraces eating matters and manners and all things epicurean — encompassing the faculty of (good) taste, the gratifications of gastronomy, and popular food philias and phobias. In closing, in Chapter 21 we consider ourselves: presenting a veritable thesaurus of trencher folk of every stripe — gourmets and gourmandisers, foodists and faddists, buzguts and belly-gods all.

All entries have been carefully selected from the most exhaustive unabridged dictionaries and extensive word troves available, as well as a wide range of specialist resources and learned monographs in both print and digital formats.

There is no scholarly apparatus — parts of speech, variant spellings, etymologies or phonetics — to burden the text. The entries are defined in the compiler's own words with economy of expression and ease of comprehension foremost in mind, seasoned with the occasional dash of wit. Any errors are his and his alone; in keeping with the spirit of the book, he humbly pledges to eat his own words in such event.

So, why not expand your vocabulary and not your waistline by taking a hearty bite from *Eat Your Words: The Definitive Dictionary for the Discerning Diner.*

Bon appétit.

Paul Convery, Glasgow, September 2019

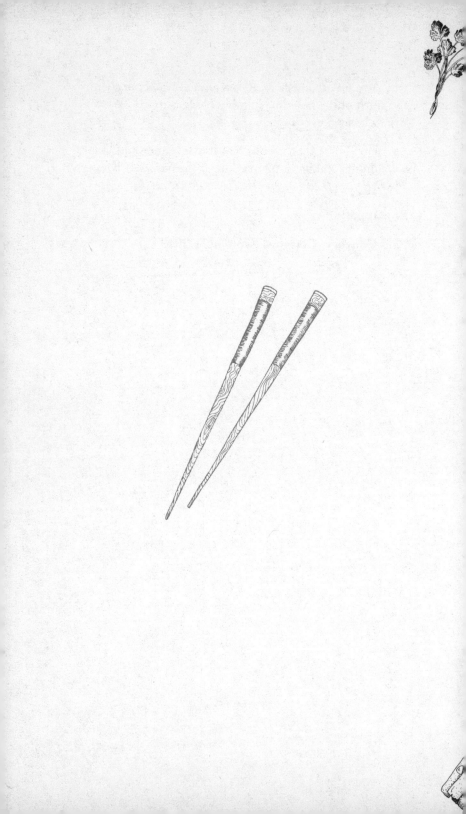

PART ONE

Food, Glorious Food

Of Flora, Fauna, and Food

CHAPTER 1

Foodstuffs: Classes and Categories

> *"There is no love sincerer than the love of food."*
> **—George Bernard Shaw**

acates * bought-in food, especially fresh or luxury provisions; catering supplies

acetaria * salad plants and vegetables, considered collectively

adipsa * foods which do not produce thirst following their consumption

aliment * food formally considered as sustenance and nourishment for the body

alternative protein * substitute meat or dairy products developed in the laboratory

ambient food * goods which retain their freshness when stored at room temperature

ambrosia * the food of the Olympian gods; to mere mortals, a bite of heavenly taste

analects * dropped or discarded morsels of food; figuratively, crumbs of wisdom

appast * an archaic generic term for food, in the sense of one's "daily bread"

assature * roasted food, especially meat

bag & bottle * food and drink, informally

bakemeat * baked food, notably pastries and pies

beefmeat * bureaucratese for the flesh of cattle, as foodstuff and agricultural product

belly-timber * grub for one's gut

bioengineered food * edible produce from natural organisms, either flora or fauna, that have undergone genetic manipulation in some form

bite & sup * something to eat

blubber-totum * food no better than thin gruel, as too watery soup or weak stew

bolus * a ball of soft, chewed food matter just prior to swallowing and digestion

breadkind * vegetables with a high starch content, such as yams and sweet potatoes

breadstuff * baked goods collectively; also, constituent items for baking such as flour

broma * an obsolete medical term for convalescent fare better chewed than supped

buckone * a mere morsel or mouthful of food

bullamacow * tinned or canned meat; also, cattle or livestock, in South Seas pidgin

bushfood * any traditional Australian Aboriginal dietary staple, normally eaten raw

bushmeat * any African wild animal hunted for food, or the flesh therefrom

butchermeat * the flesh of domesticated animals slaughtered for the table as traditionally sold by butchers, viz beef, lamb, veal, mutton, and pork

cackling-farts * eggs, in the colourful language of the erstwhile "canting crew"

cag-mag * unwholesome, spoiled, or downright bad food of any kind

calavance * edible beans, generically considered; by extension, food made from same

carbonado * grilled or barbecued food

carnish * meat, being the flesh of any animal used as food

cassan * cheese, in the vernacular of yesteryear

cerealia * cereal foods, such as corn, collectively

cetaries * a neglected synonym for seafood, being victuals sourced from open waters

champignon * a catch-all culinary term for mushrooms, notably as a delicacy food

chankings * food matter that has been chewed and subsequently spat out—olive pits, fruit stones, gristle, and the like

charcuterie * cold pork cuts as a class of meat product: includes ham, bacon, and pâté

chazerai * any truly awful food or dish; more strictly, non-kosher fare

cheeseparing * a miserly sliver or miserable scrap of food

cherishment * food in the context of nourishment or sustenance for body and soul

chewin's * chow to chew on

chompin's * chow to chomp on

chow * food, in common parlance

cibaries * food stocks; catering provisions

cibosity * food aplenty

cibus * a Sunday-best term for food used by scholars of yore, and rarely so even then

comestibles * articles of food

comfort food * richly enjoyable no-fuss fave fare that brings succour as well as sweet satisfaction to the consumer

conditement * any spice, sauce, season, or garnish used to lend pep to a dish

confectionery * foods rich in sugar and carbohydrates, chiefly candy and chocolate

confiture * the class of culinary goods made by preserving fruit with sugar

conner * canned food or service rations; an expression from the forces' lexicon

conserve * any confection or preserve of candied fruit, such as marmalade or jam

convenience food * commercially pre-prepared hence "ready to serve" easy meals

cookables * items or ingredients that may be cooked for food; stuff fit for the pot

coquillage * shellfish considered as a discrete culinary category

corbullion * stock, broth, bouillon: flavoured liquid for cooking

courtesy-morsel * a small quantity of food left on a diner's plate for manners' sake

crassing-chetes * crunchy fruits, in the bygone idiom of the Georgian underworld

creamery * dairy produce in the round, with particular reference to butter

cribbing * a now outdated colloquialism for food and sustenance

critouns * cooking refuse, notably burnt bits of fried food

crudity * food matter resting undigested in the belly

crug * food in general; bread crusts or crumbs in particular

dainties * sweetmeats; titbits or treats

dairy goods * a generic term for milk and the various food products derived from it

delicacies * dainties, fancies, and other choice or luxury viands

devilment * humorously, food flavoured with spicy seasonings or condiments

dinner-piece * food for the evening meal

dipsa * foods which produce thirst following their consumption

dish-meat * any foodstuff such as pie cooked in an open container

dollop * a sloppy, shapeless mass or serving of soft food

dressing * sauce or seasoning, especially applied as a complement to salad dishes

dulciaries * an archaic term for sweeteners or other such flavour enhancers

eatments * items of food

eattocks * Scottish dainties, sweets, and the like

edibles * articles of food, in particular snacks or nibbles

edule * edible matter

esculents * foods that may be healthily consumed, especially fresh vegetables

estables * an earlier form of eatables—items for the eating

estmete * Old English epicurean fare

exchange * a quantity of safe, alternative food for those following a diabetic diet

fameal * basic food of the nature of meal distributed for the purpose of famine relief

faring * food; fare

farsure * one of many lost soundalike synonyms for farcement or forcemeat; stuffing

fast food * inexpensive, pre-prepared, and quickly served hot food, to-go or to sit-in

finger food * light bites requiring no utensils to consume, such as canapés

fixings * garnish, in American English; more broadly, any food items or ingredients

flatogen * a "gasser," being a foodstuff notorious for producing flatulence

flavouring * any essence or extract used to impart greater flavour to food; seasoning

flesh-meat * animal flesh—in contrast to fish, fruit, or vegetables—as an article of food

fodder * grub considered so poor it would be more suitable for animal consumption

foodstuff * any substance, or class of substances, capable of providing nourishment

foodwise * with regard to food; concerning matters culinary or consumptionary

forcemeat * any ground or minced and well-seasoned food mixture used as stuffing

fosterment * food, with a connotation of virtuous eating and vital nourishment

fourment * an archaic name for cereal grains, such as wheat or more commonly corn

fowl * poultry; by extension, in cookery, the flesh of domesticated birds used as food

fragrant meat * a euphemism for the flesh of an exotic animal, or one not customarily killed for the pot; candidly put, dog meat

Frankenfoods * genetically modified foods regarded as a dietary and ecological evil

Friday-fare * fast-day food, especially fish; otherwise, plain and simple cooking

friture * fried food

frosting * iced confectionery, usually consumed in the form of trimming or topping

fruitage * food fruits, variously and collectively

fruits de mer * a culinary expression covering seafood and edible crustaceans

functional food * any consumable item purposively fortified with specific nutrients

furmage * formerly, a general term for cheese

furnitures * seasoning, in particular salad dressing

game * birds or field animals hunted or shot for the pot; hence also, the meat of same

garbage * offal; the organs and offcuts of any creature used as a source of food

garnison * victuals to support an army or sustain a population under siege

glop * unpalatable or otherwise unappetizing food

glutting * a quantity of food sufficient to fill the consumer to the point of repletion

glycosites * sweets and suchlike sugary treats

gobbet * a mouthful of semi-digested or regurgitated food

gob-meat * a coarse vernacular expression for food; grub to stuff the mouth with

gorgeful * a most immoderate amount of consumed food

goulie * food that one is unfamiliar with or perhaps unaccustomed to

grannam * an old term for the cereal staple corn, in the common tongue

greengrocery * fresh fruit and vegetables

grillade * grilled food, most notably meat, in general

groats & grits * oats and grains as one's basic food resource

groceries * those foods and goods retailed in a grocery store; loosely, fruits and vegetables

gros-gibier * big culinary game such as wild boar

grub & bub * food and drink

grubbins * food, in earlier American idiom

gruel * thin, watery fare unpleasant in both taste and texture; slops, spoon food

grunting-peck * pork or bacon; pig meat

gustables * tasty articles of food

gut-pudding * sausage or sausage meat

guttle * that which one consumes in a guttlesome, or gluttonous, fashion

gyppo * greasy food, be it gravy, stew, butter, bacon fat or other substance

halal * lawfully prepared food, according to Muslim legal and customary observance

harmalia * manna; nourishment

hastery * roasted food; alternatively, roast meats categorically regarded

health food * natural food claimed to contain superior nutritional goodness

herbage * a collective term for culinary herbs, used as garnish for prepared food

hog & hominy * spartan or simple fare

hogo * any dressing, relish, seasoning, or condiment adding piquancy to a dish

hollow * poultry, rabbit and hare; those meats not traditionally sold by butchers

infant formula * instant baby food given as surrogate breast milk

ingesta * those substances swallowed to sustain the body; in plain, food and drink

ingredients * those individual food items which together comprise any given dish

inmeat * the edible viscera of an animal slaughtered first and foremost for its flesh

inside-lining * filling food, jocularly speaking

jossop * any juicy foodstuff, as syrup, gravy or sauce

jowpment * a confused jumble of victuals or extemporized hash

junk food * high-calorie fare of little nutritional value or redeeming culinary merit

junketry * sundry candies and confections

jusculum * medicinal broth; alternatively, savoury soup

kickshaws * fancy French food, especially bonnes bouches or similar titillating bites

kitchen-physic * nourishing and restorative food for invalids and convalescents

kitchen-stuff * pan fat or dripping saved for subsequent cooking

kitchen-tillage * vegetables grown for their culinary utility

knick-knackery * assorted sweets and other light confections

lactage * dairy produce; milk and milk products including butter, cream, and cheese

larder * food laid down in store

legumes * beans, peas, lentils and pulses; collectively, edible plants or vegetables

levets * leftover food; the leavings from a dish or a meal

livenoth * in Old English, food as nourishment and the sustenance of bodily needs

long-pig * human flesh as a dietary option; cannibal fare

lubberwort * junk food; after a mystery herb imagined to render one idle and stupid

mammaday * runny food, especially pap; soft, soppy fare for weaned babies

manna * miracle food; heavenly fare

marinade * seasoned liquor for flavouring and tenderizing food prior to cooking

marrow * nourishing food

masticatory * any plant substance such as gum that is chewed for pleasure

maw-wallop * emetically foul food

meal * the edible part of any cereal grain, plant seed, or pulse ground to a powder

meat analogue * any substance designed as surrogate meat in look, texture and taste

meaties * food for infants and younger children

meatkin * food provisions; victuals

meat-ware * potatoes, pulses, and other fare of a similarly starchy nature

menavelings * food scraps, tidbits, or general odds and ends

menu-gibier * small culinary game such as partridge, grouse, and pheasant

meresauce * brine or marinade for pickling or preserving food

mess-meat * minced meat; hash

microgreens * leaf vegetable shoots used as garnish for salads, sarnies, and soups

milkness * cheese and other dairy goods made from milk

minifoods * cultures of single-cell proteins specially harvested as human food

mongee * grub, in old American hobo argot

morsel * a small "bite" of food

mouthful * a modest quantity of food, somewhat more than a mere morsel

moyse * anciently, a class of set pudding

muggings * food; informally, grub

munchable * an article of food that's good to munch on

munjary * food in Antipodean slang

musical fruit * humorously, fruit or vegetables that make one toot

mycoprotein * meat analogue grown in fermenters from fungi

natural food * prepared without artificial ingredients or known food additives

nonedibles * food items not deemed fit to be eaten; or, items not deemed fit to be food

nonperishables * foodstuffs that do not easily or quickly spoil

nourishment * nutritious food

nouriture * poetically, sustenance, food

nunyare * grub in camp theatrical argot

nutmeat * nuts as a class of food; also, that part or germ of a nut that people eat

nutrimentum * food as aliment, as nutrition

nutrition * food, especially of the wholesome and health-giving variety

nutritive * any article of nourishing food

ofett * a generic term used in Old English for fruit and vegetables

offalment * the edible waste parts stripped from the carcass of a butchered animal

offmagandy * the choicest of choice viands; top-notch gourmet grub

olitory * vegetables and herbs grown for any culinary purpose

opsony * any rich food or relish taken with bread as an accompaniment

organic food * produced or prepared holistically without chemical supplementation

orts * meal scraps or morsels; the proverbial crumbs that fall from the table

pabulum * food, feed or fodder; often used figuratively, meaning "food for thought"

packaged food * pre-prepared, wrapped commercial food, as opposed to fresh fare

panfish * fish good for simple pan-frying, especially if caught rather than bought

panmeat * food of any description cooked in a pan

pannum * bread or breadstuffs; more broadly, one's workaday staple fare

pantile * cookies or biscuits as a genre of hard-baked goods

papmeat * breastmilk; alternatively, any semi-liquid food for infants or invalids

pasternaks * culinary root vegetables, particularly carrots and parsnips

pastry-meat * pies and pasties, collectively

patisserie * pastries and cakes, collectively

peck & tipple * food and drink

peckage * food scraps or supplies

pedware * an antique culinary term embracing pulses, peas, and beans

penance * poor or paltry food; hence fare more suitable for fast days

perishables * fresh foodstuffs that all too easily or quickly spoil

pharmafoods * health food products containing bespoke nutritional enhancement

phitosite * high-calorie food

pianteric * fattening food

pig-cheer * meat products made from the inferior or interior portions of the animal

pigswill * loathsome food; originally, kitchen scraps and slops fed to the pigs

ploughmeat * cereal, in the popular tongue of yesteryear

pogeybait * a sweet treat or food package for those confined to care or convalescence

poisson * the flesh of fish used for food, in the jargon of the gastronome

porkery * pig flesh and pig meat products, collectively

potage * food cooked in the pot; thick soup or stew, generically

potherbs * culinary herbs, notably those grown in a kitchen garden

pottage-ware * those herbs or vegetables traditionally used to make soups and stews

poultry-ware * domestic fowl reared or regarded as a source of meat or eggs

prasadam * vegetarian food purified as a gift to the gods and partaken by worshippers

preserves * candied fruit stuffs all: jams, marmalades, chutneys, compotes, and more

processed food * any edible substance whose essential material or nutritional nature is altered in some way during manufacturing as a modern commercial food product

prog * food, grub, vittles

prosphagion * historically, any delicacy or luxury viand eaten with bread

provender * food, generally or jocularly speaking; elsewise, animal fodder

proviant * victuals for the catering corps; food for the forces

pullayly * an older dialectal synonym for poultry

pulment * stodge for the lower orders, typically of the nature of gruel

pulses * the edible seeds of leguminous plants as a separate nutritional category

purtenance * animal innards—organs, intestines, and all—as a class of unclassy food

purvey * the food or catering supplied on occasions such as weddings and funerals

reduction * in cooking, a concentrated stock or condensed sauce

regalo * an offering of food in the form of dainty or delicacy; a gastronomic gift

remissals * remaindered food

repasture * food for a feast

reversion * leftover food

salading * those herbs or vegetables suitable for eating raw, and so ideal for salads

salsure * any seasoning brine useful for pickling or preserving food

sampuru * false food; plastic display food (being a Japanese corruption of "sample")

saucepanful * a quantity of food or fluid sufficient to fill a cooking pan

29

saucer-meat * a lost dialectal synonym for sausage meat, or sausages generally

savouries * snack food items either salty or spicy in flavour, rather than sweet

scitament * an archaism for delicate, delicacy, or downright delicious food

scoffings * food in the vernacular

scran * grub, scoff; originally, scraps of food eaten to sustain labourers at toil

seafood * marine fish and shellfish used as food; the ocean's bounty

seasoning * any condiment, relish, or table sauce used to lend extra savour to food

shambles-meat * fresh meat, not yet salted

sheepmeat * mutton, hogget, or lamb — ovine flesh overall as a food resource

shellfish * in cookery, the meat of exoskeleton-bearing aquatic invertebrates, such as lobsters, crabs, oysters, and prawns, served as food

shmeat * meat analogue grown in a petri dish from tissue culture; lab meat

shortening * edible fat used in cooking to make baked goods light and flaky

sipperty * sauce or gravy; any relish for a dish

sirtfoods * an informal dietary class of disparate foodstuffs alleged to share the potential to activate sirtuins, or fat-burning proteins, in the body

slibbersauce * any foul, sloppy concoction ingested as foodstuff or pharmaceutical

slink-meat * generally, meat deemed unfit for human consumption; more precisely, the flesh of an aborted animal passed off as veal

slow food * quality fare carefully prepared using seasonal produce and honouring local culinary tradition

soot-meat * sweets or similar dainties

soul food * the comestibles and cuisine of Black America

sowl * highly flavoured food, typically in the form of relish for bread

space food * victuals specially prepared and processed for cosmic consumption

specery * spice and all things nice

spiceries * either spices or groceries, collectively

spissament * any thickening agent used in cookery, as flour in gravy

spoonmeat * soft or semi-liquid food taken by spoon; pap

spreadum * butter, in the vernacular of bygone days

staple * the basic foodstuff or essential dietary item of a given population

stickjaw * any foodstuff that causes the teeth to stick together when chewed

stodge * high-carb, farinaceous fare that sits heavy in the gut and is difficult to digest

street food * viands cooked and sold outdoors for on-the-spot consumption

stuffure * forcemeat; stuffing

suckabobs * a generic term denoting boiling, or suckable, sweets

suckings * any food that may be consumed by the action of sucking

sugar-work * confectionery

superfoods * nutrient-rich foods marketed on the basis of their purportedly superior health-giving properties

suppage * light or fast food; supper's fare

suppings * food that may be supped or taken by spoon, as soup or broth

surchargure * an excessive quantity of food devoured

sustenance * food as the basic sustainer of life; that which makes one hale and hearty

sweetmeats * sundry candies and confections, collectively considered

swineflesh * pork, vulgarly

syfling * in Old English coin, food eaten with bread; alternatively, salt or seasoning

taureau * beef denominated as a culinary resource; also, broadly, jerked red meat

theobroma * god-food

thickening-stuff * victuals of any description, for any diet

titbits * bites of choice food; tasty treats

toothful * the smallest quantity of anything edible, nothing more than a morsel

tracklements * savoury condiments or sauces, especially jellies, serving as an accompaniment to roast meat

tragemata * fancy sweetmeats, in particular items of confectionery best chewed

trail mix * high-energy snack food for those who enjoy the great outdoors

treif * non-kosher fare

tripes & trillibubs * offal; the edible entrails and internal organs of beast or fowl

tubers * those starchy edible vegetables that grow underground on plant roots, as potatoes, yams, beets, and such

tubesteak * in vitro or otherwise synthetic meat

tucker * as grub, prog, scran, and so forth—food, informally speaking

variety meats * a euphemism for a range of interior or inferior edible animal cuts

vegetive * a vegetable, any vegetable

vegebles

an old dialectal form of vegetables — plants used as food

venison * literally "hunted' food"; the meat of any big game beast such as boar or deer

vetches * a culinary descriptor once broadly applied to legumes and pulses

viance * food in general

viand * meat in general

viands * eatables, often with a connotation of gastronomic merit

victuallage * food held in stock or supply; catering provisions

victuals * foodstuffs fit for human consumption

victus * health-giving food

viennoiserie * baked goods made from puff pastry, such as croissants and brioche

vitafoods * foods made and marketed with the health-conscious consumer in mind

vittles * demotic victuals

vivers * Scots victuals

voidance * uneaten food or scraps such as bones cleared from plate and table

voip * tasteless food that is nonetheless filling

wafery * light pastry

washmeat * unsubstantial and unsatisfying food

waybread * food, baked or otherwise, to sustain one on a long or arduous journey

welfare * food in happy abundance

werednys * "weirdness"—sauce or spice in the early English lexicon

whitemeat * food prepared from milk; an outmoded synonym for dairy produce

wholefood * additive-free plant food grown with minimal processing or refining

wholemeal * any bread or other baked product made from the entire wheat kernel

wistfyllo * food in abundance in olden times

wistmete * aliment in older, leaner times; literally "existence-food"

wyrtmete * any Anglo-Saxon food consisting of vegetables or herbs

yarrum * milk, in old money

zuuzuus & whamwhams * vending machine confectionery, in US penitentiary slang

CHAPTER 2

Items and Ingredients from the Plant World

> *"Eat food. Not too much. Mostly plants."*
> **— Michael Pollan**

acerola * a cherry-like fruit native to South and Central America, rich in vitamin C

acetum * vinegar, historically; a pickling agent and perennial condiment favourite

achocha * a high Andean relative of the courgette, also known as stuffing cucumber

adobo * Caribbean spice mix

advieh * Persian spice mix

adzuki * a sweet red mung bean widely used in East Asian cooking

agar-agar * vegan gelatin; a culinary jelly derived from seaweed

agave * Mexican cactus nectar used to sweeten dishes as a healthy sugar substitute

ajwain * an Indian spice flavouring extracted from carom seeds

akebia * the edible fruit of the East Asian "chocolate vine" shrub

alexanders * horse parsley; the herb's stems are used as celery, its roots as parsnip

alkanet * a herb boiled to produce the red food colouring used in rogan josh curries

alphonso * a small Indian mango variety

amaranth * a peppery plant meeting fully three-quarters of human nutritional needs

ambarella * a slightly sour-tasting but versatile tropical food fruit

ampalaya * a Philippine bitter melon

ananas * a culinary synonym for the pineapple

anardana * an Indian table spice made from dried pomegranate seeds

ancho * an aromatic Mexican chilli, otherwise known as the poblano

angelica * a pot herb whose stem may be used for flavouring, but never eaten raw

anguria * a gourd, specifically the watermelon

aniseed * a popular spice plant with liquorice flavoured seeds

annatto * a natural orange-red food colouring also widely applied as a condiment

apple-John * any apple somewhat shrivelled with age yet considered to be at its best

arborio * speciality risotto rice

armorace * horseradish, a root vegetable used in cooking as a spice

arrowroot * a versatile edible starch used internationally as a food thickening agent

arugula * rocket, a peppery salad leaf vegetable belonging to the cabbage family

asafoetida * a culinary herb of the celery family; once known as the "food of gods"

atemoya * a tropical fruit cross popular from Taiwan to the Levant to Brazil

avocado * from an Aztec word meaning "testicle"; the fruit highest of all in energy-rich protein and oil

azarole * the Naples medlar, used in Mediterranean cooking for many centuries

baharat * Arabian spice mix

bambara * the Congo goober or groundnut; a traditional African food crop

bananino * a small, sweet ladyfinger cultivar of the dessert banana

barberry * a tart, edible berry; it figures most prominently in modern Iranian cuisine

basmati * literally "fragrant rice"; a long-grained variety originating in southern Asia

batata * West Indies sweet potato

batavia * a variety of endive with qualities similar to the lettuce; also called escarole

berbere * East African spice mix

bergamot * a name for both a sweet dessert pear and the dwarf Seville orange

biffin * a cooking apple

bigaroon * the Royal Anne cherry; eaten in the hand or reserved for making fruit pie

bignay * a small Southeast Asian fruit used to make jams, jellies, and such

bilberry * an edible berry often mistaken for its cousin the blueberry or blaeberry

blackbutter * a gourmet seaweed from the shores of Cornwall

blewit * a palatable fragrant mushroom of the agaric family

boletus * a mainly edible genus of mushroom-producing fungi

boniato * a Cuban sweet potato with characteristic white flesh

borage * a garden herb ideally dried for use in salads and garnishes

borecole * a rarer, alternative name for kale

bostongurka * Swedish gherkin pickle

bouquet garni * a classic French herb bundle added to stocks, sauces, and soups

boysenberry * a large four-way hybrid bramble fruit

brassica * cabbage or kale as food; cruciferous vegetables in general or aggregate

breadfruit * a tropical staple; the texture of the cooked fruit is similar to fresh bread

broccoflower * a vegetable cross between broccoli and cauliflower

brunion * another name for a nectarine, being a hybrid of plum and peach

buckwheat * a "pseudo-cereal" flour used especially in Eastern European cooking

buffaloberry * a sour berry with assuredly spurious claims to be a "superfruit"

bulgur * a Levantine cereal food made from the parboiled groats of durum wheat

bullace * a small wild English plum

burdock * a root vegetable relative of the artichoke, with wide culinary application

burnet * a pot herb traditionally used as an item in salads and dressings

butterbeans * lima beans as grown in the Southern US, notable for their large flat edible seeds

cabelluda * an exotic yellow food fruit indigenous to Brazil

calabash * a fleshy bottle gourd squash of both cultural and culinary significance

calamint * a herb and condiment often appearing in Middle Eastern za'atar spices

calamondin * a Southeast Asian citrus fruit usually cooked or used as a preserve

cale-flory * the original English-language name for the cauliflower

calendula * a genus of edible flowers also known as pot marigold

cambuca * the edible "flying saucer fruit" of the Brazilian rainforests

candlenut * a nut used in Indonesia and Malaysia as a thickening agent in curries

canella * a now obsolete term for cinnamon

canistel * a widely cultivated food fruit known in Taiwan as "peach of the immortals"

cannellini * a type of large white kidney bean frequently used in Italian cooking

canola * a variety of oilseed rape yielding a palatable and healthier cooking oil

cantaloupe * a small muskmelon, informally classified as a "fruit-vegetable"

capers * pickled flower buds or young shrub berries used as a flavouring or garnish

capsicum * a genus of chillies including especially the milder sweet bell peppers

carambola * a juicy tropical fruit enjoyed fresh or cooked; also known as the starfruit

caraway * Persian cumin, an everyday culinary seed-spice

cardamony * an older variant spelling of cardamom, an expensive yet popular spice

cardoon * a thistly plant whose roots, stalk, stems and buds alike are entirely edible

carob * the "locust bean," trumpeted as a healthy substitute for cocoa in chocolate

cascabel * a moderately pungent chilli pepper cultivated across its native Mexico

cassabanana * a sweet, fragrant melon fruit containing nary a hint of banana

cassareep * a West Indies condiment made from the bitter root of the manioc tuber

cassonade * unrefined, or brown, sugar

cedrate * a variety of citron fruit much used in jams

celender * Old English coriander, the oldest of all the culinary herbs

celeriac * celery knob; an aromatic root eaten either raw or cooked

celtuce * stem lettuce; a celery-like cultivar of lettuce with edible stalks and leaves

chanterelle * a class of wild, woodland mushrooms, widely consumed

charlock * a wild mustard green and common cornfield weed, it was a widespread food source of last resort during the years of Ireland's "great hunger"

checkerberry * an edible American fruit sometimes called the teaberry or boxberry

cherimoya * a conical, white-fleshed food fruit known to some as a "custard apple"

chervil * French parsley seasoning; etymologically, it means "the happy herb"

chibol * a dialectal term for the sybee, or spring onion

chilgoza * an edible Himalayan pine nut, and rich local source of carbohydrates and proteins

chiltepin * a Texan chilli pepper packing significantly more intense heat than its state neighbour the jalapeño

chinkapin * the "dwarf chestnut," an edible nut gleaned or foraged gourmet-style

chipotle * smoked jalapeño, a popular Mexican culinary spice and sauce base

chives * the smallest members of the onion family used in the kitchen

chokecherry * an edible fruit requiring to be cooked well due to its cyanide content

choricero * a fleshy red pepper with an important role in northern Spanish cuisine

cicely * any of several culinary herbs of the celery family, most notably sweet cicely

cilantro * coriander, as it is better known stateside

cipollini * the "wild onion" bulbs of grape hyacinth, a staple of Italian gastronomy

citrangequat * a trigeneric citrus fruit hybrid, crossing the citrange with the kumquat

clavers * white clover when used as a salad ingredient

clitocybe

a genus of agaric mushrooms seldom consumed owing to the difficulty of distinguishing those that are poisonous from those that are safe to eat

clementine * a citrus fruit cross between the Seville orange and the tangerine

cloudberry * a northern bramble fruit popular across Scandinavia as a base for jam

coco de mer * the sea coconut, often encountered as a flavouring in Cantonese soups

cocoa * the fermented seed of the cacao tree, and basis of all chocolate preparations

cocoyam * a common name for the taro and malanga tropical root vegetable crops

colewort * an older name for the cabbage, notably young cabbage reserved for salads

collards * kale leaves, eaten as a vegetable; a staple of Southern US "soul food"

colombo * West Indies curry powder

coloquinty * an edible gourd variously known as "bitter apple" and "vine of Sodom"

colythron * a ripe fig

copra * coconut oil, a versatile if high-fat, high-calorie cooking product

cornflour * corn meal or starch ground to a powder for use as a thickener in cooking

cornichons * immature cucumbers or miniature gherkins, pickled French-style

costard * an ancient British ribbed cooking apple

costmary * a popular medieval pot herb prized for its spearmint astringency

cottonfruit * a.k.a. santol, a fruit used in numerous Thai salad and curry dishes

couverture * cooking chocolate, made with added cocoa butter for extra gloss

cowcake * an old Scots dialectal term for the wild parsnip

cowcumber * the cucumber of yore, the fruit being regarded as mere animal fodder

crabapple * any small sour apple, better cooked than eaten in the hand

cremini * a meaty immature button variant of the portobello mushroom

crestmarine * a rare culinary herb also referred to as sea fennel or rock samphire

crookneck * a sweet-fleshed yellow summer squash

cubanelle * a long, thin sweet pepper much used in Caribbean and Italian cuisine

cumin * a popular kitchen spice ground or whole; known in its native India as jeera

cush-cush * tropical American yam tuber, consumed as a vegetable

cydon * the quince, or "apple of Cydonia"

cymling * the pattypan squash, in American English

dactyl * a date, in older coinage

daikon * cooked radish, a popular item in East Asian cuisine

damascene * an earlier name for the damson, the "plum of Damascus"

dasheen * the edible starchy corm of the taro plant

demerara * natural, unrefined crunchy cane sugar; known in the US as turbinado

dewberry * the edible blueish-black fruit of the eponymous bramble

dilex * seaweed as a food resource, specifically dulse

dillseed * a pungent seed used to spice and season numerous dishes

dittander * a historical mystery herb; variously pepperwort, dittany of Crete, or cress

duqqa * Egyptian spice mix

duracine * a firm-fleshed peach

durian * a tasty tropical fruit notorious for its foul and off-putting aroma

durum * a hard wheat whose flour is used to make premium breads and pastas

earthapple * a term variously denominating the potato, cucumber, or artichoke

edamame * a foodstuff prepared from fresh green soybeans boiled in their pods

eddoes * edible taro tubers or cormlets

eggplant * the aubergine, in American English; so named for the vegetable's shape

einkorn * man's first wheat, indeed one of the earliest food plants ever cultivated

elderflower * a British berry fruit primarily used today to produce juices and jams

elecampane * a root used in classical times as a condiment, and latterly as a candy

emblic * the edible fruit of the Indian gooseberry tree

emmer * a hulled wheat in the style of farro; one of the first crops to be domesticated

endive * a leaf vegetable called chicory in its curly form, and escarole when broad-leaved

enokitake * golden needle mushrooms, a mainstay of East Asian gastronomy

epazote * an aromatic herb strongly featured in traditional Mexican cuisine

eryngo * the sea holly parsley plant, especially its edible root which is often candied

farina * a fine carb-rich cereal food made from milled wheat or other vegetable meal

faverel * an old English provincial term for the onion

fecula * powdered starch extracted from food plants, used in cooking as a thickener

fenugreek * a herb whose seeds are typically ground as a spice for curry powder

fenwort * an archaic term for the cranberry

fiddleheads * the edible tips or fronds of certain ferns, consumed as a vegetable

filberts * large, cultivated hazelnuts

fines herbes * a classic balanced fresh herb mix, integral to French haute cuisine

fingerroot * a gingerish culinary herb perhaps better known as Chinese keys

finocchio * Florence fennel, a herb with a bulbous stalk base eaten as a vegetable

five-spice * Chinese spice mix

flageolet * the common French kidney bean

flaxseed * edible linseed oil, used culinarily in Europe to lift the flavour of quark

floweret * the clustered flowering head, or floret, of such as broccoli or cauliflower

forastero * an inferior cocoa bean often used to produce commercial-grade chocolate

frais * strawberries, in the formal context of cookery

framboise * raspberries, in the formal context of cookery

freekeh * a cereal food made from unripened durum wheat, roasted and rubbed

frijoles * any beans, such as the pinto, commonly featured in Tex-Mex cuisine

funori * an Asian aquatic plant food, or polysaccharide extract of edible seaweed

galangal * a generic term for a group of aromatic spice roots found in Asian cuisine

gamboge * a fruit used as a condiment in the preparation of Thai sour curries

garam masala * Indian hot spice mix

garbanzo * the humble chickpea

genipap * the succulent fruit of a Caribbean evergreen, useful for making preserves

gillyflowers * a once-popular name for cloves

gingelly * sesame oil, variously used to cook with or as a table condiment

glycyrize * "sweet root"; liquorice as a confectionery flavouring or culinary spice

gochugaru * a smoky red pepper spice from Korea

goji * a native Asian berry lately promoted in the West as a purported health food

granadilla * a somewhat larger, sweeter, and more exotic cousin of the passion fruit

greengage * a small dessert plum

grisette * a common edible woodland toadstool

grysmolle * an archaic name for either apricot or quince

guava * a pink-pulped tropical food, designated the national winter fruit of Pakistan

gurgeons * coarse bran flour or similar cereal meal

habanero * the "Scotch bonnet," a famously pungent chilli pepper from the Amazonas

hackberry * an astringent though edible berry fruit

haricot * a type of French kidney bean; an old dish of mutton bore the name first

hautboy * an archaic synonym for the strawberry

hedge-mustard * a bitter salad leaf formerly also known as English rocket

heirloom * any "heritage" or non-hybridized tomato cultivar

hemidesmus * Indian sarsaparilla, a herbal root pickled and served with rice

hericium * a family of fleshy edible mushrooms, distinctive for bearing no caps

hickory * loosely, the pecan; a nut with a tough outer shell and edible inner fruit

hindberry * an archaic synonym for the raspberry

hominy * a gritty foodstuff made from coarsely ground and soaked maize kernels

honeybell * another name for the tangelo, a citrus cross of grapefruit and tangerine

horehound * a herb traditionally candied in lozenge form and taken to aid digestion

horse-gog * a lost regional expression for a plum that is tart to the taste

huckleberry * an edible bramble fruit akin to the blueberry

huitlacoche * a flavoursome fungus, or corn smut, dubbed the Mexican truffle

hulkage * miller's bran, being the husks of cereal grains, rich in dietary fibre

ilama * a compound tropical fruit of the Americas, best served and eaten chilled

inkcap * a common name for multiple genera of mostly edible toadstools

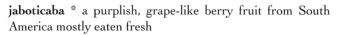
jaboticaba * a purplish, grape-like berry fruit from South America mostly eaten fresh

jaca-dura * a hard variety of the exotic jackfruit, the largest of all tree-borne fruits

jaggery * Indian palm sugar

jalapeño * a hot green chilli pepper, much used in Mexican cooking

jambolan * the Malabar plum, an edible fruit long used too in Eastern medicine

jargonelle * an early ripening pear

jenneting * an early ripening apple

jicama * the "Mexican potato," a root vegetable eaten raw in salads or boiled in stews

jostaberry * a unique gooseberry and blackcurrant cross, good for chutneys and such

kabocha * a sweet winter squash, colloquially referred to as Japanese pumpkin

kalamata * a meaty brine-cured black olive grown in the Greek Peloponnese

kalumpang * the "Java olive," in actuality an oily cashew-like edible nut

kari patta * curry leaves, a key item in much of the cookery of the Subcontinent

kastainy * an older name for the chestnut, a nut traditionally roasted for edibility

ketambilla * the Ceylon gooseberry, a somewhat acidic fruit often made into jam

khorasan * oriental wheat, a large-grained ancestral alternative to modern wheat

king stropharia * a gourmet agaric mushroom, cultivated for food

kiwano * an exotic edible fruit cross known as the "horned" melon or cucumber

kiwifruit * the Chinese gooseberry, as cultivated commercially in New Zealand

kohlrabi * a popular European cabbage with an edible stem resembling the turnip

kombu * East Asian kelp, used fresh in sashimi or as a seasoning for broth, or dashi

kumquat * a mini orange, citrus-like fruit typically eaten preserved or candied

lablab * a species of African bean cultivated across the tropics as a local food source

laminaria * an edible seaweed with postulated efficacy against "diabesity"

langsat * a tart, fibre-rich berry fruit native to the East Indies

lemandarin * a hybridized lemon and mandarin citrus fruit, also called the rangpur

lemongrass * a herb used to impart subtle citrus tones to Southeast Asian dishes

lingonberry * a popular Scandinavian cooking berry; also called mountain cranberry

loganberry * a raspberry-blackberry cross, interchangeable with either in recipes

lombia * a widely cultivated edible bean better known as the black-eyed pea

longan * a small pulpy food fruit related to the lychee, grown throughout Asia

loomi * a Middle Eastern lime sun-dried as a souring agent or powdered as a spice

loonzein * brown, or hulled, rice

loquat * the Japanese medlar, a plum-like exotic fruit often used to make preserves

lovage * a pot herb notable as a celery-like flavour enhancer; also called sea parsley

lovi-lovi * a fruit of the Philippines, chiefly reserved for producing jams and syrups

lychee * a sweet fleshy tropical fruit, best eaten fresh for full flavour

macadamia * a round white common edible nut, extensively cultivated

madrean * a gingerish spice formerly much used in conserves

malagueta * a hot chilli favourite across the cuisines of the lusophone nations

maligar * a type of eating apple, recorded long ago but perhaps now lost

mameyito * a small sour-sweet tropical fruit usually eaten fresh

mamoncillo * the Spanish lime, a tangy Caribbean fruit eaten like grapes

mandarin * a small, sweet orange with a thin skin that peels away effortlessly

mangetout * the sugar, or snap, pea; a variety consumed pods and all

mangosteen * an exotic fruit with a flavour hinting at peach and pineapple alike

maraschino * a preserved cherry and essential component of ice cream sundaes

marionberry * a highly productive American crop cultivar of the blackberry

marjoram * a general term covering a number of aromatic herbs, oregano included

marsall * any compound of complementary culinary spices as a powder or paste

masa harina * dough flour obtained from maize, used to make tortillas and tamales

massecuite * a semi-solid mix of sugar cane juice obtained during refining

matoke * a green cooking banana found in Uganda; also, the flesh of same as food

maypops * the edible fruit of the passionflower vine, native to the United States

mazagan * an early variant of the broad, or fava, bean

mazzard * a wild sweet cherry

mealie-meal * coarse South African corn meal, a staple; a mealie itself is a corncob

medjool * a large moist date, widely harvested and highly prized

medlar * a small stone fruit which only becomes edible once it has started to decay

melopepon * literally "apple-gourd," a cover term for any of various kinds of squash

millet * a Eurasian cereal grass producing small grains used chiefly to make flour

mirasol * a mild to medium strength chilli pepper, no stranger to Mexican cuisine

mirliton * a succulent tropical "fruit-vegetable," known as chayote in Cajun cooking

miso * fermented soybean seasoning paste, a mainstay of Japanese gastronomy

mizuna * edible salad "water greens," a variety of oriental rape

molasses * concentrated sugar cane syrup or treacle; useful in cooking and baking

mongcorn * an old mix of rye and wheat grains reserved for making the best breads

morello * a sour cherry cultivar, more often dried and cooked than eaten in the hand

morels * a genus of gourmet sac fungi, especially prized in Provençal cuisine

mousseron * an edible bonnet or button "fairy ring" mushroom of the agaric family

mugwort * a bitter herb used as a flavouring agent, more rarely as a dish ingredient

munyeroo * a salad vegetable and enduring staple of the Aboriginal Australian diet

muscovado * raw brown sugar suffused with flavour through contact with molasses

muskmelon * essentially a large, sweet cantaloupe with a distinctive musky aroma

myrobalan * a cherry plum usually prepared for eating in preserves and compotes

naga jolokia * the "ghost pepper," a fearsomely fiery chilli registering one million units plus on the Scoville heat scale

nameko * a nutty "butterscotch" mushroom, ideal for traditional Japanese stir-fries

nannyberry * a rare wild edible berry native to North America

naranjilla * literally "little orange," an edible citrus found in South American uplands

navew * an obscure English word referring to a variety of small, wild turnip, or rape

neeps * Scots turnips, especially when consumed with haggis and tatties as a supper

nigella * cookery's "blessed seed," the pungent seeds of the black cumin spice plant

nopales * the edible fleshy pads of the prickly pear cactus

nostoc * a genus of jelly-like algae eaten historically in China as famine fare

nuciprune * an early modern name for the walnut, being "betwixt a plum and a nut"

oatmeal * a flour prepared from ground or rolled oats, as typically used in porridge

ogbono * the African wild mango; alternatively, the aromatic oily nuts of said fruit

oilberry * an Old English olive

okra * edible mucilaginous seed pods, also known as bhindi, gumbo, or ladyfingers

oleaster * any wild-growing olive or one of markedly inferior palatability

orangelo * a naturally occurring orange and grapefruit, or pomelo, citrus fruit cross

orgament * a bygone name for oregano, the popular culinary herb

oronge * Caesar's mushroom, an edible fungus for the connoisseur

ortanique * a Jamaican food fruit, promoted as a "unique" orange and tangerine cross

palmetto * palm hearts eaten as a vegetable

panch phoron * a five-way whole spice masala of fenugreek, fennel, cumin, and nigella with either mustard or radhuni seeds from the Indian Subcontinent

pandan * "Asian vanilla," an aromatic leaf widely used as a flavouring ingredient

paprika * a ground table spice obtained from sun-dried sweet and hot red peppers

paranut * the Brazil nut, an oily edible seed and common ingredient in mixed nuts

partminger * a Nigerian culinary herb with qualities similar to basil

passata * Italian tomato purée

passionberry * a sweet wild tomato bushfood found in the arid parts of Australia

pastillage * a thick sugar-based setting paste ideal for decorating or sculpting pastry

pawpaw * the "hillbilly mango," an American fruit often confused with the papaya

pearmain * any of a range of red-skinned English dessert apples, of ancient lineage

peasemeal * flour derived from roasted field peas, a staple of old Scots cookery

pekmez * Turkish molasses; a cooking syrup derived from grape must or carob pods

pellitory * a herb used by the pinch in medieval cooking to lend spice to bland meals

peppercress * an edible mustard grass, typically sautéed or eaten raw in salads

pepperoncini * chilli peppers in general, as featured in Italian cuisine

pepyn * an archaic name for the common pea

perdrigon * a long-established variety of culinary plum

perilla * the name in English for the Japanese mint herb shiso

persic * an archaic name for the common peach

persillade * parsley and garlic prepared as a garnish

persimmon * a succulent super-sweet fruit, also known as the kaki

petersilie * "rock celery," as parsley was first known in early English

phaselles * kidney beans

phyllo * filo pastry, a very thin unleavened confectioner's dough

physalis * an exotic winter cherry from Peru, both sweet and sour to the taste

picholine * a French cocktail olive of medium size

pignolia * the edible seed of certain pine tree cones

pimento * a sweet red pepper offering mild heat, often used as a stuffing or relish

pinder * the humble peanut

pippin * a term for any apple cultivated from seed

pisang * either banana or plantain, as featured in South Asian cuisine

pistace * the pistachio nut, in its earliest anglicized form

pitahaya * the dragon fruit, an edible exotic originally from Mexico

pitanga * the Surinam cherry, a spicy red berry fruit used as a base for conserves

pitomba * a palatable fruit abundant in the Amazonas, usually eaten fresh

plantain * a cooking banana

plumcot * a natural fruit cross blending elements of the plum and the apricot

pokeweed * a plant traditionally eaten in the Appalachians though toxic if uncooked

polypores * a genus of bracket fungi including the "chicken of the woods" mushroom

pomato * a plant chimaera produced by grafting tomato scions onto potato roots; cherry tomatoes appear on the vine while potatoes grow underground

pomegranate * literally "seedy apple"; a juicy berry fruit with a long culinary history

pomodoro * the plum tomato, as used extensively in Italian cookery

pompion * an older name given to the pumpkin or any large melon

poppyseeds * tiny seeds used as topping, filling, or flavouring for baked goods

porcelana * a highly coveted cocoa bean, produces the most expensive chocolates

porcini * ceps, or flavoursome wild boletus mushrooms, in culinary parlance

portobello * a "meadow mushroom" that has matured past its bonnet or button stage

praty * an old vernacular term used in Ireland for the potato

pregnada * a type of "pregnant" lemon, one enclosing a similar smaller fruit within it

prewyn * an archaic variant spelling of prune, being a dried plum

prickpear * the Indian fig, from a cactus with the same title bearing edible fruits

puffballs * a group of edible wild mushrooms requiring to be picked with care

pulasan * an ultra-tropical fruit and sweeter close cousin to the rambutan

purslane * a peppery leaf vegetable and commonplace ingredient in medieval sallets

quandong * the Australian "wild peach," a staple food of the indigenous population

quarrenden * an ancient English dessert apple, best eaten straight off the tree

quassia * an aromatic bark eaten as an aid to digestion and stimulant to the appetite

quatre-épices * the classic four-spice blend of pepper, cloves, nutmeg, and ginger

querdling * any hard, elongated cooking apple, most usefully roasted over the fire

quibibz * the spice berries of the cubeb pepper shrub, long used as a condiment

quickening * leaven or yeast; a ferment added to dough causing bread to rise

quinoa * a traditional Andean edible seed staple, now faddish modern health food

radicchio * a chicory cultivar with variegated leaves consumed raw as a salad green

raffinade * top-quality refined sugar

rambutan * a subacid tropical berry fruit known informally as the hairy lychee

rampion * the bellflower consumed as a vegetable, with leaf and root good for salads

ramsons * the wild garlic, a plant with a bulbous root eaten as a relish

rapadura * low-grade unrefined whole cane sugar

rapeseed * an alternative vegetable oil growing in popularity with health-conscious modern consumers

ras el hanout * Moroccan spice mix

redcurrants * small sweet berries often jellied as a condiment to complement lamb

rocambole * a loose cover name for a range of full-flavoured gourmet garlics

romaine * the North American cos lettuce, the classic choice for Caesar salad

romanesco * a visually striking variety of cauliflower with fractal-like conical florets

rosmarine * an older name for rosemary, a time-honoured culinary herb

russet * any of various dessert apples with a distinctive rough, reddish-brown skin

rutabaga * the cruciferous vegetable known outside of North America as the swede

ryfart * old Scots horseradish, a corruption of the original French

safflower * a cooking and salad oil also useful for making soft margarines

sago * a primary food product prepared from the pith of tropical palm stems

salep * a starchy powdered foodstuff obtained from dried orchid tubers

saligot * the water-chestnut, a plant cultivated for millennia for its edible seeds

salsify * the "oyster plant," a tasty dandelion taproot eaten as a vegetable

samphire * "poor man's asparagus," a sea herb also known as papwort or pickleweed

sapodilla * the edible fruit of a tropical tree which also yields chicle, or chewing gum

sargassum * a genus of harvested edible microalgae

saskatoons * a.k.a. juneberries, a North American fruit species similar to the blueberry

sassafras * filé powder, a spicy herb serving as a base for Louisiana Creole gumbos

satsuma * a small, seedless Japanese version of the mandarin orange

saturege * Old English savory, a culinary herb of the mint family

sauce-alone * garlic mustard, a pot herb used as a condiment and salad component

sauerkraut * German pickled cabbage; formerly known in the US as "liberty cabbage"

savoy * a hardy cabbage with a compact head of densely crinkled leaves

schorchanarrow * a rare root vegetable treated and served up in the style of parsnips

scurvygrass * any of a variety of greens eaten by sailors of yore to prevent scorbutus

seakale * a maritime pot herb cultivated for its succulent young shoots

seitan * "wheat meat," a protein-rich Asian foodstuff made from wheat gluten

semolina * coarse grains of milled durum wheat, used to prepare pudding and pasta

sentynode * knotgrass, recorded in Elizabethan England as a culinary herb

serrano * a Mexican "mountain" chilli pepper, mostly eaten raw despite its pungency

shaddock * the pomelo, a fruit closely related to the pamplemoose or grapefruit

shichimi * Japanese spice mix

shiitake * a species of edible lentinula mushroom, essential to Japanese cuisine

silphion * a yet unidentified table condiment mentioned in classical cookbooks

skirret * water parsnip, a now neglected sweet Tudor root vegetable

smallage * wild celery, formerly used as a food flavouring

smeddum * an old Scots term for any finely ground meal or flour

songrong * an aromatic mushroom highly prized in East Asian gastronomy

sorghum * a cereal grass native to Sub-Saharan Africa, widely cultivated for grain

sorrel * a somewhat sour-tasting dock leaf used to prepare salads and sauces

sourdough * a leaven for making bread, consisting of actively fermenting dough

soybeans * the protein-packed edible seeds of a leguminous East Asian crop plant

sparassis * the "cauliflower mushroom," a fungus of modest culinary utility

sparrowgrass * a dated vernacular form of asparagus, or edible vegetable spears

spearmint * a leafy herb found in vegetable salads and health food products alike

spelt * an ancient wheat crop recently popularized as a gluten-lite alternative food

spinogre * an archaic variant spelling of spinach, a leaf vegetable and source of iron

spirulina * a nutrient-rich algae variously used as a foodstuff and food additive

squaghetti * an edible marrow, also dubbed vegetable spaghetti or spaghetti squash

squashberry * an American viburnum bearing edible fruits good for making jam

star-apple * a tropical American food fruit with a star-shaped arrangement of seeds

succory * an alternative version of chicory, a salad plant with edible leaves and root

sultana * a type of raisin, or seedless dried grape, cooked in cakes and puddings

sumac * a red shrub fruit commonly used as a sour spice in Mediterranean cookery

sunchoke * the Jerusalem artichoke, especially with reference to its edible rootstock

susumber * the gully bean, a bitter Jamaican berry boiled and cooked with codfish

sweetsop * a West Indies heart-shaped custard apple

sybow * a Scots sybee or shallot, a spring onion with green leaves

synamoun * early English cinnamon, an aromatic spice of powdered tree bark

tabasco * a variety of chilli pepper and basis of the hot table sauce of the same name

tahini * a raw condiment dip or spread made from toasted sesame seeds

tamarillo * an exotic tropical food fruit otherwise known as the tree tomato

tamarind * the pulp of pea tree seed pods, used as a souring agent in Asian cuisine

tangerine * any of various commercial cultivars of the mandarin orange

tapioca * a grainy, starchy primary food product extracted from cassava root

tartufo * the white truffle, a highly expensive epicurean fungus

tatsoi * a native Chinese green, now widely cultivated for both its stems and leaves

teff * a fine cereal grain and staple foodstuff in the cuisine of the Horn of Africa

tempeh * Indonesian fermented soybean cake, used as a substitute for meat

tengusa * a red seaweed plant food used in Japan to make jelly noodle dishes

tepary * a hardy American edible bean harvested since pre-Columbian times

theriac * black treacle or molasses — a byproduct of the sugar-refining process

thevethorn * the original English-language name for the thorn-grape, or gooseberry

thimbleberry * a North American black raspberry, palatable raw or prepared as jam

thoory * the commonest variety of dry date; possibly the first food cultivated by man

tofu * curd made from mashed soybeans; now a standard item in vegetarian cooking

tomatillo * a Mexican "fruit-vegetable" favourite, mostly eaten cooked in salsa verde

topitambo * an indigenous Trinidadian root vegetable and minor food crop

tormarith * an archaic variant spelling of turmeric, a powdered yellow curry spice

tragonia * an archaic name for tarragon, a perennial Old World pot herb

tremella * "snow fungus," a mushroom family highly esteemed in Chinese cuisine

trick-madame * an astringent herb nowadays only rarely consumed as salad leaf

trigonella * a genus of legumes, with particular culinary reference to blue fenugreek

Trinidad scorpion * a weapons-grade capsicum cultivar; strictly for aficionados of hotter-than-hot chilli sauces, or the foolhardy

triticum * a generic term covering the many species of wheat, a global cereal staple

tsampa * roasted barley flour, a primary foodstuff of many Himalayan communities

tuckahoe * a starchy rootstock and formerly a staple plant food of Native Americans

tummelberry * a large Scottish hybridized raspberry, new to the market

urad * the mungo bean, an Indian pulse commonly used in the preparation of dhal

vadouvan * a masala paste featuring curry spices aromatized with garlic and shallots

vanaspati * a thick Indian vegetable oil used as a substitute for butter and ghee

vergaloo * a variety of white pear noted for its soft flavoursome flesh

verjuice * a condiment for the epicure, being the pressed sour juice of unripe fruit

vincotto * "boiled wine," a thick kitchen stock obtained by cooking down grape must

wakame * "sesame seaweed," an edible kelp skilfully exploited in East Asian cuisine

walmore * a dated name for the parsnip, carrot, or similar tuberous vegetable

wampee * the "yellow skin," a citrusy food fruit cultivated widely throughout Asia

wardon * an ancient English cooking pear formerly renowned for its use in pies

wasabi * Japanese horseradish paste, a pungent accompaniment to sushi dishes

watercress * a peppery herb nowadays typically used as a garnish in sandwiches

waxpod * an edible dwarf French bean

wheatmeal * flour from whole wheat grains, with some loss of bran and germ

wineberry * a contender for the earliest word for grape in the English language

winter banana * an apple cultivar recommended for eating fresh in the hand

witherslacks * a Northern dialectal term for damsons

witloof * the Belgian endive, a type of chicory mostly grown as a salad green

xocolatl * chocolate, or "bitter water" in the original Nahuatl; a plant food produced from roasted cocoa beans and spices given to Aztec warriors as a reward for bravery

yatsufusa * a hot speciality chilli pepper native to Japan

ynneleac * an Anglo-Saxon onion; as the name suggests, onions and leeks are alliaceous vegetable cousins

youngberry * a raspberry, blackberry, and dewberry triple-hybrid food fruit

yuca * cassava or manioc root, an edible tuber rich in starch

yuzu * a fragrant Japanese citrus fruit; the rind is a garnish and the juice a seasoning

za'atar * Middle Eastern spice mix

zahidi * a common semi-dry date; it "dates" as a human food crop to 4000 BCE

zedoary * white turmeric, an aromatic culinary root with qualities similar to ginger

zenvy * ground wild mustard seeds used as a food spice in West Country patois

zerumbet * Indian "bitter ginger," a rare traditional spice and flavouring agent

zinziber * an archaic name for ginger

zizypha * a cover term for a range of sweet edible berries or dates, or "jujubes"

zucchini * the courgette as it is known stateside, a popular summer squash

CHAPTER 3

Items and Ingredients from the Animal World

> *"Nothing helps scenery like ham and eggs."*
> **— Mark Twain**

abalone * a species of edible marine snails, enjoyed raw or cooked

acacia * the most popular variety of honey among modern consumers

aileron * in culinary parlance, poultry wings or fish fins used as food

aitchbone * a beef cut lying over the buttock, or rump bone, of cattle

albacore * a commercially important table fish, being the chief source of canned tuna

albondigas * small Spanish or Latin American-style meatballs

alecs * herring; a name also sometimes given to pickled anchovies

amberjacks * a genus of food and game fish found in temperate and tropical waters

andouille * a spicy smoked pork and tripe sausage popular in Cajun cooking

angelot * a soft, rich cheese from Normandy

animelles * a culinary term for testicles, most especially from oxen and sheep, cooked and served as food

anthotyros * a fresh, "flowery" traditional Greek whey cheese

appetitost * a nutty semisoft Danish cheese made from sour buttermilk

asadero * a flavourful semisoft white cheese from Mexico

asetra * a highly prized type of caviar, obtained from the Ossetra sturgeon

asiago * a many-textured Italian cow's milk cheese

aspic * a clear jelly obtained from meat stock used to glaze cold savoury dishes

Australorp * a breed of chicken with a reputation as a copious egg producer

axayacatl * "Mexican caviar," aquatic insect eggs enjoyed since Aztec times

ayren * hen's eggs, as they were known in days of yore

baconer * a pig reared solely to produce bacon

barramundi * the Asian sea bass, a popular item in Thai cuisine

bêche-de-mer * the flesh of the sea-worm, esteemed in the Far East as a delicacy

beefalo * a bovine-bison hybrid; its meat is lower in fat and cholesterol than beef

beestings * the protein-rich super-milk yielded by a cow or goat upon giving birth

beluga * the world's most expensive type of caviar, from the fish of the same name

bierkase * a semisoft "beer cheese" originating in Germany

biltong * "buttock-tongue," strips of lean, cured meat eaten as field rations in the veld

bindenfleisch * an air-dried beef product from Switzerland

blacang * a Malaysian fermented shrimp paste, also known as terasi

bloater * a whole herring soaked in brine before being smoked

blutwurst * German "blood" or black pudding

bockwurst * traditional German sausage made from ground veal

boerewors * South African spicy sausage

boloney * Bologna sausage

bonito * the flesh of a tunny-like food fish—a cheap substitute for skipjack tuna

bonnyclabber * a thickly clotted sour milk, somewhat akin to cottage cheese

botargo * mullet roe pressed to form rolls of fish paste or relish

boudin * French black pudding

boulette * a whiffy Flanders cheese

Boursault * an internationally popular modern French cheese made from cow's milk

Brangus * a hardy trademarked beef cattle cross

branzino * the flesh of the sea bass used as food

bratwurst * German fresh link sausage, usually made from pork

braunschweiger

spicy smoked liverwurst, a sausage meat speciality of Brunswick

brawn * cooked meat from the head of a pig or a calf, pressed and potted in jelly

bresaola * Lombardy air-dried salted beef

Brillat-Savarin * a triple-cream Brie named for one of the great historical gourmets

brisket * one of the nine primal beef cuts, taken from the breast of the animal

brisling * the Norwegian sprat, an abundant and versatile food fish

brynza * a feta-like cheese produced throughout Eastern Europe and Asia Minor

bucheron * a semi-aged goat's cheese from the Loire

buckling * smoked and salted herring, gutted and throated but leaving the roe

bummalow * the "Bombay duck," a lizardfish whose dried flesh is eaten as a relish

burrata * an Italian buffalo milk cheese, essentially a creamed mozzarella

busycon * a genus of edible sea snail; the term originally denoted a large fig

butterine * an artificial butter manufactured from animal fat with milk intermixed

caciocavallo * a semisoft, stretched-curd cheese made historically from mare's milk

calamari * meaning "inkpot," squid considered as a culinary resource

calico * a type of edible scallop harvested in open Atlantic waters

calipash * turtle meat, specifically the gelatinous green upper-shell portion

calipee * turtle meat, specifically the gelatinous yellow lower-shell portion

cambozola * a German blue cheese cross between Camembert and Gorgonzola

capocollo * a traditional rustic Italian-Corsican pork cold cut

capon * a rooster castrated and fattened for the pot

carcass * the bones of a cooked bird used to make stock

Caribbean lobsterette * a genus of Atlantic lobster; also, sardonically, the humble prawn as consumed by the poorer folk of the region

carnitas * "little meats," bites of crisp Mexican pulled pork

caviar * salt-cured edible sturgeon roe; long regarded as the ultimate status food

Cayuga * a North American domesticated utility fowl bred for its eggs and meat

cervelat * the national sausage of Switzerland, a smoked pork and beef product

cervelle * the brain matter of livestock animals, cooked and served as food

chapulines * gourmet edible grasshoppers, a popular Mexican snack food

chateaubriand * a beef cut taken from the thickest part of fillet steak

cheesine * an imitation cheese product manufactured in the nineteenth century

cherrystone * a commercial denominator for an edible clam smaller than the quahog

chevaline * horse meat

chevon * goat meat

chevrotin * a soft goat's milk cheese from Savoy

chicharrón * Mexican fried pork crackling

chicken-fixings * chicken, in part or whole, prepared as food

chine * a joint of meat comprising all or part of the animal's backbone

chipolatas * Italian "little fingers" or pork sausages

chitterlings * pig or hog intestines prepared as food

chorizo * a smoky flavoured, paprika-spiced Iberian pork sausage

churnmilk * as buttermilk in bygone times; nowadays more properly a thin yoghurt

clochette * a textured French goat's milk cheese distinctively shaped like a small bell

cobblecolter * turkey, in the "vulgar tongue" of yesteryear

cockles * small edible shellfish often enjoyed as a seaside snack

codfish * the flesh of the cod or similar marine fish as food

contrefilet * a steak cut, variously sirloin, striploin, or tenderloin

coral * the unfertilized roe of lobster or scallop used as food

cotechino * a large Italian pork sausage

cowheel * a beef offcut; "sole food"

crackling * in cookery, crispy pork rind; popular as either snack or side dish

crappies * edible sunfish, more often caught for home-cooking than fished as such

crawdaddies * freshwater crayfish, or rock lobster; considered a Louisiana delicacy

crème fraîche * a soured cream dairy product, heavier than plain sour cream itself

crespine * forcemeat wrapped in pork or veal caul, or omentum

crevette * shrimps or prawns as a gourmet food item, cooked and served unshelled

crottin * "horse stool," an unpasteurized goat's milk cheese from the Loire

crowdie * an ancient fresh cheese from the Scottish Highlands, eaten with oatcakes

crubeens * Irish pig's trotters, traditionally boiled, battered, and fried

culatello * "little ass," an Italian cured meat similar to prosciutto di Parma

cutlets * thin slices of meat commonly breadcrumbed prior to grilling or frying

dab * an edible flatfish, akin to the flounder, found prolifically in British waters

derma * a food product derived from animal intestines, stuffed with meal and meat

dogdrave * historically, a deep-sea food fish, most likely cod

dorado * the meat of various marine fishes, including the mahi-mahi and orata

dripping * the fatty exudate from roasted meat, occasionally eaten cold as a spread

drisheen * gelatinous Irish blood pudding

drumstick * the meaty lower portion of a chicken's leg

duckling * the flesh of a tender young duck cooked and served as food

Dungeness * a large American crab enjoyed for its sweet and tender meat

ecrevisse * a gastronomical term for edible crustaceans, notably crayfish

eelpout * the burbot or "poor man's lobster," a freshwater codfish

elder * in butchery and cookery, cow's udder in its regard as a "variety meat"

elvers * young eels fried in the manner of whitebait

Emmental * a traditional Swiss unpasteurized hard cheese

emperors * a family of tropical food fish, chief among them the pigface bream

engraulids * anchovies, in all their variety

entrecôte * a premium boned beef cut used for rib steaks

escalopes * thin slices of boneless meat for frying, typically veal

escargot * snail food as customarily denominated on posh menus; "edible snaildom"

eucalyptus * a monofloral honey best eaten raw for fullest health benefits

extrawurst * a parboiled sausage, and most popular of all Austrian cold meat cuts

faggots * traditional British minced pork offal meatballs

falsomagro * Sicilian stuffed meat roll

fatback * chunks of adipose tissue cut from a pig's back as an article of charcuterie

feta * a rather salty and crumbly white Greek cheese made from ewe's or goat's milk

fiambre * Argentinian cold meat cuts

filet mignon * a lean beefsteak cut taken from the narrow end of the tenderloin

fingerling * a small or young fish, especially salmon or trout parr

finnan haddie * Scottish smoked haddock

fisnogge * in Ashkenazi cuisine, a confection or deli cut of calves' feet in aspic

flanksteak * a cheap beefsteak cut from a cow's side muscle; also known as bavette

fleed * internal pig fat as a food resource, before being rendered and melted into lard

flitch * a side of bacon, or occasionally salmon

flounder * a group of non-sole flatfish, at risk of overfishing and overconsumption

foie gras * a luxury meat product made from the liver of fattened domestic fowl

fondue * a sauce or dip of melted cheese

fontina * a mild Italian cheese made from cow's or, originally, ewe's milk

foreshank * the toughest of all beef cuts, also known as shin

frankfurters * slim cured beef and pork sausages, skinless or encased; hotdogs

frikadeller * Danish meatballs

fromage frais * a low-fat, fresh white cheese with the creamy consistency of yoghurt

fumet * reduced and seasoned game or fish stock, used as a flavouring for sauces

galena * an older popular term for salted pork

galotyri * an ancient, naturally fermented "milk cheese" from mainland Greece

gammelost * a smelly Norwegian "old cheese" made from skimmed cow's milk

gammon * the lower portion of a bacon flitch, hind leg included; ham more generally

geoduck * neither duck nor terrestrial animal — rather, a large edible saltwater clam

ghee * Indian clarified butter, a core item in the authentic cuisine of the Subcontinent

giblets * edible fowl offal, including the gullet and guts as well as the major organs

gigot * a leg of mutton or lamb for cooking

gizzards * the stomach parts, notably the gastric mill, of a bird used as food

glair * egg white; "gleyres of ayrenn" is the term found in medieval cookery books

goldenrod * a full-bodied honey made from the nectar of the solidago plant genus

Gorgonzola * a blue-veined Italian cheese, one of the oldest of its type in the world

gosling * the flesh of a tender young goose cooked and served as food

goujons * strips of processed fish or chicken

graviera * a common Greek cheese, second in domestic popularity only to feta

gravlax * Scandinavian cured salmon, typically served sliced as an appetizer

griskin * a lean cut or portion of pork loin

grunion * a small fish species found in Californian waters, best grilled like sardines

gubbins * edible fish scraps or offal

gurnard * an edible fish option; until recently, used more often as bait than table fare

haddock * the flesh of the eponymous, commercially-important, northern food fish

haggis * a Scots savoury meat product made from the pluck and purtenance of sheep

haimation * an antique culinary sauce prepared from animal blood

hákarl * Icelandic fermented shark meat; as pungent to taste as it is putrid to smell

halibut * "holy fish," formerly any flatfish partaken on Christian feast days

halloumi * a traditional firm white Cypriot cheese, useful for frying or grilling

hartshorn * gourmet deer antler shavings

haslet * a meatloaf of cooked hog testicles or entrails, traditionally wrapped in caul

hastelings * the major organs—heart, liver and lungs—of a pig, as used for roasting

Havarti * a porous semisoft Danish table cheese

headcheese * a somewhat euphemistically named jellied meat product

hindsaddle * a wholesale cut of mutton or lamb, including loin, leg, and rump

hogget * the flesh of a juvenile sheep used for food

honeycomb * tripe from the second stomach of a ruminant, such as a cow

honey-rore * honeydew or nectar; a sweet substance secreted by aphids, inter alia, of both medicinal and mythological repute as a wholesome source of nutrition

hough * a widespread dialectal variant of hock, being a knuckle of ham or pork

hypenemy * a "wind-egg," one in some way addled or rotten

ikary * caviar; unfertilized fish eggs salted and prepared as a luxury food item

inchpin * select deer organ meats or "sweetbreads"

ireness-bag * curdled milk from the stomach of a calf, used in cheesemaking

isinglass * a form of gelatin obtained from fish bladders, used to make fruit jellies

jabugo * the signature ham of Huelva, and best-known variety of *jamón ibérico*

jambonneau * a deboned chicken leg filled with forcemeat to resemble a mini ham

Jarlsberg * a hard, yellow Norwegian cheese of global market reach and renown

jerky * jerked meat; typically lean beef cut into strips and cured in the hot open air

jibbings * the last strainings of Scottish milk

John Dory * a widely distributed and popular white-fleshed table fish

kabanos * Polish smoked pork sausage

kasseri * a rather rubbery Greek-Turkish cheese, though ideal for melting

katsuobushi * blocks or flakes of Japanese tunny, dried, fermented, and smoked

kebbuck * a Scottish cheese wheel

keema * Indian minced meat

kefalotyri * a salty, white Greek-Cypriot cheese, especially suited for grating

keftedes * Greek-style meatballs

khorovats * Armenian barbecued meat, or shish kebabs; a national dish

kielbasa * Polish ground pork sausage

kippers * smoked herrings

klipfish * a codfish, split, salted, and sun-dried

knackwurst * a highly seasoned, shorter, and plumper version of the frankfurter

köttbullar * Swedish-style meatballs

krautfurter * a frankfurter dressed or drilled with sauerkraut

kumminost * Swedish "cumin cheese"

labneh * a Middle Eastern soft cream cheese made from strained yoghurt

lachsschinken * smoked and rolled double pork loin; a German butchery product

lactoline * an early, though now long vanished, evaporated milk product

ladotyri * a Lesbos cheese preserved in extra-virgin olive oil, made since antiquity

laitance * a culinary term for soft roe, ripe fish sperm or testes served as a delicacy

langoustines * Dublin Bay prawns, prepared and cooked as an item on a menu

lardoon * a sliver of bacon inserted into another meat in the process of larding

lavignon * an edible French mollusc

leghorn * a Mediterranean chicken renowned for its egg production capacity

lights * the lungs of game or livestock animals used as food

Limburger * a surface-ripened Belgian cheese, notorious for its pungent odour

Liptauer * a spread of Hungarian soft cheese seasoned with paprika

littleneck * a young quahog clam, quite edible raw

Livarot * an appellation-controlled ripened soft cheese from Normandy

livermush * a coarse pâté of pig liver and head parts from North Carolina

lomo * Spanish beef tenderloin

longhorn * a Texas beef cattle breed; alternatively, a variety of American cheddar

loukaniko * Greek pork sausage

lox * Jewish smoked salmon

luderick * a herbivorous Australian food fish, also known as the black bream

lutefisk * Nordic dried whitefish softened in lye prior to boiling and serving

mahi-mahi * the flesh of the common dolphinfish; loosely, dolphin meat

mako * the flesh of the shortfin mackerel shark; loosely, shark meat

mananosay * an edible soft-shelled clam

manchego * cheese of La Mancha

manuka * a monofloral honey with many alleged health benefits for consumers

manzo * beef, in gastronomic parlance

margarine * a substitute butter spread prepared from vegetable oils and animal fats

marsoline * historically, a Florentine cheese esteemed the best in all Italy in its day

mascarpone * a mild and easy-to-spread Italian cream cheese

mashonzha * gourmet edible caterpillars widely enjoyed across southern Africa

matambre * an Argentinian speciality beef cut, thinner than the American flanksteak

matjesherring * young herring, salted and soused

medallions * small, flat, usually round cuts or servings of either meat or fish

megapodes * Australasian scrubfowl; their eggs and meat serve human consumers

merguez * a heavily spiced Maghrebi sausage made with beef or mutton

merrythought * the wishbone of a chicken

micklewame * in cookery and butchery, the stomach or "big belly" of an ox

milkfat * the natural fatty portion of milk from which butter is chiefly made

milt * the seminal fluid and ripe testes of a male fish, prepared as a culinary resource

miltz * in Jewish cuisine, animal spleen prepared as an item of food

Mimolette * a French cheese notable for being intentionally exposed to mites

monkfish * the angel shark as food; only the meaty white tail flesh is edible

Monterey Jack * a Californian cow's milk cheese, widely used in Mexican cuisine

morcilla * Spanish black pudding

moretum * a herb cheese spread eaten in classical Roman times with bread

mort * pig fat, or lard; rendered and clarified, it is a useful cooking product

mortadella * authentic Bologna sausage

morwong * an Australian perch-like marine fish, commercially harvested for food

moscardino * baby white octopus, commonly used as food in Italian cuisine

mozzarella * a traditional Italian buffalo milk cheese, often used in pizzas

muktuk * frozen whale skin and blubber—a staple of Inuit cuisine

mullet * any of various small sea fish widely cooked and eaten

mulloway * a well-regarded Antipodean table fish

mussels * edible bivalve molluscs; they can be cooked first or eaten from their shells

mutton * the flesh of mature domestic sheep eaten as food; also, in India, goat meat

mysost * a Norwegian whey cheese product, originally made from goat's milk

myzithra * a Cretan ricotta-style unpasteurized cheese

nerka * sockeye salmon

Neufchâtel * an ancient French soft cow's milk cheese, similar to cream cheese

noisette * a small, usually round, portion of lamb loin or beef cut from the rib

nostrano * an appellation accorded to any homemade Italian cheese

onglet * a prime French beef cut, or hanger steak

Orloff * a long-established chicken breed primarily suited to meat production

ortolan * the flesh of a small songbird once prized as a delicacy, but now protected

oxtail * a beef cut taken from the beast's tail, used for making stew or meat soup

oxygala * literally "sour milk," the original, classical-era Greek yoghurt

paillard * a boneless portion of meat pounded thin before rapid grilling at high heat

pancetta * Italian cured pork belly

paneer * Indian milk curd cheese

pastrami * spicy, smoked brisket of beef, thinly sliced and eaten cold

pâté * a cold savoury meat paste prepared from offal, notably liver, or fish flesh

pecorino * a family of traditional Italian ewe's milk cheeses

pemmican * a highly concentrated and calorific dried bison meat product, traditionally carried by Native Americans as iron rations

pepperette * a spicy mixed meat product resembling sausage that may be eaten cold

pepperoni * strongly peppered Italian salami

percoid * any edible fish of a group including the perch, bass, snapper, and bream

pettitoes * pig's trotters as an article of food

pickerel * in cookery, the meat of a young pike

picorocos * edible giant barnacles, as featured in Chilean cuisine

piddocks * gourmet edible molluscs, also known as angelwings or rock oysters

pilchards * small, oily, shoaling food fish; essentially sardines, but older and larger

pinjane * Manx curds and whey, or cottage cheese

pismo * a large North American coastal clam exploited extensively for food

pluck * the major internal organs—heart, liver and lungs—of an animal as food

pollock * a commercially significant North Atlantic food fish of the cod family

polpettone * Italian meatloaf

pomfret * a family of open seas fishes, valued as a food resource

pompano * a common name given to a number of food fishes and edible clams

porterhouse * a large, choice beefsteak cut taken from the short loin, or sirloin

Port-Salut * a mild whole-milk cheese, originally produced by Trappist monks

poussin * a chicken specially raised for eating at around six weeks

prosciutto * a generic term in Italian cuisine for dry-cured salted ham, sliced thin

provolone * a mild cheese from southern Italy, moulded in the shape of a pear

pufferfish * a.k.a. fugu; a fish whose prized flesh can prove fatally toxic for some

pullet * in cookery, the flesh of a young hen

pulpo * octopus meat or octopus as an item appearing on a menu

qaymaq * Afghani clotted or sour cream

quail * the flesh of any of several genera of galliform game birds, cooked and eaten

quark * a fresh German soft cheese product made with skimmed milk but no rennet

quarter-pounder * any standard hamburger weighing four ounces prior to cooking

rabbitfish * a commercially significant marine food fish

reblochon * a variety of soft cow's milk cheese from Savoy

rib-eye * a large cut of tender beefsteak taken from the outer side of the rib

riblets * processed strips of boneless rib-end meat

ricotta * a soft white unsalted and unripened Italian cheese; often used as a filling

rillettes * a highly seasoned potted meat product; prepared in a similar way to pâté

roaster * any animal suitable for roasting, especially chicken

rollmops * uncooked herring fillets pickled in brine

Romadur * a smear-ripened German cheese somewhat similar to Limburger

Roquefort * a strong French ewe's milk blue cheese, matured in limestone caves

rouget * a cookery term for the red mullet, considered as a table fish

salami * spiced and salted sausage meat served in slices and eaten cold

salpicon * French forcemeat; in particular, a chopped meat stuffing for legs of veal

saltfish * dried and salted cod; a hugely popular item in Caribbean cooking

salumi * Italian cured meat appetizer bites; salami is hence a kind of salumi

sapsago * an ancient Swiss hard cheese flavoured with clover or fenugreek

satay * Malaysian skewered meat bites, served with a signature peanut sauce

saucisson * a large garlicky sausage of ground pork

saveloy * a smoked pork sausage, highly seasoned and coloured red with saltpetre

scallops * edible saltwater molluscs; a highly popular article of seafood

scaloppini * veal cutlets, served coated with flour and sautéed in a reduction

scamorza * an unfermented Italian "beheaded" cheese, shaped like a small gourd

scampi * in cookery, Norwegian lobsters prepared and served as food; a.k.a. langoustines

schlagobers * German whipped cream

schmaltz * rendered and clarified poultry fat, useful as a frying medium

schnitzel * a fillet of seasoned and garnished veal

scratchings * crisp, cooked scraps of pork fat, eaten as a snack

scrod * any young whitefish prepared as food

scungille * mollusc or conch meat, regarded as a gastronomic delight

serate * sour milk; a term from Norman times

sevruga * "stellar sturgeon," noted for the pricey, grey caviar processed from its roe

sewin * Welsh sea trout harvested as food

shad * a food fish, part of the wider herring family

shashlik * Georgian mutton kebab

shawarma * an Arabic take on the Turkish doner kebab, a processed meat product

sheftalia * Cypriot crépinettes, or skinless sausages

shimesaba * Japanese pickled mackerel

shirako * the sperm sacs of the male cod, served both raw and cooked across Japan

shortplate * a cut taken from the belly of a cow, arguably the best cut of beef ribs

shottsuru * a pungent, salty Japanese paste of fermented sandfish

siffleur * marmot meat

silverside * a hindquarter beefsteak cut, usually prepared as a roasting joint

sinarapan * a species of freshwater goby, notable as the world's smallest commercial food fish

sirloin * a quality beefsteak cut taken from the loin, just in front of the rump

siskebap * lamb spiced, spitted, and sliced; better known to diners as shish kebab

skipjack * a major species of tuna, accounting for most of the tinned meat sold

skyr * an Icelandic cultured dairy product with qualities of both cheese and yoghurt

slipcote * an organic ewe's milk cheese from Sussex

smearcase * sour cottage cheese, easily spread or eaten with a spoon

smetana * traditional Eastern European sour cream

smokies * Scottish smoked haddock

sobrasada * Balearic pork sausage

sockeye * a commercially important salmon species, popular with consumers

soft roe * the semen and reproductive organs of a male fish, used as items of food

souse * pig's ears or trotters, pickled and prepared as a culinary treat

souvlaki * Greek kebab meat, served in bite-sized chunks on a skewer

sowbelly * salted pork or bacon from the belly of a hog

spalderling * any fish split, cured, and dried for eating

spam * a tinned meat product made with spiced ham

spareribs * ubiquitous cooked pork ribs

spermyse * a soft summer cheese not made since the Middle Ages

squab * the meat of fledgling pigeons or doves

squeakers * freshly made cheddar cheese curds, or "squeaky cheese"

squeteague * the weakfish, a marine food fish native to North American waters

Stilton * a mouldy, wrinkly, rinded, and notoriously pongy Leicestershire cheese

stockfish * unsalted cod allowed to dry by the action of cold air and wind

stracchino * an Italian soft cheese, eaten on its own or used as a bread filling

suet * hard white internal beef or mutton fat, used to make puddings and so forth

suine * an old butter substitute, made from an admixture of oleomargarine and lard

surimi * a bland fish paste from processed pollock, used to make surrogate crabmeat

surströmming * fermented Baltic herring; a contender for the world's smelliest food

sweetbreads * in cookery, the pancreas and thymus glands of animals used as food

swine-grease * pig fat or lard

taleggio * a square semisoft Lombardy cheese made from whole cow's milk

tasso * speciality Cajun spiced smoked ham

tawari * a mild-tasting gourmet honey from New Zealand

tenderloin * fillet steak, a premium beef hindquarter cut

tendron * in culinary idiom, the rib cartilage of deer or cattle prepared for the table

thrutchings * a vivid dialectal term for the last pressings of curdled milk, or whey

thuringer * a speciality German smoked summer sausage

thymus * in cookery, the gullet sweetbread; an organ meat of either calf or lamb

tilapia * an African freshwater fish, now raised for food in many parts of the world

Tillamook * an Oregonian cheddar variety

Tilsiter * a mild to sharp, semisoft porous cheese originally produced in Prussia

tomalley * the gooey digestive gland of the lobster prepared as a gourmet paste

topside * a British beef joint cut from the upper portion of the leg

toro * the fatty belly meat of the tunafish, widely used in sushi and sashimi bites

torrentine * a long-lost name for the common trout

torsk * a variety of edible whitefish, also known as codling

tournedos * a thick round beefsteak cut taken from the tenderloin

trevally * a large edible fish of the jack family

tri-tip * an inferior triangular muscle cut of beef taken from the bottom sirloin

tunny * tuna meat

tupelo * a high-grade, uniquely non-crystallizing honey suitable for diabetics

turbot * a commonly eaten European flatfish; flounder flesh

tushonka * Soviet-era bully beef or tinned meat; a regular Red Army field ration

tvorog * soft Russian cottage or curd cheese

twizzler * a turkey-based formed meat product, now withdrawn from the market

Tybo * a mild Danish cow's milk cheese, frequently flavoured with caraway seeds

umbles * the edible innards of a deer; whence "humble pie"

vacherin * a family of soft Franco-Swiss cow's milk cheeses

veal * calf meat

veggieburger * a surrogate burger made from vegetable protein instead of ham

vendace * the UK's rarest freshwater fish, edible though classified as "endangered"

verivorst * Estonian "black pudding," a traditional Christmas pig's blood sausage

volute * an edible deep-water sea snail

wahoo * a large gourmet relative of the mackerel

walleye * a North American freshwater pike, valued as a food fish

wallfish * a British edible snail

weisswurst * traditional mildly spiced Bavarian veal sausage

Wensleydale * a flaky Yorkshire white cheese now in widespread production

wesson * a beast's windpipe or gullet considered as a culinary resource

whelks * large, edible sea snails found abundantly in UK and Irish coastal waters

whiting * any commercially valuable cod-like marine fish with delicate white flesh

wienerwurst * literally "Vienna sausage," a product akin to the frankfurter

witchetty * edible Australian grubs with high-protein flesh; an old Aboriginal staple

wolffish * any of a family of carnivorous food fishes found in North Atlantic waters

wombclout * tripe or omentum; the stomach matter of a ruminant cooked for food

wrasse * a family of percoid marine fishes, a good number being valued as table fare

wyandotte * an American domestic fowl breed raised for both its meat and eggs

yakitori * Japanese "grilled fowl," or skewered chicken kebabs

Yarg * a modern Cornish nettle-wrapped cheese

yoghurt * a popular dairy product prepared from milk fermented by bacterial action

zampone * spicy Italian pork sausage meat stuffed inside the skin of a pig's trotters

zander * a European freshwater pikeperch, valued as a food fish

CHAPTER 4

Fishing, Farming, and Food Production

> *"If you tickle the earth with a hoe, she laughs with a harvest."*
> —**Douglas William Jerrold**

abattoir * a facility where farm animals are sent to be slaughtered for food

acclimatization * a vogue among affluent Westerners in the later 1800s for importing, cultivating, and breeding exotic plant and animal species for human consumption

aeroponics * the practice of growing plants in a soil-free air environment; nutrients are delivered in solution in the form of a fine spray

affinage * the process of maturing cheese in a climate-controlled closet or cellar

agribiz * the commercial production and distribution of field crops and farm products

agricolation * the husbandry of the fields—that is, the practice of agriculture

agriculturalist * a hifalutin term for a humble farmer

agrihood * an urban green space where residents can grow food or raise animals

agrology * the application of science and technology to agriculture

agromotor * a motorized farm machine, such as a tractor or combine harvester

agronomy * the study of land productivity with special reference to crop output

algaculture * the farming of algae such as giant kelp, either directly for food or for nutritional supplements such as omega-3 fatty acids

alveary * an apiary, apifactory, or beehive; a repository for harvested honey

animaliculture * stock-raising; the rearing of animals for the table

anthroponics * a method of growing plants in nutrient solution rather than soil, using filtered and dissolved human waste as the fertilizing agent

apiculture * commercial beekeeping for the production of honey

aporkalypse * jocularly, dread at the prospect of a global dearth of bacon

aquaculture * the husbandry of marine life including fish, crustaceans, molluscs, snails, and prawns for the food trade

aquafarm * a managed body of water wherein aquatic flora and fauna are reared for consumption

aquaponics * a symbiotic animal/plant food production system wherein wastewater byproducts from farmed fish break down into nitrate nutrients fed to crop plants

arable * land suitable for growing food crops, or the crops themselves so produced

arbustum * a plot of land set aside for the cultivation of fruit or nut trees; an orchard

aucupation * the practice of "fowling" or snaring wild birds, including for the table

biofortification * the strengthening of food crops to increase their nutritional value

boar-frank * a fattening pen for pigs

boviculture * the domestication of cows for either meat or milk

breadbasket * a region with a reputation for growing wheat and grain in abundance

broilerhouse * a building where chickens are raised for slaughter and the plate

cannery * a manufactory where processed food is packaged into cans or tins

caprification * an artificial fruit-ripening process aiding the pollination of edible figs

caseiculture * the making or manufacturing of cheese

cheesery * a commercial enterprise or establishment where cheese is produced

chinampa * a Mesoamerican "floating garden" used to produce various food crops

citriculture * the cultivation of citrus fruits, chiefly oranges, lemons, and limes

condensery * a facility dedicated to the preparation of condensed milk

confectory * an abattoir or slaughterhouse

crop-dusting * the aerial spraying of large agricultural acreages with pesticides

cultivage * agriculture; the production of food by preparing land to grow crops

cuniculture * the breeding and rearing of rabbits as livestock, including for the pot

deesing-room * a place where newly landed herrings are dried out and dressed

delvage * the ploughing or harrowing of land in preparation for sowing food crops

deyhouse * a dairy

dude-hamfatter * a wealthy pig-jobber, or livestock merchant trading in baconers

ecofarming * broadly, sustainable agriculture operating on organic principles

electrofishing * a method of stunning and harvesting fish by application of weak electrical currents to the marine environment

enrober * a contraption for coating foodstuffs with chocolate on a production line

entoleter * a sorting machine used to separate insects and their eggs from grain

escargatoire * a snail nursery, where the gastropod delicacies are reared for the pot

estantion * a cattle farm, especially one found in Mexico or Central America

eventilation * in farming, the act of vanning or winnowing — exposing cereals to draughts of air to remove the inedible chaff

farination * the process of milling or grinding grain to produce flour

farmageddon * apocalyptic paranoia about the development of GM food crops

farmerage * farmers, considered collectively as a body with common interests

farmership * the business or occupation of a farmer

farmery * agriculture

farmhold * an archaic term signifying land for cultivation

farmtoun * a Scottish farmhouse with its outbuildings; a farmstead

fat-ware * cattle or other livestock fatted for the food market

feedlot * a confined space within which beef cattle are fattened up prior to slaughter

fertigation * a term combining fertilization and irrigation, whereby water and nutrients are put to work together in the field to boost crop production

fertilage * the act of fertilizing and so enriching agricultural soils

fisherfolk * poetically, people or a community who catch fish for a living

fishgarth * a seashore or riverine enclosure for garnering and taking fish

flake-yard * a space put aside for variously drying, curing, or smoking fish

fogponics * a specialized form of aeroponic food production utilizing vapour to deliver nutrients and oxygen to enclosed suspended plant roots

foison * a bountiful crop or harvest

foodscaping * the transformation of lawns into kitchen gardens for city dwellers

foodshed * the local geographical area where metropolitan food stocks are produced

foraging-expedition * a quest to scavenge food from the land

frigorifico * a South American packing and freezing plant for meat exports

fructuation * the process of producing fruit; also, the end product—a fruit crop

fruticulture * pomology; the production and marketing of stone fruits

fungiculture * the cultivation of mushrooms and other fungi for food or medicine

galaxy * a collective noun for milkmaids

geopony * the practice of growing crops in earth, or similar solid rooting medium

georgics * the work of agriculture, notably the physical labour of tilling the land

gleaning * the practice of collecting leftover crops and food scraps following harvest

grainage * a grain crop or harvest

guttery * an establishment for gutting and processing freshly caught fish

haaf * a deep-sea fishing ground or station in northern waters

halieutics * the art and activity of fishing; the work of fishermen

harrowing * the practice of scraping ploughed land to loosen the soil and cover seed

harvestry * the action of reaping, or gathering crops; also, the crops so gathered

herbary * a kitchen garden growing pot herbs or vegetables

hoggery * a piggery; a place where hogs are housed and bred as livestock

horticulture * the cultivation of plants, including vegetables

hortyard * a plantation of fruit trees, or orchard

hummelling * the action of thrashing barley, rye, or oats to remove bristles or beards

husbandry * in farming, the care, cultivation, and raising of both crops and animals

hydroculture * the cultivation of crops in an inert porous medium, without any soil; synthetic fertilizer in a water solvent is transported to the roots by capillary action

hydroponicum * a farm or facility where plants are grown on a supporting bed of clay pebbles or gravel, with their roots drawing on dissolved mineral nutrients

increment * sustenance from the soil, hence crops — vegetable products in particular

kailyard * a Scottish kitchen garden or plot for growing herbs, vegetables, or fruit

lactarium * a dairy farm or commercial milking operation

laetation * the action of manuring or fertilizing soil to enhance crop yields

livestock * domesticated animals, especially ruminants such as cattle, raised for food

lobster-hatchery * a place used to rear lobsters and boost stocks by artificial methods

magnetoculture * the hypothesized channelling of earth energies to enhance soil fertility, stimulating plant growth and increasing crop yield

manurance * the enrichment of arable land using either animal waste or fertilizer

mariculture * the open-ocean cultivation of marine organisms for food

market-gardening * small-scale agricultural production, notably of cash crops

meatpacking * the business of processing and packaging meat for the retail market; the wholesale meat trade, in short

mellation * the activity of gathering honey from beehives

melliturgy * the work of keeping honeybees and producing honey

melonist * a melon grower

micro-farm * a market garden, where produce is grown and sold direct to the public

microponics * the hybrid integration of fish, other marine life, plants, and microlivestock in a partially controlled food production environment

milkmadge * a dairymaid

millerator * a double-sieved grain sifter and wheat-cleaning machine

minilivestock * insects and edible arthropods cultivated for human food

monocropping * the practice of perennially growing a single crop species on the same plot of land without rotation or variation

monoculture * in farming, the raising of one crop or rearing of one stock only

muckspreading * the action of distributing manure over fields to fertilize the soil

nessotrophium * a yard where ducks are reared and fattened for market

nutriculture * hydroponics—the growing of plants in special nutrient solutions

nuttery * a plot of land put aside for growing trees that bear nuts; a nut orchard

occation * the harrowing of ploughed land ahead of sowing crops

oleiculture * the production, processing, and marketing of olives

olericulture * the science and practice of growing leafy vegetables or herbs for food

oligoculture * the raising or rearing of a restricted variety of crops or animal stocks

olivet * an enclosed grove dedicated to growing olives

orangery * a hothouse purposed for growing oranges in a cool climate

orcharding * the cultivation of fruit trees in plantations or walled gardens

organoponics * a system of urban agriculture using organically sustained gardens

ormering * the practice of fishing for ormer, an edible sea snail and prized delicacy

ostreiculture * the breeding and harvesting of oysters for the food market

oysterage * a commercial oyster bed

paddy * a field reserved for growing rice

pascuage * the grazing or pasturing of livestock, especially cattle

pastination * the digging of virgin soil preparatory to planting and cultivating crops

pastoralism * the practice of rearing grazing livestock like sheep, cows, and so forth

peachery * a peach grove or garden

peasecod-time * the agricultural season for gathering peas

pecudiculture * the farming of cattle or similar ruminants

periwinkling * fishing for periwinkles, a species of edible whelk

permaculture * the practice and principles of sustainable agriculture

pining-lair * a "hunger-house," or pen where cattle are kept prior to their slaughter

piscatology * the practical study and applied science of commercial fishing

piscicapturist * a fisherman; one who takes fish in the open sea

pisciculturist

a fish-farmer; one who breeds, hatches, and harvests fish in pens

plansifter * a powered flour-mill riddle which oscillates to separate and grade grain

plantage * a farm or estate dedicated to the purposes of agricultural production

polyculture * the farming of multiple crops or livestock breeds simultaneously

polytunnel * a protective plastic structure acting as an extended greenhouse for growing fruits and vegetables outdoors in often inclement weather conditions

pomary * an orchard or fruit garden

pomiculture * the horticultural science and practical activity of growing fruit

pomology * the art and science of cultivating fruit, with special reference to apples

porculation * the feeding or fattening of swine for the pot or the meat market

porkopolis * historically, any city such as Cincinnati or Chicago noted for being a major pork-packing centre

poultrycide * humorously, the slaughtering of domestic fowl for market or table

praedial * pertaining to the cultivation of land

primices * the first fruits or produce of the harvest

purse-seining * a method of fishing for tuna using a purse seine or wall of netting

quahogging * the action of fishing or digging for edible clams

riviation * trawling for fish or hunting for waterfowl on an inland watercourse

rotavation * the mechanical action of tilling soil or breaking up land for cultivation

rotolactor * a machine for mass-milking cows using a special rotating platform

saginary * a compound where livestock may be specially fattened for market

saladero * an abattoir where the meat is further dried or salted before dispatch

salmonization * the introduction of salmon to a fish farm or river

saltery * a salt-works; also, a factory where fish are salted ahead of storage

sarrition * the hoeing or harrowing of fields for agricultural development

sature * the planting or sowing of crop seeds

scaphage * the act of digging to prepare soil for sowing seeds, herbs, plants, or trees

scarificator * a device for loosening soil or breaking land for cultivation

scrumping * the practice of stealing fruit, especially apples, from an orchard

sea-fishery * the action, occupation, or business of fishing at sea

semence * the act of sowing seeds or crops

shechita * the ritual slaughter of cattle and poultry according to Jewish dietary law

skeo * a stone shed used in the Orkney and Shetland isles for drying fish or meat

slaughter stock * domesticated animals set aside to be slaughtered for food

slaughterage * the full business involved in killing and processing animals for food

smokery * a house or other establishment for the curing of meat or fish

sodbuster * colloquially, either farmer or farmhand—food growers both

spaliard * a lattice or frame for training fruit trees

spice-isle * an island where spices abound and are exported in great quantity

starve-acre * a tract of agricultural land producing a meagre yield of food

stercoration * the action of spreading manure on fields as fertilizer for crops

stockbreeding * the raising of animals domesticated to serve as primary food sources or secondary food producers

swidden * forest land cleared for agricultural production by way of slash-and-burn

sybotism * the rearing and herding of pigs as livestock; the activity of a swineherd

tank-farming * hydroponics; the soilless cultivation of crop plants in an aquatic environment enriched with mineral nutrient solutions

terraculture * a rarely used synonym for agriculture

thremmatology * the controlled breeding of animals, such as by means of artificial insemination, to improve livestock quality and numbers as food demand rises

tilth * agricultural work or field labour ahead of sowing and growing crops

tonnara * a special fishing ground where bluefin tuna may be snared en masse

trapiche * a sugar-cane plantation; alternatively, a mill for extracting olive juice

trepanging * the harvesting of sea-cucumbers, considered a delicacy in the Far East

trufflery * a cultivated mushroom or truffle ground

vaccarage * a near-archaic term for a dairy farm

vaccimulgence * the action of milking cows

vanchase * the hunting of wild animals for sport or the pot

vegeculture * the cultivation of root vegetables, such as carrots, yams, and beets

vertilage * the action of digging, tilling, or otherwise preparing agricultural ground

vindemy * the harvesting of fruit; rarely, the gathering of honey from a beehive

viticulture * the practical science of growing grapevines and harvesting the grape

vivier * a fish farm or other controlled reservoir devoted to aquacultural production

votator * a machine used to process margarine and condition it prior to packaging

weequashing * the art and practice of spearing fish or eels from canoe by torchlight

wheat-belt * a bountiful wheat-growing region, reliably producing surplus grain

whorting * the action of picking edible berries

wildcrafting * the harvesting of herbs from their natural or wild habitat

yabbying * fishing for prawns, shrimp, or crayfish

zero-grazing * fattening penned cattle on cut fodder rather than grass out in pasture

zootechnics * the art and science of animal husbandry, or breeding and improving stock

Dainty Dishes
and Choice
Cuisine

CHAPTER 5

A Cornucopia of Culinary Delights from the English-Speaking World

> *"A cheerful look makes a dish a feast."*
> — **George Herbert**

abyrtaca * an old salad said to comprise chiefly leeks and cress in a sour sauce

ackempucky * any gelatinous hillbilly hash of mixed mystery ingredients

alamagoozlum * a nineteenth century maple syrup recipe from New York state

alderman * a bygone dish of roast turkey "hung" with link sausage chains

alker * a pudding featuring fruit pieces set in a base of rice flour and almond milk

allemain * historically, a huge sculptured pudding concealing jugglers or acrobats

allsorts * a type of confectionery comprising assorted liquorice flavoured dainties

alows * spit-roasted steaks of meat, cooked with complementary herbs and spices

alphabetti spaghetti * novelty letter-shaped pasta pieces served in a spaghetti sauce

ammy-dammy * a colonial-era New England bread of cornmeal, flour, and molasses

angels on horseback * a hot savoury bite of shucked oysters baked in a bacon wrap

Anzac tile * army biscuit, as distributed to Empire forces at Gallipoli

apetito * an old dish of chopped goose offal and offcuts fried with eggs

applemoyse * a traditional stewed dessert of sweet apple pudding and almond milk

aquapatys * garlic boiled in oil and served sprinkled with saffron, salt, and spices

bacon floddies * Northumberland breakfast patties of potato, onion, and bacon

balourgly * a lost medieval fish stew

bannock * a round flat loaf of unleavened bread, found in Scotland and the North

barapicklet * historically, a dark Welsh "pitchy bread" made of fine flour yeast-raised

barmbrack * a soft spiced Irish fruit cake or loaf

Bartlemas beef * a spiced beef dish prepared to celebrate the feast of Saint Bartholomew

Bath chap * a regional speciality of pickled pig's cheek chops coated in breadcrumbs

battenberg * a light sponge cake revealing a chequerboard motif when sliced

bennets * an old dessert dish of battered eggs fried in clarified butter then sugared

Bermuda witches * thin slices of sponge cake sandwiched with jam and coconut

blackeyed Susan * a plum or raisin pudding, split and filled with butter and sugar

blancmange * "white food," originally, a mild chicken dish with rice boiled in milk

blaundsore * a medieval meal of eels; else, a white broth dish served at Christmas

blobsterdis * a mystery food from the Middle Ages; the wonderful name alone survives

bonbons * small sugary confections, generically

boudoir biscuits * sponge fingers — sweet dry biscuits of the dimensions of a digit

bourreys * in medieval cookery, small pastry pouches filled with hot sauce

bow-wow mutton * dog flesh in naval slang, as in a meal-ration of the foulest meat

boxty * traditional Irish potato pancakes

brains & bacon * a sauce of calves' brains in bacon caul, baked in a dish with sherry

brandysnaps * brittle confectionery snacks, or caramelized biscuits

brasey * an old pouring sauce for fish consisting of wine, stock, ginger, and sugar

brewet * an earlier meat soup or broth, thickened with a variety of ingredients

Bronx vanilla * American diner slang for garlic

Brown Betty * a dessert close to a cobbler, made from apples and a sweet crumb mix

bryndons * anciently, small cake treats served in a sauce of wine, fruit, and nuts

bubble & squeak * a dish formerly made with cold meat and cabbage fried in butter

bukkenade * a sweetly seasoned medieval meat stew with the addition of egg yolks

bummer's custard * in reality, a style of cheese sandwich from a century or so ago

Burlington whimsey * a dish of brawn set in a mould with appropriate spices

bursews * formerly, gobbets of minced pork and eggs, rolled in flour and fried

busbayne * a chicken nugget and pork meatball stew made with fruits and spices

butterscotch * a popular toffee-like confectionery made from brown sugar

by-dish * any dish of marked complexity, requiring extra skill on the part of the cook

cabobs * a dated linguistico-culinary take on "kebabs," being bites of skewered meat

Caesar salad * a classic modern salad of cos and croutons with a special dressing

camelyn * a bread sauce for quail dishes, featuring cinnamon, ginger, and mustard

candyfloss * a popular carnival treat of spun sugar, also known as cotton candy

cecils * early English fried meatballs or patties of seasoned beef

chardequynce * quince pulp prepared in sweet paste, purée, or preserve form

charlet * an old savoury custard of milk and eggs with cooked pork and seasoning

chawdron * a sauce of chopped entrails or other organ meats soused in vinegar

chewitts * miniature pies, as known in traditional English cookery

chireseye * a pudding of puréed cherries, breadcrumbed and garnished with cloves

chocolate nemesis * a variant "death by" chocolate cake made without flour

chow miaow * cooked meat of dubious quality or provenance, in Antipodean wit

chowder * a North American fish soup, notably one prepared with fresh clams

chudleigh * a small round Devon cake typically eaten with clotted cream or jam

chutney * a pungent sweet and sour relish made of fruits, vinegar, spices, and sugar

civey * a historical sauce or broth made from hog entrails

clams casino * a New England appetizer of clams with breadcrumbs and bacon

clapshot * tatties and neeps mash, the classic savoury accompaniment to haggis

clootie dumpling * Scottish suet pudding, customarily consumed at Hogmanay

coaxyorum * a cake baked by a mother-in-law to-be for her daughter's intended

cockagrice * a dish once made of an old cockerel and a piglet spit-roasted together

cock-a-leekie * Scottish chicken and leek soup

colcannon * an Irish favourite of potatoes and green vegetables creamed together

coleslaw * cabbage salad

collops * a plate of bacon and eggs of yore

corat * offal stewed in verjuice; a long-neglected dish, perhaps unsurprisingly so

crabcake * shredded crabmeat cooked with breadcrumbs, mayo, and pickled eggs

cranachan * cream crowdie; a traditional Scottish summer harvest dessert

crappit heid * a boiled fish head stuffed with oats, suet, and the fish's own liver

craytoun * a former well-seasoned pottage in which game or fowl was boiled

croutons * "little crusts" of hard cubed bread, for use with salads, soups, and stews

cruller * a small curled fried pastry, popular throughout North America

cryspels * medieval fritters

cullen skink * a thick Scottish soup featuring smoked haddock, potatoes, and onions

cullis * a savoury sauce or gravy; alternatively, a meat broth or beef-tea for invalids

Cupid hedgehogs * almond candies of the eighteenth century, often set in a dessert

dagwood * a multi-layered sandwich filled with multiple meats, cheeses, and relishes

dandyfunk * a dessert at sea of powdered ship biscuit baked in grease and molasses

desdemona * a bygone Australian tartlet filled with white vanilla custard

diacydonium * late Elizabethan quince marmalade

dilligrout * a spiced chicken porridge anciently prepared for coronation banquets

divinity * an American confection similar to nougat

dogsbody * naval service pease pottage

dolly mixture * an assortment of selected small fondant sweets

dorcake * an early kind of cracknel biscuit, dating from the 1500s

dormers * fried patties of hashed meat, suet, and rice, rolled in egg and crumbs

dough Jehovahs * a nineteenth century American meat stew of poor reputation

dowsett * an old sweetened egg custard tart containing minced white meat

drowsen * an oatmeal porridge or broth of yesteryear

Dublin lawyer * a historical Irish luxury dish of lobster cooked in whiskey

dumpsy-deary * a preserve of apples, pears, and plums with ginger and lemon zest

dunelm * a rare regional concoction of braised mutton or veal with mushrooms

eggalourie * in old Orkney and Shetland, a dish of eggs and milk boiled together

elegant economist's pudding * boiled pudding remains reheated with custard

entrayle * cooked sheep's womb stuffed with chopped meat, cheese, eggs, and spices

Eton mess * a dessert of broken meringue with whipped cream and strawberries

fackle * a traditional Yorkshire savoury pudding of boiled mutton and cabbage

fadderless stew * a poor meal of potatoes stewed on their own, without meat

fairy butter * a table sauce of egg yolk beaten with orange-water, sugar, and butter

farls * triangular oatcakes or flatbreads, common to Lowland Scotland and Ulster

farts * spherical light pastry titbits, or tiny spheres of minced mutton and fruit

fat rascals * large rich buns with cream, candied peel, and currents intermingled

figgyhobbin

a richly sweet plain pastry treat "figged" or specked with raisins

fauntempere * a fifteenth century dessert of carnation flowers and cloves

figgie-dowdie * an old West Country plum pudding much favoured by sailormen

flammick * a lost confection made with butter, eggs, and cheese

flathon * variously, a type of custard flan, cheesecake, or pancake

flaumpens * medieval pies or tarts ornamented with pointed pieces of pastry

flickermeat * Devon and Somerset whitepot, being a porridge of flour and milk

florentine * a meat pie with the crust formed only on the top

fluff-duff * any poorly prepared steamed fruit pudding

fluffernutter * a sandwich of peanut butter and marshmallow crème

flummadiddle * historically, a bake identified with the fishermen of New England

flummery * a starchy semi-set dessert pudding of stewed fruit and cream

fonnell * an old roast of small birds and shredded meat, decorated with boiled eggs

foreign entanglements * spaghetti, in the lexicon of the short-order cook

franchemyle * a savoury dish of various ingredients cooked in a sheep's stomach

frawsey * an early version of the modern pancake; by extension, any "treat to eat"

frians * medieval fried filled pasties, similar to samosas

frumenty * a staple medieval pottage of grains boiled in milk, similar to couscous

funistrada * a phoney food "created" by the US military as a culinary survey control

galandine * an old bread sauce spiced with galingale, served with meat and fish

galantine * a dish of bread sops and chopped white meat set in or glazed with jelly

gallimaufry * originally, any hodge-podge of leftover liver and other organ meats

gansel * a forgotten sauce of milk and garlic, served especially with goose

garnade * an ancient dish of chicken in pomegranate sauce

gaylede * formerly, a sweet dessert of figs, grapes, and croutons in almond sauce

geograffy * a concoction of boiled burnt biscuits served on sailing ships of old

girty-milk * porridge made with milk rather than water

glycipricon * any bittersweet culinary curio

gobbet-royal * a medieval sweetmeat; literally "a mouthful fit for a king"

gobstoppers * large balls of hard multi-coloured candy; also known as jawbreakers

godivoe * a former forcemeat pie of chopped veal and suet, seasoned

Gotham pudding * a Notts steamed sponge pudding studded with sugared peel

granola * a breakfast cereal of rolled oats and so forth, dating from the late 1800s

gravy bastard * any inferior cooking sauce or one containing incongruous elements

groaty dick * a Black Country beef and onion stew thickened with hulled oats

gumdrops * a confectionery item consisting of selected small chewy candies

gyngawdry * an ancient dish of chopped fish livers and other edible innards

gyngener * an old table sauce of grated bread mixed with vinegar and ground ginger

hamkin * an obscure historical mutton dish from Devon, probably a type of pie

hanoney * a medieval omelette made with chopped fried onions

hardtack * any cookie or cracker consumed as rations by members of the military

hashmagandy * any basic stew served up at Australian sheep stations and the like

Hawkshead whigs * small oval teacakes or buns made with lard and caraway seeds

hell balls * cayenned meatballs with chutney and minced olives, crumbed and fried

hendhoven-bread * Lancashire oatmeal cake

herbelade * an early dish of egg and pork sausage baked with finely chopped herbs

hodge-pudding * a general term for any pudding of many and varied ingredients

hogling * an early version of apple turnover

hogmanay * a dark fruity bun offered as a "first-footing" gift on New Year's Day

hokey-pokey * colloquially, either inexpensive ice cream or honeycomb toffee

hokum-snivvy * any foul stew or boiled meal of indeterminable ingredients

hotchpotch * a thick stew of diced hog with mixed vegetables dating from the 1400s

hotpot * a cover term for British meat stews, most famously that from Lancashire

howtowdie * a traditional Scottish dish of boiled chicken, poached eggs, and spinach

hucklebuck * Amish lunch cake or "whoopie pie"

huffkin * rich Kentish roll or teacake

humbugs * a confection of hard-boiled but soft-centred mint candies

hundreds & thousands * a decorative confection of myriad miniature comfits

hushpuppies * "corn dodgers," Southern deep-fried cornmeal balls

impossible pie * a dessert pie mix which forms it own crust and layers as it cooks

jammy marse * the humble jam butty in older colloquial Cornish

jance * a versatile late medieval warm ginger wine sauce for use with fish or fowl

jannock * a "genuine" Northeast England leavened oatcake or loaf

jellybabies * a selection of shaped soft sweets; a British confectionery classic

jessamy chocolate * chocolate flavoured with jasmine

johnnycake * traditional American cornpone flatbread, or "journey cake"

jujubes * fruit flavoured gumdrops or similar confectionery lozenges

jumbal * a sweet cake or cookie shaped like a ring

jumboburger * an outsized American ground meat patty slapped in a bap

juncate * cheesecake, or any sweetened curd delicacy food

jussell * an old meat broth or soup, occasionally thickened with eggs

karibat * "curry and rice," or modern-day Anglo-Indian cuisine more generally

ketchup * an all-purpose tomato-based table sauce

kissing comfit * any small item of confectionery taken to sweeten the breath

kixsies * Isle of Wight sloe jam or jelly

knickerbocker glory * an opulent layered sundae adorned with fruits and nuts

knotty-tommy * a North Country breakfast plate of oatmeal drenched in warm milk

lamington * an Australian sponge cake coated in chocolate sauce and grated coconut

laverbread * a traditional Welsh breakfast dish of seaweed mush fried with oatmeal

lechefryes * a fifteenth century milk pie containing fruit and almonds

lenten-kail * Scottish meatless broth, suitable for consuming during Lent

lethelory * a medieval milk custard with added fat; or, possibly, scrambled eggs

leveredge * an early liver sausage, often made with egg yolks and sundry spices

loblolly * any gruel standardly including common vegetables and meat scraps

lobscouse * a Liverpool sailor's stew of red meat, root veg and pickled cabbage

loseyns * in early English cuisine, shaped pasta lozenges if not lasagna as a dish

love in disguise * the heart of a calf or lamb stuffed and baked; an offal delicacy

lumpytums * an old oatmeal porridge eaten at breakfast or later as a milky dessert

macaroon * a dense chewy cookie most often made with coconut

maconochie * a tinned stew of poor repute formerly serving as an army field ration

macrows * a macaroni cheese dish from the Middle Ages

manchet * a premium wheaten yeast bread of yesteryear

marchpane * marzipan, a confection of ground almonds, egg whites, and sugar

marmulate * an archaic variant spelling of marmalade; citrus fruit preserve

marquise * a rich chilled chocolate dessert or mousse

marshmallows * a popular confection of spongy cylindrical sweetmeats

mawmenny * a forgotten dish of spiced ground capon in almond milk sauce

mealy-crushy * oatmeal fried in dripping; an old regional favourite

meatloaf * a savoury dish of ground meat, shaped and baked to resemble a loaf

mellinder * a sweet pastry of the early modern era, now lost to cookery

mellorine * a 1950s frozen dessert manufactured as a cheap facsimile of ice cream

meltaway * a general type of shortbread cookie intended to melt easily in the mouth

merribowk * literally "merry-belly," a pleasant dish much as a posset or syllabub

meselade * an early omelette or dinner of scrambled eggs

midshipman's nuts * broken ship's biscuit, eaten as dessert

millionaire shortbread * a supremely rich patisserie item, also called caramel slice

mimpins * a nineteenth century "mystery" confection, or American plum cake

mincemeat * the meatless contents of a dried fruit pie, spiced and laced with spirits

mitchkin * historically, a small cake or loaf

mock turtle soup * a stew using calf brains and brawn as surrogate turtle flesh

monamy * a lost dish of Old England

monchelet * another lost dish of Old England

moonshine * an Elizabethan dish of egg yolks cooked on a sweet base

moreta * salad with garlic

mortress * an old terrine of pounded meat cooked to the consistency of thick custard

muffuletta * a Louisiana sandwich based on traditional Sicilian sesame bread

mulligan * an American stew of odds and ends; a veritable hodgepodge of a hotpot

murrey * formerly, a veal stew prepared and coloured red with mulberries

musculade * a mussel sauce or dish cooked with mussels, from the fifteenth century

mylate * a medieval baked dish of pulled pork, eggs, and cheese, well-seasoned

nettle haggis * an austerity meal of boiled nettles in oatmeal with crispy bacon atop

ninety-nine * an ice cream cone with a stick of flaky chocolate inserted as a treat

noteye * a bygone dish of ground spiced meat, garnished with blanched nuts

nysebek * a type of medieval fritter or pasty

olycook * a doughnut, in the Hudson Valley vernacular

orgmount * a historical Scottish porridge of boiled pearl barley

oyster-chevit * a bite-sized pie case filled with spiced fruits topped with oyster meat

pamperdy * essentially eggy bread with sweet spices; a meal from the early 1600s

panackelty * a casserole of corned beef and sliced potatoes; Sunderland hotpot

panade * a culinary paste or sauce of stale bread boiled in milk with seasoning

pandewaff * a pan-baked dish of boiled oatmeal mixed with fat, from Yorkshire

pandowdy * a dessert of stewed apples baked under a broken crust; akin to a cobbler

panhaggerty * a pot meal of cheese upon onion upon potato, cooked with dripping

panjotheram * a rare Durham dish of lamb chops with sliced onions and potatoes

papelote * the original English-language word for porridge, being a mess of oatmeal

papyns * a historical milk pudding enhanced with honey and saffron

parkin * Northern gingerbread cake, a traditional Bonfire Night treat

parlies * Scottish gingerbread biscuits, or "parliament cakes" for the gentry

partan bree * Scottish crab bisque, a speciality seafood soup

pastelade * a fancy pastry of sorts mentioned in fifteenth century cookbooks

patum peperium * an old anchovy paste commonly known as Gentleman's Relish

pavlova * a twenties Australian meringue dessert named for a famous ballerina

payndemayn * "panis dominicus," or quality white bread fit for the lord of the manor

pease pottage * a savoury pudding of boiled split peas often cooked with a ham joint

penny puzzle * a sausage, in jocular reference to its often mystery ingredients

pepperpot * a hugely popular Caribbean-style stew of vegetables with meat or fish

petypernaunt * a modest medieval pasty containing ginger, dates, and raisins

Philly cheesesteak * a hoagie of chopped beef, grilled onions, and melted cheese

pickalilly * a relish of pickled vegetables in vinegar with mustard and turmeric

pinionade * any candy, conserve, or confection formerly made from pine nuts

pionade * any candy, conserve, or confection formerly made from peony seeds

po' boy * a Louisiana submarine sandwich, typically containing fried seafood

pochee * a lost dish of poached eggs coated in an egg yolk sauce, milk, and spices

pokerounce * a dessert of thick toast spread with hot spiced honey and pine nuts

pommedorry * an old dish of pork meatballs glazed so as to resemble golden apples

poplolly * a lollipop or ice lolly

porray * a simple leek stew widely eaten throughout the Middle Ages

poterons * a forgotten preparation of "pot eggs" soft-cooked in a mound of hot salt

potlikker * a Southern US soup of seasoned vegetable stock with cornpone croutons

potwise * forcemeat baked in an earthen pot which is then broken to access the food

poverroy * an old pepper-based pouring sauce for pheasant and other fowl dishes

powsowdie * sheep's head broth, a speciality of Scottish cuisine

pozzy * British forces' slang for jam or marmalade

prawling * a dated variant spelling of praline, a small sweetmeat based on nuts

pufftaloons * in Australian cookery, fried or puffed scones, usually eaten hot

pulpatoon * a pie encasing small items of wild game within a thin forcemeat crust

punchnep * a Welsh dish of mashed potatoes and root vegetables, with added cream

purloo * a Southern US savoury stew of rice and chicken

quiddany * a sweet pink marmalade made from quince

quiver & shake * Australian rhyming slang for steak

raisinet * a winter preserve of peeled mixed fruit, from the nineteenth century

ramolade * a sauce for fish salad, consisting of parsley, onions, anchovies, and capers

rapeye * a thick peppered table sauce from dried fruit boiled in wine; mostly for fish

rattoon * baked cheesecake

raynolls * fried patties of ground pork cooked with a medley of further ingredients

resurrection pie * humorously, any pie or similar meal made from leftovers

revalenta * a Victorian lentil and barley flour gruel specially prepared for invalids

rishews * medieval fruit balls fried in oil; modest progenitors of the modern burger

Rocky Mountain oysters * a dish of bull's testicles; a deep-fried Western delicacy

roly-poly * a sweet steamed pudding made from suet pastry spread with jam

roseye * historically, a creamy almond sauce for fish perfumed with rose petals

Ruby Murray * British rhyming slang for curry, arguably the new national dish

rumbledethumps * a Borders mess of mashed potatoes and cabbage

rumble-tumble * an Anglo-Indian dish of scrambled eggs

sallet * salad, in the original; a cold variety dish of mostly dressed mixed vegetables

salmagundy * a centrepiece salad dish of layered miscellaneous mixed ingredients

salomene * a light fish dish prepared with wine and spices, dating from the 1400s

saltine * an American soda cracker, or salted savoury biscuit

sambocade * a kind of curd tart or cheesecake fragranced with elderflowers

sambouse * a hashed meat pasty of yesteryear

sassengers * American sausages

saunders * a prototype cottage or shepherd's pie, popular in the nineteenth century

sawgeat * a medieval plate of egg-fried pork balls specially wrapped in sage leaves

scranchum * gingerbread in the North Country style, baked as brittle wafers

scrapple * a pan rabbit dish similar to the "pannhaas" of the Pennsylvania Dutch

scripture cake * a confection made using only ingredients mentioned in the Bible

scroggin * Antipodean trail mix for going walkabout in the Outback

scrotchat * an obscure Scottish sweetmeat recorded in the sixteenth century

shagapenter * Devon roasted shoulder of pork with the blade bones cut into it

shit on a shingle * "SOS," American chipped beef in milk gravy, served on toast

shoofly pie * molasses crumb cake, a traditional favourite among the Amish

simballs * an old New England Puritan term for doughnuts

simnel * a marzipan bun or fruit cake traditionally eaten during Lent

singing hinny * a honey cake emitting sizzling sounds while cooking on the griddle

sippid-puddin * a pudding made of alternate layers of buttered bread and currants

skensmadam * a show dish, one set upon the table as a spectacle rather than a meal

skillygalee * a thin broth or gruel of soaked sea biscuit fried with pork fat

skuets * early British kebabs, or skewered gobbets of bacon and various organ meats

slumgullion * informally, any insipid US hash or stew of cheap meat and vegetables

slut's pennies * hard lumps of baked bread or loaf caused by imperfect kneading

smatchcock * a forgotten chicken dish, mostly likely to have been fried or roasted

smiggins * poor-quality "hulk" soup or cold slops served up to Victorian-era convicts

s'mores * a marshmallow dessert treat by tradition cooked at night over a campfire

smotheration * historically, a sailors' repast of meat smothered in potatoes

snickerdoodle * a whimsically named North American cinnamon sugar cookie

snowcone * a shaved ice and sugar syrup dessert served in cones of paper or foam

sonofabitch stew * an old cowboy savoury dish of beef stewed with calf offal

soor plooms * Scottish boiled sweets, somewhat sharp or "sour" to taste

soup-meagre * traditional meat-free Lenten soup, using early season vegetables

sowans * a Lowland Scottish porridge or pudding of fermented oat bran or husks

sowpes dorry * "golden sops," an old broth of toasted bread sweetened with saffron

spiced fizzer * a dialectal term for currant teacake

spotted mystery * tinned beef: who knows what the ingredients truly are?

spynee * a thickened cream dessert garnished and flavoured with hawthorn flowers

squichanary pye * a lost pie made of boiled turnip roots soaked in wine with fruits

stargazy pie * a favourite Cornish bake made with projecting whole small silver fish

stirabout * Anglo-Irish porridge

stovies * a Scottish savoury meal ideally of leftover meat, vegetables, and potatoes

stromboli * an American-style turnover filled with Italian cheeses and cold cuts

sturmye * a medieval dish of chopped pork done in almond milk and spices

succade * fruit crystallized in sugar or syrup, especially sweets of candied citrus peel

sugarolly * a traditional Scottish confection of liquorice sticks

sugarplums * small roundish hard-boiled dainties available in various fruit flavours

sundae * a rich ice cream dessert served in a glass with syrup and other toppings

suppawn * American hasty pudding, being a mush or porridge of boiled cornmeal

swainloaf * bread of inferior quality, formerly reserved for the servant class

swarry * bygone street slang for boiled leg of mutton with all the trimmings

syllabub * a sweet frothy dessert of whipped cream, sherry, sugar, and lemon juice

tadago pie * an old Cornish pie said to have been made from aborted piglets

talmouse * a type of cheesecake or cheese-filled triangular pastry

tantadlin * a tartlet or other whimsical item of light pastry

tartan purry * a Scottish pudding of boiled oatmeal and chopped kale

tartine * an open sandwich spread with butter or jam

tartlettes * medieval meat dumplings featuring pork with raisins and spices

tavorsay * a lost delicacy of spiced cod's head and liver

temperade * a bygone fowl dish

thorcake * a seventeenth century flatbread or flapjack, popular around Halloween

Thousand Island dressing * a salad dressing and table condiment from New York

thunder & lightning * a slice of bread topped with clotted cream and golden syrup

tiddy-oggy * a variation on the standard Cornish pasty containing bacon and cheese

tipsycake * cake heavily saturated with wine or liqueur

toad-in-the-hole * a savoury dish of sausages baked in Yorkshire pudding batter

tofurkey * a tofu loaf formed like turkey, once much in vogue with vegetarian diners

tom-trot * a hard, brittle, stretched toffee traditionally home-made for Bonfire Night

tostee * a simple medieval dessert dish much resembling ginger syrup toasties

triple-decker * an extended sandwich with three layers of bread and two of filling

trogalion * some dainty, dessert or other sweet confection

tuftafetta * a frothed cream formerly cooked to a custard for pouring over fruit

turducken * a deboned chicken inside a deboned duck inside a deboned turkey

turtulong * a special breakfast biscuit enjoyed in Georgian times

tuskyn * medieval meatballs of minced pork, sweetened and spiced

tutti-frutti * an ice cream or confection of mixed candied fruits

Ugley duckling * an Essex in-joke and dish of roast duck with herb stuffing

uvate * conserve prepared, unusually, from grapes

uzzle-pye * a medieval pastry spectacular containing singing blackbirds and all

vantage loaf * the thirteenth and free loaf in the proverbial baker's dozen

vaunts * little fruit tart favourites of yesteryear, enriched with bone marrow

vegelate * faux chocolate with cheaper vegetable fat substituting for cocoa butter

vertsauce * an early salsa verde, or culinary sauce chiefly prepared with green herbs

viper broth * an eighteenth-century soup or stew of skinned and chopped snakes

wangrace * in old Scots, a bland broth or flummery dish intended for convalescents

washbrew * oatmeal boiled until it becomes a stiff jelly; a most gelatinous porridge

wastel * historically, a loaf of only the finest white bread

waterloo * a stew, or stewed food generally considered, in rhyming slang

water-souchy * formerly, a dish of perch stewed and served in its own liquor

Welsh rarebit * toasted cheese

wet nelly * Liverpool bread pudding

whangby * coarse cheese, or cheese gone hard; an old Lancashire expression

whey-wullions * a poor peasant's supper of leftover porridge

whim-wham * an elementary trifle, fool, or similar sweet dessert

whistleberries * American diner slang for baked beans

whitepot * milk pudding or custard, especially as traditionally made in Devon

Wigan slappy * a meat pie served between the covers of a sliced barm cake or bun

wild willies * a.k.a. pigs in blankets; cocktail sausages wrapped in bacon or pastry

yrchins * an ancient pork dish bristling with almonds on the surface, sea-urchin style

zephyr * any dish or delicacy that is whipped or frothed, as with a soufflé

zeppelins in a cloud * bangers and mash

CHAPTER 6

A Cornucopia of Culinary Delights from the Rest of the World

"Life is a combination of magic and pasta."
— Federico Fellini

achaar * hot Desi-style vegetable pickle; "achaari" curries are dishes cooked with such

acitrón * "cactus candy," a Mexican dainty consisting of crystallized cactus leaf

acquacotta * "cooked water," an ancient bread soup and staple of Tuscan peasant fare

æbleskiver * Danish pancake puffballs, customarily enjoyed at Christmas time

afelia * a Greek Cypriot dish of pork braised in red wine with coriander seeds

affogato * an Italian dessert of vanilla ice cream "drowned" in espresso

agemono * a Japanese culinary category embracing deep-fried dishes

agnolotti * Piedmontese mini ravioli pockets stuffed with roasted meat or vegetables

aligot * a rich purée of mashed potatoes, cream, and cheese, from the Auvergne

allemande * a classic continental velouté sauce enriched with egg yolks and cream

allioli * Catalan garlic dip

almavica * a sweet Italian dessert somewhat akin to semolina pudding

almondine * a style of dish garnished atop with toasted almonds, whole or flaked

amandine * a traditional Romanian chocolate layered cake

amatriciana * a pasta sauce recipe of cured pork cheek, pecorino cheese, and tomato

anchoyade * Provençal anchovy purée

apfelstrudel * a Viennese pastry filled with cooking apples, raisins, sugar, and spice

aphraton * an old Byzantine soufflé made from chicken and egg whites

arepa * a versatile corn pancake or sandwich bread widely consumed in Venezuela

argenteuil * denotes a plate of food prepared with asparagus as a side garnish

arrabbiata * spicy or "angry" pasta sauce, made with garlic and hot chilli peppers

ashure * Noah's Ark pudding, a Turkish dessert favourite

atmit * a nutritious Ethiopian porridge distributed as famine relief food

avgolemono * a Greek soup or sauce of egg yolks and lemon juice mixed with broth

awwamath * Lebanese doughnuts

baba ghanoush * a popular Levantine eggplant dip with a famously smoky taste

bacalhau * Portuguese salted cod; considered to be the nation's signature dish

baguette * a breadstuff otherwise known as a French stick

baklava * the classic phyllo pastry sweetmeat of Balkan and Middle Eastern cuisine

ballottine * a French hot dish of boned poultry or fish rolled round various fillings

balti * a Punjabi "one pot" meat curry prepared and presented in a wok-like bowl

baozi * steamed Chinese meat buns or dumplings, often eaten for breakfast

barfi * fudge-like flavoured dessert bites, prized in the cookery of the Subcontinent

barigoule * a Provençal speciality preparation of in-season globe artichokes

basundi * an Indian confection of sugared condensed milk garnished with nuts

bavarois * "Bavarian cream," a cold whipped cream pudding thickened with gelatin

baveuse * denotes a style of omelette with a purposely soft or undercooked middle

béarnaise * a classic French steak sauce notable for the use of tarragon

béchamel * white sauce, one of the five so-called "mother sauces" of French cuisine

berlingot * a hard continental caramel bonbon, typically pyramidal in shape

beshbarmak * "five fingers," a boiled meat noodle mainstay of Central Asian cookery

bestilla * Moroccan pigeon or poultry pie

bhaji * a spicy vegetable fritter and ubiquitous Indian street food

bhuna * a concentrated curry dish with dry-roasted spices, originally from Bengal

biberot * an old French seigneurial luxury dish based on minced partridge breast

bibimbap * literally a "mixed meal" of assorted rice, meat, and vegetables, from Korea

bibingka * a Philippine rice cake, cooked by tradition between banana leaves

bigarade * a French culinary sauce prepared with bitter Seville oranges

bigos * a traditional Polish "hunter's stew" of cabbage and meat

biryani * a popular Indo-Pak dish of seasoned mixed rice, lamb, and vegetables

bisque * a smooth French shellfish soup, usually consisting of crayfish or lobster

bisquotins * bygone sweetmeats, said to have first been confected by the Huns

bitsu-bitsu * deep-fried Philippine doughballs with sugar and coconut

bitterballen * beef croquettes, a common savoury bar snack in the Netherlands

blanquette * a French ragout of white meat, particularly veal, in a white sauce

blintz * in Jewish cookery, a thin pancake folded to encase a filling prior to baking

blitztorte * a German quick and easy to make, hence "lightning," butter cake

bobotie * South African curried mincemeat baked with a savoury custard topping

bolognese * both a signature Italian sauce and dish, known domestically as ragù

bordelaise * denoting a dish served with a Bordeaux sauce of red wine and onion

borodinsky * a Russian sourdough rye loaf sweetened with molasses

borscht * a sour beetroot soup widely regarded as the national dish of Ukraine

bouillabaisse * a highly seasoned stew of various seafoods, originating in Marseilles

boulanee * an Afghani flatbread baked or fried with any of various available fillings

boureki * courgette, curd cheese, and potato pie; a self-crusting Chaniot speciality

bourguignon * a rich casserole featuring beef braised in red Burgundy wine

bozbash * a soup of fatty lamb or mutton breast consumed across the Caucasus

brandade * puréed salt cod, olive oil, and milk; a speciality dish of Nîmes

brioche * a favourite continental breakfast bun, unmistakably sweet and rich

brunoise * a garnish of diced butter-fried vegetables for flavouring soups or sauces

bruschetta * an Italian appetizer of brushed toast topped with tomatoes and herbs

bucellatum * a hardtack biscuit and iron ration of the Roman legions on campaign

bulgogi * Korean "fire-meat," a dish of shredded prime beef marinated and grilled

buraniyyah * an elaborate medieval Arabian dish of stewed meat and fried eggplant

burrito * a Tex-Mex tortilla wrap typically containing minced beef or refried beans

callaloo * a quintessentially Caribbean leaf vegetable soup or stew

calzone * a variant turnover-style "trouser leg" pizza, of Neapolitan origin

capellini * extra fine Italian pasta strands; finer still is capelli d'angelo, or "angel hair"

capilotade * in French cookery, a hash typically composed of multiple minced meats

capirotada * a sweet Mexican bread pudding customarily eaten during Lent

caponata * Sicilian ratatouille, normally served cold as an appetizer

caprese * denotes food prepared in the Capri fashion, most famously salad

carbonara * a distinctive modern Roman spaghetti sauce and dish; rich and creamy

carpaccio * in Italian cuisine, an antipasto fillet of raw meat or fish served with sauce

cassata * a sweet liqueured sponge cake or trifle originating from Palermo

cassoulet * a classic ragout of pork or game with haricot beans, from the Languedoc

ceviche * a fresh raw fish dish widely consumed across Ecuador and Peru

chakalaka * a piquant all-purpose South African mixed vegetable relish

chalupa * a Mexican fried corn tortilla served with a spicy or savoury filling

chapati * a flat pancake of unleavened wholewheat flour; an Indian bread staple

chapelures * dried breadcrumbs, as used in French cooking as ingredient or coating

char siu * a popular Cantonese dish of barbecued pork in a sweet and savoury glaze

charoseth * a Jewish fruit paste of chopped apples, nuts, and spices eaten at Passover

chasseur * an old French dish of game or poultry cooked in a forest mushroom sauce

chaudfroid * in French cuisine, a jellied sauce used to garnish plates of meat or fish

chermoulah * a special Maghrebi marinade or seasoning for fish or seafood dishes

chilaquiles * a Mexican breakfast food of tortilla chips topped with salsa and cheese

chimichanga * a deep-fried, wet burrito, usually containing a savoury filling

chimichurri * a spicy condiment cum marinade used with Argentinian grilled meats

chiquetaille * traditional Haitian herring or cod salad, often eaten as a starter

chłodnik * cold Polish beetroot soup; a summertime favourite

cholent * a Jewish casserole prepared on the Friday for consumption on the Sabbath

chop suey * a Chinese-style meal of stewed meat chunks with stir-fried vegetables

chouquettes * light and fluffy French choux pastry bites topped with pearl sugar

chow-chow * variously, a Chinese mixed fruit preserve or US mixed pickle relish

christopsomo * sweet Greek Orthodox Christmas bread

churek * traditional Azeri or Armenian flatbread

churros * Iberian fritter fingers, now a ubiquitous Latin American street food too

ciabatta * a flattish Italian white loaf or baguette made with olive oil

cioppino * a home-style seafood stew created by Italian immigrants in California

clafoutis * a French cherry flan baked in a topping of sweet batter

cocido * a name for any main dish stew served in Spain, Portugal or Ibero-America

coliphia * classically, penis-shaped bread baked by prostitutes as a token of business

compote * broadly, any continental-style dessert of fruit stewed in sugar syrup

conchiglie * Italian pasta "shells," ideal for working with the fullest range of sauces

confit * in French cookery, a dish of whole duck cooked slowly in the bird's own fat

congee * Chinese rice soup or gruel

consommé * a French culinary broth prepared from concentrated or clarified stock

coulibiac * Russian fish pie, traditionally made with salmon or sturgeon

couscous * a North African savoury staple of steamed semolina served with stew

craquelins * Belgian-style brioche buns or cream puffs with a sweet crispy topping

crêpes suzette * French dessert pancakes in an orange liqueur sauce, served flambé

croquembouche * a continental dessert spectacular made to "crunch in the mouth," a "profiterole mountain" or pyramid of patisserie items bound with spun caramel

croque-monsieur * an iconically French sandwich of boiled ham and cheese, toasted

croustade * French pie crust; a pastry or perhaps potato case filled with savouries

csöröge * crisp Hungarian "angel wing" cookies, traditionally served at weddings

curanto * a native Chilean feast of meat, seafood, and potatoes cooked in a fire pit

currygewürz * German spicy ketchup

dacquoise * a nutty, layered French dessert cake normally served chilled with fruit

dafina * a slow-cooked Moroccan Jewish stew traditionally eaten for Sabbath lunch

dampfnudeln * German "steamed noodles," in fact, a dish of sweet dumplings

daqqus * a popular Gulf chilli sauce; of Yemeni origin, where it is known as *zhug*

dariole * a French open-crust custard tart, prepared in a mould of the same name

datemaki * sweet Japanese egg roll; a favourite of New Year festive fare

dauphinois * denotes a French gratin dish of sliced potatoes baked in milk or cream

dhal * a South Asian spiced lentil soup

dhansak * a traditional Parsee mutton curry cooked with lentils and served on rice

dhosa * a savoury South Indian crêpe, often served stuffed with various ingredients

diablotins * little continental dainties or delicacies, notably chocolate confections

dinuguan * a Philippine stew of pig's guts simmered in a dark gravy of pig's blood

ditalini * a variety of Italian macaroni pasta in the form of tiny tubes or "thimbles"

dolmades * in Greek gastronomy, rolled vine leaves stuffed with rice and herbs

donburi * a culinary cover term for a range of Japanese easy one-bowl rice meals

dopiaza * a speciality "double onions" meat curry, consumed across the Subcontinent

drachena * a soufflé-like egg pudding common to Russian and Ukrainian cookery

dumboy * a doughball prepared from fresh cassava; the national foodstuff of Liberia

duxelles * in French cuisine, a paste of sautéed mushrooms used as stuffing or sauce

eclair * a "lightning bolt," or oblong cream and chocolate pastry of French invention

empanada * a South American turnover invariably stuffed with savoury foods

enchilada * a Mexican meal of a meat or cheese filled tortilla baked in chilli sauce

ensaïmada * a spiral of sweet pastry coated with powdered sugar, from Mallorca

epigramme * in classical French cookery, lamb chops or cutlets done two ways

escabeche * a Mediterranean cold dish of marinated fried meat, or more often fish

escudella * a signature Catalan combination soup and stew, popular in wintertime

espagnole * brown sauce, one of the five so-called "mother sauces" of French cuisine

estragon * denoting a French chicken dish made with sprigs of fresh tarragon

étouffée * a spicy Cajun and Creole stew of shellfish served over white rice

fajitas * Tex-Mex tortilla wraps typically containing meat strips with cheese and vegetables

falafel * deep-fried Middle Eastern patties made from mashed chickpeas and pulses

faloodeh * a cold vermicelli sorbet or dessert, of Persian origin

fanchonnette * in French cookery, a custard tartlet covered with meringue

farfalle * Italian pasta "butterflies"

fårikål * a casserole of boiled "mutton in cabbage," Norway's official national dish

fasolada * the quintessential rustic Greek soup, made with haricot beans

fastnacht * a German festive fried doughnut, enjoyed especially on Shrove Tuesday

fattoush * crunchy Lebanese pita bread salad

faubonne * vegetable purée soup; a dish from classic French gastronomy

feijoada * a signature Brazilian stew of black beans and pork, served with rice

fesenjan * an Iranian poultry stew flavoured with pomegranates and walnuts

fettuccine * a type of ribboned pasta, favoured in Roman and Tuscan cuisine

feuillantine * a French puff pastry tart containing layers of alternating ingredients

fillozes * Portuguese-style doughnuts

financière * denotes a rich haute cuisine meal prepared in a suitably opulent style

focaccia * a flat Italian "hearth bread," baked with olive oil and herbs

fondant * a continental candy consisting of a thick paste of boiled sugar and water

foofoo * a West African staple of doughballs made from boiled plantain or cassava

forestière * indicating a particular method of garnishing French game fowl dishes

fra diavolo * "devil monk," a piquant sauce used with Italian pasta and seafood fare

frangipane * a creamy almond flavoured cake or pastry, of Italian invention

fregola * Sardinian pasta, consisting of small oven-toasted semolina doughballs

fritessaus * Dutch "fries sauce," a popular mayonnaise-style condiment for chips

ful medames * Egypt's national dish, a fava bean dip commonly eaten for breakfast

fungee * a Caribbean cornmeal dish, similar to polenta; typically made with okra

fusilli * Italian corkscrew pasta pieces, produced in a variety of flavoursome colours

gado-gado * an Indonesian egg and vegetable salad with peanut sauce dressing

galaktoboureko * a sweet Greek custard pie, made with phyllo pastry

galette * a savoury Breton crêpe or pancake, made with buckwheat flour

ganache * a creamy chocolate filling or frosting, used in continental confectioneries

garbure * a rich Gascon broth of bacon, cabbage, and other available vegetables

garganelli * a penne-like Italian egg pasta variety

gastrique * a redux of vinegar and sugar used as a flavouring for French sauces

gâteau * French sponge cake

gaufrette * a crisp Belgian-style waffle

gazpacho * a classic cold soup of chopped salad vegetables, from Andalusia

genoise * a light but rich French butter cake, typically layered and filled

ghorayebah * traditional Middle Eastern shortbread, or butter biscuits

gnocchi * Italian potato dumplings

gooksu * Korean noodles generally; more specifically, a special occasion noodle soup

gordita * a "chubby girl," small Mexican corn cake stuffed with a savoury mix

goulash * an iconic Hungarian ragout of "herdsman's meat"

granita * a Sicilian semi-frozen fruit dessert, somewhat similar to a sorbet

gratin * in French cookery, a dish encrusted with raspings of toasted bread or cheese

gremolata * a zesty Italian garnish of select chopped herbs and, optionally, anchovy

grissini * Italian-style breadsticks

guacamole * a traditional Mesoamerican chunky avocado-based spread or salad

gulaman * a jelly-like Philippine flan made from bars of dried seaweed

gumbo * in Creole cuisine, a soup or stew such as of shrimp with greens and okra

gyros * a classic Greek fast food of lamb, tomato, onion and yoghurt on pita bread

hagebuttenmark * a rose hip preserve; part of the culinary heritage of Switzerland

haleem * a thick slow-cooked stew consumed across the Levant and Central Asia

halo-halo * a Philippine dessert of sweetened beans and fruits served in crushed ice

halvah * a crumbly Turkish sweetmeat made from ground sesame seeds and honey

hamantaschen * in Jewish cookery, three-cornered filled cookies baked for Purim

harissa * a piquant North African paste used as both condiment and flavouring

harusame * Japanese-style cellophane noodles, or vermicelli

hasenpfeffer * a highly seasoned German rabbit stew, garnished with sour cream

hoisin * a renowned reddish-brown Chinese dipping sauce and meat glaze

hollandaise * a classic French culinary sauce of eggs and butter with lemon juice

hoosh * the "cuisine of the Antarctic," a pemmican stew eaten by the early explorers

horiatiki salata * the iconic Greek salad of tomatoes, olives, onions, lettuce, and feta

huevos rancheros * "ranch eggs," a traditional morning meal of Mexican farmhands

hummus * a smooth Middle Eastern chickpea spread or dip, often taken with pita

incaparina * a Guatemalan vegetable protein food for the nutritionally impoverished

injera * an Ethiopian teff flatbread with all the taste and texture of carpet underlay

involtini * Italian "little bundles," being a dish of various bite-sized savoury wraps

jäger-eintopf * a German "one-pot hunter's stew," made with coarsely ground beef

jalebi * a popular South Asian dessert of coiled or pretzel-shaped sweetmeats

jalfrezi * a medium to hot Indian curry cooked with abundant fresh green chillies

jambalaya * a classic Cajun casserole of rice with meat or seafood, not unlike paella

jardinière * variously, a French soup, sauce or garnish of mixed spring vegetables

jollof rice * West Africa's favourite stew of long-grained rice, tomatoes and chillies

joshpara * an ancient Persian dish of little dumplings filled with lamb and onions

julekake * Norwegian Christmas bread, baked with candied fruits and cardamom

kaisersemmel * Viennese "emperor roll," a crusty roll displaying a crown-like motif

kapitan * "captain's curry," a creamy Malaysian chicken dish

kasha * buckwheat porridge; a staple of Central and Eastern European cookery

käsknöpfle * a dish of soft egg noodles and melted cheese, from Liechtenstein

kavourma * an ancient Armenian and Turkish dish of lamb cooked in flank fat

kazmag * a gourmet "bottom pot" crust commonly found in Azeri and Uzbeki dishes

kedgeree * originally, as "khichri," and properly, an Indian dish of rice and legumes

kelewele * a popular Ivorian snack food or appetizer of spicy fried plantain

khachapuri * molten cheese bread topped with an egg; a signature Georgian dish

kibbeh * savoury Lebanese patties made from minced meat, bulgur and local spices

kimchi * a Korean side dish of spicy fermented vegetables, principally napa cabbage

kleftiko * a classic Greek-Cypriot dish of "stolen" lamb cooked in parchment paper

knäckebröd * Dutch rye crisp bread

koeksister * a highly sweet and sticky plaited Afrikaner doughnut

kokoretsi * a dish of lamb guts and offal prepared across the Balkans and Near East

kolacky * a sweet Czech yeast bun variously filled with fruit pulp, jam or nuts

koulourakia * Greek butter biscuits, by custom baked and eaten around Easter time

kreplach * in Jewish cuisine, small ravioli-like dumplings served with chicken soup

kromesky * a Russian-style croquette wrapped in bacon, then battered and fried

krupnik * traditional Polish pearl barley soup

kugelhopf * in Alsatian cookery, a sweetened Bundt cake flavoured with raisins

kulfi * an Indian flavoured frozen dairy dessert, akin to a cone of dense ice cream

kushari * a rich Egyptian vegetarian dish featuring mixed rice, macaroni, and lentils

ladikanee * an Indian sweet named in the 1850s after then vicereine Lady Canning

larb * a spicy and aromatic Laotian minced meat salad

lasagne * an Italian casserole of layered pasta sheets alternated with various fillings

lavash * a widely consumed Middle Eastern cracker bread

lebkuchen * German gingerbread cookies or cake; a traditional Christmas treat

linguine * thin flat Italian pasta strands, or "little tongues"

linzertorte * a jam tart encrusted in a lattice of spiced nut pastry, from Austria

liquamen * a fermented fish sauce used as a relish in classical and Byzantine cuisine

lokshen * noodles, in Jewish cookery; typically used to make egg noodle soup

loukoumi * Greek-style Turkish delight, or cubes of jellied candy

lumpia * a popular Indonesian spring roll appetizer

lyonnaise * denoting a style of fried potato dish done with onions or in onion sauce

macaroni * curved narrow tubes of short-cut Italian pasta

macédoine * a salad mix or cocktail of diced vegetables or fruit, of French origin

machbous * a dish of meat and mixed rice widely enjoyed across the Gulf states

madeleine * a small rich distinctively shell-shaped sponge cake, from the Lorraine

madrilène * a French consommé flavoured with tomato; frequently served chilled

mafrooda * a near-white Arabian flatbread, similar to pita but without a pocket

majoun * an intoxicating Moroccan cannabis leaf candy made with ghee and honey

malloreddus * Sardinian pasta dumplings made from besaffroned semolina flour

mamaliga * a Romanian polenta dish, often garnished with cheese or sour cream

mandelbrot * "almond bread," a cookie in the Ashkenazi Jewish culinary tradition

mansaf * the national dish of Jordan; lamb cooked in yoghurt sauce on a bed of pilaff

margherita * a Neapolitan pizza variant suitable for vegetarians

marinara * a Neapolitan pasta dish in "sailor's sauce," though sans seafood content

massaman * a mild Thai curry with origins in Muslim Malaysian cuisine

mayonnaise * a cold and creamy culinary dressing, of French or Menorcan invention

mazamorra * "Moor's dough," a milky Latin American maize pudding or porridge

mazurek * a traditional sweet Polish shortcake, baked on high days and holy days

melitzanosalata * Greek aubergine salad

mendiant * a hard French chocolate confection studded with nuts and dried fruits

menudo * a highly seasoned Mexican tripe soup

meringue * in French cookery, a crisp yet chewy dessert topping and delicacy

mesclun * a Provençal salad consisting of mixed young leafy greens and herbs

meunière * denotes fish done in flour and butter, "in the style of the miller's wife"

mignonette * a French cracked pepper sauce best served with raw oysters

millefeuille * French custard slice; sheets of puff pastry with sundry sweet fillings

minestrone * a rich Italian soup of meat stock thickened with vegetables and pasta

mirepoix * in French cuisine, an aromatic three-vegetable seasoning and sauce base

mohinga * a Burmese street food favourite of rice noodles in a spicy, fish-based broth

mole poblano * the quintessential Mexican "people's sauce"— thick, dark, chocolatey

molokhia * an Egyptian stew named for the "vegetable of kings," its main ingredient

mondongo * a basic stew of diced offal and vegetables, eaten across the Spanish Caribbean

monokythron * historically, an extravagant "one pot" Byzantine fish soup

montelimar * a regional French speciality nut confection or nougat

moules-frites * classic Belgian mussels and fries

moussaka * a signature Greek lamb bake prepared with aubergines and cheese sauce

mousseline * Chantilly sauce; hollandaise frothed with whipped cream or egg white

muesli * a Swiss breakfast dish of rolled oats, nuts, and dried fruits, taken with milk

muhallabia * a creamy Middle Eastern dessert flavoured with rose or orange water

mulligatawny * "pepper water," a spicy Eastern Indian meat soup

mushimono * steamed dishes or foods, with reference to Japanese gastronomy

mustaceus * an ancient Roman wedding cake, customarily baked on laurel leaves

mutabbal * Near Eastern "spiced" baba ghanoush, or purée of chargrilled aubergines

napoleonshat * a triangular Danish cake made with marzipan and chocolate

nasi goreng * Indonesian-style mixed "fried rice," the nation's signature dish

navarin * a French casserole of mutton and root vegetables, most especially turnip

ndolé * a Cameroonian spinach and peanut stew with, optionally, seafood or beef

nesselrode * a frozen Russian dessert with chopped chestnuts and candied fruits

nightingales' tongues * a dish reputedly served at sybaritic Roman banquets of old

nigiri * a Japanese sushi dish consisting of sliced raw fish served atop sticky rice

nihari * a popular Pakistani lamb shank stew of royal Mughal culinary heritage

nockerln * in Austro-Bavarian cookery, little light dumplings; northern gnocchi

nougat * a chewy continental sweetmeat made with roasted almonds and egg white

oenogarum * an ancient Roman condiment of fish sauce diluted with boiled wine

olla podrida * Andalusian "rotten pot," a spiced stew of mixed meat and vegetables

omelette * French egg pancake

orangeat * an archaic French sweetmeat of candied orange peel

orzo * tiny pellets of Italian pasta shaped like grains of rice or barley

oshizushi * Osaka "pressed sushi," the rice and toppings being compressed then cut

ossobucco * a slow-cooked veal shank stew, from the kitchens of Lombardy

oxoleum * early European salad dressing; a precursor of the modern vinaigrette

paella * a classic Valencian rice dish, suffused with saffron; the contents are simmered and served in a special large pan

pakora * a spicy savoury fritter enjoyed across the Subcontinent as a snack or starter

palacsinta * a Hungarian filled crêpe, variously eaten as a main course or as a sweet

pampushky * traditional Ukrainian doughnuts, prepared with a variety of fillings

panettone * a rich Milanese brioche, customarily consumed at Christmas as a dessert

pankarpia * a honey-soaked Hellenistic Greek "all-fruit" cake, offered up to the gods

pannacotta * an Italian "cooked cream" dessert, served chilled with sauce or syrup

panzanella * a Tuscan bread salad made with tomatoes and chopped greens

papadzul * "the food of the master," an enchilada-style mestizo dish from Yucatan

pappardelle * a type of broad ribboned pasta, typically served with a meat sauce

paprikash * a family of creamy paprika flavoured white meat stews, from Hungary

paratha * a popular and versatile unleavened Indian flatbread, usually pan-fried

parmentier * denotes a dish prepared or garnished with potatoes; French cottage pie

parmigiana * denotes a dish prepared or garnished with Parmesan cheese

pasanda * a mild and creamy lamb curry made with almonds; of Mughal origin

pastasciutta * Italian commercial dried pasta; also, any basic pasta first course plate

pastizzi * Malta's signature savoury pastries, invariably filled with ricotta or peas

paximathia * Greek-style biscotti or rusks

payasam * a sweet Sri Lankan sago dessert prepared especially for festive occasions

pelmeni * Russian ravioli, or dumplings with a thin dough shell and savoury filling

peperonata * Sicilian ratatouille; a dish of stewed peppers, tomatoes and onions

pepparkakor * Swedish gingersnap biscuits; a seasonal Christmas treat

pezzoccheri * a style of long thick buckwheat noodles, from the north of Italy

pfeffernüsse * German Yuletide gingerbread cookies, iced, and spiced

phal * a Bangalore curry consisting of mutton or lamb cooked in a coriander gravy

pho * Vietnamese rice noodle soup; now a global byword for the nation's cuisine

piccata * an Italian dish of veal escalopes done in lemon, parsley, and butter sauce

pilaff * a South Asian savoury dish based around rice steamed in a seasoned broth

piperrada * a favourite Basque side dish of peppers, scrambled eggs, and tomatoes

piri-piri * a Portuguese hot red chilli pepper sauce, with origins in colonial Africa

pirogi * in Polish, Russian, and Ukrainian cookery, small pastry turnovers or pies

pissaladière * Provençal pizza; a very Nice dish indeed

pistolet * a small round Belgian bread roll

pistou * Provençal pesto, sans nuts; also, a thick vegetable soup made with the same

pithivier * a distinctively decorative French almond tart

pizzella * a small pizza; alternatively, a traditional round Italian wafer biscuit

plombière * a classic French ice cream dessert, originally made in lead moulds

plumpy * an enriched peanut paste distributed internationally during famine crises

pôchouse * a stew of freshwater fish poached in local white wine, from Burgundy

poffertjes * traditional sweet Dutch mini puffed pancakes

polenta * a rustic Italian porridge of boiled cornmeal, also edible baked as a loaf

polkagrisar * Swedish peppermint candy stick twists

poppadom * a crispy round Indian cracker, served as an accompaniment or snack

poshintang * "body preservation stew," a Korean state euphemism for dog soup

pot-au-feu * a famous home-cooked French beef stew; anciently called pot-pourri

poulette * a special velouté with added egg yolks for use with chicken and poultry

poutine * a Quebecois dish or "mess" of chips and cheese curds in gravy

pretzel * in German cookery, a brittle salted biscuit shaped after a loose knot

primavera * denotes a style of pasta dish made with assorted fresh spring vegetables

printanier * denotes a French soup or casserole made with diced spring vegetables

profiterole * a small French cream puff typically topped with chocolate sauce

puchero * a stew of meat and vegetables consumed the length of Latin America

pumpernickel * "devil's fart," a dark, dense, and difficult to digest German rye bread

pupusa * a thick Salvadorean corn tortilla stuffed with various savouries, then fried

puttanesca * denoting a pasta dish cooked with a sauce containing anything to hand

pyramous * an ancient Greek speciality wheat cake made with sesame and honey

quadrefiori * meaty Italian ruffled pasta "squares," ideal for capturing sauces

quenelle * a poached forcemeat ball formerly used as a garnish in haute cuisine

quesadilla * a popular Mexican-style cheese toastie snack, pan-fried or grilled

quiche * an open egg flan containing assorted savoury fillings, from the Alsace

quoorma * a creamy mild Indian curry, traditionally cooked with lamb or mutton

raclette * a Franco-Swiss cheese dish, usually eaten with boiled potatoes and pickles

ragù * a well-seasoned Italian meat and tomato sauce—the authentic bolognese

raita * in Indian cookery, a cooling side salad of yoghurt and chopped cucumber

ramen * Japanese white noodles and key item in a savoury broth of the same name

rasam * a thin, highly spicy southern Indian soup prepared with tamarind juice

rasgulla * a favourite Bengali dessert consisting of curd cheese cooked in syrup

rassolnik * an old Russian soup of pickled cucumbers with giblets, notably kidneys

ratafia * a small sweet almond macaroon of Creole French invention

ratatouille * a classic Provençal vegetable stew, served and eaten hot or cold

ravigote * a herby, heavily seasoned French culinary sauce and dressing

ravioli * small square parcels of Italian pasta containing various savoury fillings

refritos * Mexican refried beans, served as a main hash or as an accompaniment

religieuse * a French patisserie item resembling a double, conjoined profiterole

rellenos * Mexican stuffed poblano chilli peppers, battered in egg, and deep-fried

rémoulade * a mayonnaise-style sauce used as a dressing for salad or seafood dishes

rendang * an Indonesian curry prepared by stewing beef in coconut milk and spices

reshteh * a hearty soup in Iranian cuisine, made with abundant thin egg noodles

ribollita * reheated Tuscan minestrone made with leftover bread and vegetables

rigatoni * a type of Italian pasta in the form of short macaroni tubes

risotto * a creamy northern Italian dish based on arborio rice cooked slowly in stock

rockahominy * Native American trail food made from parched or roasted cornmeal

rogan josh * a Kashmiri dish of lamb or mutton prepared in a rich red curry sauce

rojak * a tangy Southeast Asian salad of mixed sliced fruit and vegetables

romazava * the national dish of Madagascar; a one-pot beef broth

romesco * a Catalan nut and red pepper sauce, traditionally eaten with fish

rösti * Swiss-style potato hash browns, eaten for breakfast or as a side dish

rotkohl * a ubiquitous German side dish of sweet and sour red cabbage

roulade * a term from French cuisine indicating a cooked dish of filled rolled meat

rubaboo * formerly, a French-Canadian potage of boiled pemmican or peas and corn

rugelach * a popular Jewish fruit and nut pastry resembling a croissant

rumaki * a Polynesian-style bite of bacon-wrapped chicken liver and water chestnuts

sachertorte * a Viennese speciality chocolate gateau, served with whipped cream

sagamité * an old Native American porridge of boiled hominy and animal fat

saganaki * a Greek mezze plate of pan-seared breaded cheese, with lemon juice

saltah * a rich Yemeni soup or stew, taken for lunch; considered the national dish

salteña * a Bolivian pastry turnover filled with a hot and typically meaty broth

saltimbocca * an Italian dish of veal rolled in prosciutto and sage leaves, marinated

sambal * a signature Southeast Asian hot sauce or relish

sambhar * a Tamil dish of dhal and vegetables cooked in a spicy tamarind chowder

samosa * an Indian fried pastry case normally containing a savoury vegetarian mix

sancoche * a thick Caribbean soup consisting of meat and local root vegetables

sandesh * a popular sweetmeat or milk dessert in Bengali cuisine

sarladaise * a dish of potatoes cooked in duck fat, from the Périgord

sashimi * a Japanese dish of fresh raw fish sliced thin, eaten with soy and wasabi

sauerbraten * a German pot roast traditionally prepared with marinated horse meat

savarin * a light ring-shaped cake named in honour of a famous French gastronomer

semifreddo * a term for a class of partially frozen Italian ice cream cakes or desserts

sfogliatelle * shells of puff pastry filled with various candied fruits, from Campania

shabu-shabu * a Japanese culinary take on the iconic Mongolian hotpot

shariyya * vermicelli or little noodles, in Arabian cookery

shchi * the quintessential Russian cabbage soup

shirumono * a culinary category denoting Japanese soup meals

shrikhand * a sweet western Indian pudding made of strained dahi or yoghurt

sillsillat * a bygone Swedish pickled herring salad with beets, onions, and eggs

sinigang * a notably sour Philippine stew, best matched with fish sauce

skorthalia * Greek-style garlic dip

smørrebrød * "butter and bread," an elaborate Danish open rye bread sandwich

soba * traditional thin Japanese buckwheat noodles

soccarat * the caramelized crust of gourmet crunchy rice adhering to a paella pan

sofrito * in Spanish cuisine, an aromatic base sauce used in many savoury dishes

solimeme * "sun and moon," an old Alsatian brioche not unlike a Sally Lunn teacake

solyanka * a chunky Russian beef soup, characteristically sweet and sour to taste

sopaipillas * sweet Spanish American-style fritters; a highly popular snack food

soubise * French onion sauce, often served over fish or eggs

spanakopitakia * Greek spinach pie

spätzle * German baby egg noodle dumplings

speculaas * highly decorative Dutch spiced shortcrust Christmas cookies

springerle * highly decorative German anise-flavoured Christmas cookies

spumoni * a colourful Italian layered ice cream dessert studded with candied fruits

stamppot * mashed potatoes and vegetables; a classic recipe from the Netherlands

stifado * a Greek stew featuring beef braised in wine with onions, tomatoes, and herbs

spaghettini
fine southern Italian pasta strings, often served with a piquant sauce

stollen * a traditional German festive sugared fruitcake

strangoloprevete * "strangle-priest," an Italian viand of gnocchi with tomato sauce

streusel * in German cookery, a crumbly bread topping or cake baked with same

stroganoff * a classic Russian dish of beef cooked with sour cream and mushrooms

stroopballetje * a Dutch butterscotch confectionery

struffoli * Neapolitan doughballs sweetened with caramel, honey, or the like

subgum * any Chinese dish, as chow mein, of noodles with assorted vegetables

succotash * a First Peoples potluck stew of sweetcorn, pulses, and other vegetables

sufganiyot * in Jewish cuisine, special, jelly-filled doughnuts served on Hannukah

suissesse * denoting a particular gastronomic method of preparing cheese soufflé

sukiyaki * a favourite Japanese one-pot dish of beef simmered in a sweet soy broth

sushi * a family of light Japanese "vinegared rice" dishes, variously garnished

tabbouleh * a Levantine Arab vegetarian salad; widely consumed as a mezze dish

tafelspitz * an Austrian dish of beef boiled in broth with horseradish and applesauce

tagliatelle * a type of narrow ribboned pasta; associated with the cuisine of Bologna

tamago * Japanese "cooked egg" sushi, consisting of squares of omelette on rice

tamale * a Mexican dish of seasoned meat and masa steamed or baked in corn husks

tamari * gluten-free soy sauce, from Japan

tapenade * a Provençal culinary dip made from puréed black olives and capers

tarallucci * ring-shaped lemon crackers; a traditional snack food in the south of Italy

taramasalata * a classic Greek spread of carp or cod roe, often served as an appetizer

tarkhana * a special chicken noodle soup common to Turkish and Armenian cookery

tartare * of a fish or meat dish, sliced fine and served raw with sauce and seasoning

tartiflette * a hearty wintertime dish of potatoes, cheese and bacon, from the Savoy

tempura * Japanese-style seafood or vegetable fritters

teriyaki * in Japanese gastronomy, glazed and grilled food; also, a sauce for same

termites on toast * a popular street food snack in Kenya, by numerous accounts

tharid * a historic Arabian stew of lamb and vegetables served over crispy flatbread

thermidor * a lobster dish prepared and cooked according to a method created by the "king of chefs," Auguste Escoffier

thieboudienne * "rice and fish," a one-pot meal considered Senegal's national dish

tikka * in Punjabi cuisine, a dish of meat cutlets prepared in an aromatic marinade

tindaloo * a super-hot Bangladeshi curry recipe, heavy on habanero chillies

tinola * a Philippine chicken and ginger soup, often served as a main course dish

tiramisu * Tuscan trifle; a modern, classic "pick-me-up" dessert

tortellini * small Italian pasta rounds folded to encase a filling, as of meat or cheese

tortilla * Spanish omelette

tortoni * an Italian frozen cream cake, topped with chopped cherries and almonds

tostones * Latin American twice-fried green plantain fritters, served with garlic dip

totopos * Mexican tortilla chips

tourteau * French cheesecake

tsukemono * in traditional Japanese cuisine, a side dish of choice pickled vegetables

tum-tum * a West Indies dish of boiled pounded plantain, eaten like potato pudding

turbigo * a classic lamb kidney dish, from Lombardy

turrón * Spanish nougat; a popular Christmas treat

tzatziki * a fragrant Greek mezze dip of yoghurt with cucumber, garlic, and mint

tzimmes * in Ashkenazi Jewish cookery, a sweet root vegetable and dried fruit stew

udon * thick and chewy Japanese wheat flour noodles, often served in a light broth

ugali * a starchy cornmeal mush prized as a versatile side dish in Kenyan cookery

ultra-pizza * any avant-garde Italian pizza prepared with non-traditional ingredients

uthappam * a thick, South Indian breakfast pancake topped with various vegetables

varenyky * classic Ukrainian boiled and filled dumplings, similar to Russian pirogi

vasilopita * a speciality Greek New Year's cake concealing a lucky gold coin

velouté * a velvety French savoury sauce built from stock, cream, butter, and flour

vermicelli * "little worms," long slender strands of pasta, popular in Italian cooking

véronique * denotes a dish served in a cream sauce containing seedless white grapes

vichyssoise * in French cuisine, a cold cream soup made with potatoes and leeks

vinaigrette * the quintessential French salad dressing

vincisgrassi * a luxurious baked lasagne first course dish from the Italian Marche

vol-au-vent * a light, French puff pastry titbit enclosing a savoury mix with sauce

warqa * a paper-thin Moroccan pastry used to make signature dishes such as bestilla

wienerbrød * "Vienna bread," a Danish pastry

wonton * a soup served with small savoury Cantonese-style dumplings

wott * a spicy, Ethiopian red stew, emblematic of the broader regional cuisine

yawarlukru * "blood soup," an Ecuadorean winter stew of lamb's offal and entrails

yeyebessissi * a mystery main dish from Togo; one for readers to research

youvetsi * a Greek recipe of beef or lamb cooked with orzo in a rich tomato sauce

zabaglione * a sweet Italian "egg punch" dessert; known in France as *sabayon*

zarzuela * a hearty seafood variety stew in Catalan gastronomy

zegeni * an Eritrean beef stew cooked with a piquant tomato and berbere sauce

zeppole * a deep-fried southern Italian sweetmeat similar to a doughnut or churro

zuccotto * "little pumpkin," a semi-frozen sponge cake dessert of Florentine origin

zwieback * in German cookery, rusk or "teething toast" made from egg bread

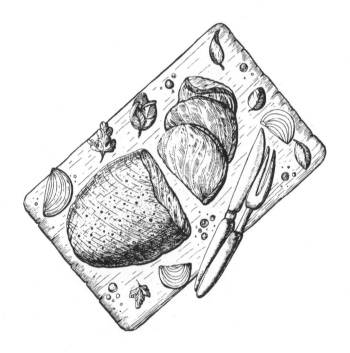

What's Cooking?

Culinary Arts and Artisans

> *"In France, cooking is a serious art form and a national sport."*
> **— Julia Child**

à la * of a dish, prepared in the manner of, or by the method of, or after the style of

aboyeur * a clerk or "barker" in the French restaurant brigade system, responsible for apportioning orders from the waiting staff to the correct station within the kitchen

acidulate * to make slightly sour, as by flavouring a dish or food item with vinegar

ad gustum * "to one's taste," an instruction to be as generous or sparing as one desires in complementing a dish with condiments

aerate * in baking, to raise bread by introducing air or other gas to the process

alecize * to season or sauce with herring or anchovy pickle

alimentary * culinary; pertaining to matters of the kitchen and the stomach

alla casalinga * of a dish, prepared home-cooking style

allay * to carve up a bird for cooking, notably pheasant

alliate * to flavour with garlic

allumette * to cut hard vegetables into matchsticks for ease of even cooking

arch-magirist * a head cook

aromatizate * to season with spice or impart a spicy flavour to a dish

artisanal * of bread or cheese, crafted in small batches using traditional techniques

assation * the action of roasting or baking

asweeten * to infuse or impart an element of sweetness to a dish

attire * to dress deer for the table

autocondimentation * the gratuitous addition of condiments to a dish or meal

baconize * to smoke food, as per bacon; to prepare pork belly or loin as bacon

bain marie * a style of gently warming sauces and so forth, or melting ingredients

bake-off * a baking competition, especially between amateur doughbangers

bakership * proficiency as a baker

barbecute * to grill or cook on the barbecue

barding * the practice of larding meat or game to prevent drying before cooking

bebaste * to apply gravy, fat, or the like to meat while cooking to maintain moisture

besaffron * to stain or season an ingredient or dish with saffron—the most expensive spice, indeed foodstuff, in the world

bias-slice * to slice food crosswise at a 45-degree angle

bishop * to inadvertently allow milk or cream to burn and ruin while cooking

blanching * cooking nuts or vegetables by plunging into scalding then iced water

blitz * to blend or purée food in a processor

bloating * the action of curing fish by smoking until semi-dried

bobachee * an Anglo-Indian term for a male cook

bombard * to stuff meat or game, especially fillet of veal with the bone removed

boucher * a resident butcher or poulterer working in a large professional kitchen

boulanger * a resident baker working in a large professional kitchen

brasill * braising, being a form of stewing meat in a tightly closed pan

brittling * butcher work, notably dressing venison or boar for the table

broasting * a method of cooking, chicken in particular, using a pressure fryer

brûlée * to coat food with a sugary crust by use of a chef's torch; to caramelize

buccaning * the act of barbecuing, or exposing meat to fire or smoke

butchery * the craft of working with knives and tools to strip meat from a carcass

butterfly * a technique whereby meat cuts are split in two for ease of grilling

calver * to prepare salmon, while still living or freshly caught, for the table

candify * to preserve or encrust fruit in boiled sugar so as to make sweetmeats

caramelization * in cooking, the stage in boiling syrup when the sugars turn brown

carbonadoing * the action of grilling or broiling scored meat over a charcoal fire

caryophyllate * to flavour with cloves

caveach * to pickle filleted mackerel in vinegar—a style popular in the West Indies

chargrilling * the action of searing meat or fish quickly using intense direct heat

chef de cuisine * a senior or executive chef

chef de partie * a station chef, in charge of a particular area of a commercial kitchen

chef traiteur * a chef who prepares meals to be served in another establishment

chefdom * the domain and occupation of a professional cook

cheffing * cooking in a professional capacity

cheffy * proficient, though perhaps somewhat pretentious, in cooking

chiffonade * a technique for finely slicing herbs and leafy greens into long thin strips

clarify * to melt butter in order to obtain milk fat free from solids or impurities

cocture * the practice and process of cooking; also, a synonym for the act of digestion

cokysse * a female cook in days of yore

comfiture * the process of preserving fruit for culinary purposes

commis chef * an apprentice or junior chef

communard * a cook who prepares meals for other restaurant staff

concasse * to dice or rough-chop peeled and seeded vegetables, notably tomatoes

conching * the process, invented by Rodolphe Lindt, of kneading, mixing, and aerating heated chocolate in liquid form to produce a smooth, rich final product

concoct * to boil, bake. or simmer a number of ingredients together; to cook creatively

concoction * any act of culinary creation

conditure * the act of preserving, pickling or seasoning food

confectionate * to prepare candied delicacies with sugar or syrup

confiseur * a cook who prepares candies and petits fours in a professional kitchen

consewe * anciently, a method of cutting up and cooking fowl, especially capons

convection * a mode of oven-cooking food with a high liquid content

cookbook * a reference work for the kitchen, containing recipes, tips, and much else

cookee * an assistant or rookie camp cook

cookery * the action of preparing food by the agency of heat or fire

cookics * a Thackerean nonce word for cooking as a special sphere of human activity

cookly * after the manner or in the style of a skilful cook

cookment * an old regional expression for cookery

cookprint * the aggregate energy and other resources expended preparing meals

cook-ruffian * an unskilled or indifferent cook

cookship * the office or function of a cook

coquicide * the killing of a cook

coquinate * to perform as, or pass oneself off as, a cook

cordon bleu * denoting the highest class or foremost quality in cooking

cosyner * formerly, a head cook or culinary supervisor in a priory kitchen

coupage * the action of cutting or carving meat at the dinner table

credenziero * a cold food cook who prepared delicacies at medieval Italian banquets; perhaps unsurprisingly the term also denoted one who foretasted food for poison

cryovacking * a sous-vide cooking technique wherein vacuum-packed food is gently cooked in warm water

crystallize * to preserve fruit by way of coating or impregnating it with sugar

159

cuisine * a distinctive regional or national method, manner, or style of cooking

cuisine bourgeoise * simple home-cooking; good plain fare

cuisine classique * a refined version of canonical cooking in the grand French style

cuisine minceur * lighter gourmet cooking for those eager to become or remain thin; dairy and high-calorie foods in particular are avoided

cuisinier * a cook, especially one within the French brigade de cuisine hierarchy

cuisson * allowing meat to stew in its own juice; literally "cooking" or "baking"

culinarian * jocularly, a cook or chef

culinarious * pertaining to cooking and affairs of the kitchen

culinary constructivism * molecular gastronomy, where chemistry meets cuisine

curry * to render a dish more intensely flavoursome or fiery by the use of hot spices

cury * the standard Old English term for cookery, as well as cooked food itself

custron * a menial assistant to a chef or cook; a scullion or kitchen servant

decoct * to extract a flavour essence by way of heating or boiling; loosely, to cook

décorateur * a chef devoted to preparing showpiece fancies and speciality cakes

deglazing * the practice of dissolving the residual browned cooking juices or meat particles deposited in a cooking pot to produce a rich gravy or sauce

demi-chef * an assistant station chef within a large commercial restaurant

deplumation * the action of preparing a fowl for the pot by first plucking its feathers

despumation * the action of skimming or clarifying honey

devein * to remove a prawn's intestinal tract before cooking

disgarbaging * the butchering and disembowelment of fowls destined for the table

disscale * to remove the shell or other carapace from shrimp, crayfish, and the like

disseason * to render a dish tasteless or ruin the eater's sense of taste

dissweeten * to deprive a dish of its sweetness; to make sour or unpalatable

domestic goddess * a female household cook possessed of surpassing culinary flair

domestic science * the study of household skills, notably cooking; home economics

deep-frying

a form of cooking food, be it chips or — infamously — chocolate bars, immersed whole in sizzling fat or oil

doughbanger * an Australian vernacular expression for a humble cook

drizzle * to finely pour or trickle oil or syrup over the surface of food

drudge-pudding * a lowly kitchen staff member or scullion

dulcescate * to sweeten food

dulcification * the action of sweetening, as with molasses and such

dumple * humorously, to make a dumpling

dumpoke * to cook mutton *dum pukht* style, slowly in a sealed pot over a low flame

edulcorate * to make a dish sweeter or more palatable

egotarian cuisine * an unwelcome trend toward culinary self-indulgence and competitive showing off in the professional kitchen

elixation * the process of boiling or stewing, as of fish guts

embitterment * the action of imparting a bitter flavour or taste

embroche * to skewer an animal or otherwise prepare meat for the spit

emulsification * in cooking, the blending and binding of immiscible ingredients to make silky sauces and creamy dressings, such as mayonnaise from oil and vinegar

engastration * the act of stuffing one bird inside another, as in preparing turducken

entremetier * a chef who prepares entrées within the brigade de cuisine system

estouffade * a variant braising technique, from the rich brown stock of the same name

exossation * the action of pitting stone-fruit

expediter * a kitchen clerk who organizes the dispatch of plated food to the table

fabrication * the process of boning and trimming beef carcasses for sub-primal cuts

flamb * to singe or baste food with flaming gravy or lard

flash-fry * to sizzle food at a very high temperature for a short period of time

flavourist * a chemist cum culinarian employed in the food industry to synthesize new flavours or reinvigorate natural ones

flensing * cutting up seal or whale meat for the pot

fleshing * the art and practice of butchery

flitching * the process of cutting up halibut into steak sides or "flitches"

food stylist * a skilled cook; also, one who arranges the food for a gastroporn shoot

foodpairing * the art of matching up innovative yet flavoursome food combinations

formula * a recipe, or full inventory of the ingredients comprising a prepared dish

fraisage * a means of obtaining a flaky pie crust by smearing butter pieces into flour

frenching * the action of slicing vegetables lengthwise into long, thin slivers

fricandeau * to dress meat, especially veal cut, in fine strips from the leg

fricasseer * one who serves up fowl or rabbit sautéed and braised in a white sauce

friturier * a dedicated deep-fry cook within the classic restaurant brigade system

frizzle * to fry or grill food with considerable spitting and spluttering from the pan

furnage * the craft of baking

garde-manger * a cook with expertise in preparing cold food dishes; a pantry chef

frush

to carve chicken for the table

garnish * to dress a dish with decorative trimmings or touches

garniture * the act and art of adding savoury embellishments to a prepared dish

gastrogigantism * the cooking of stunt, supersized dishes; off the scale culinary showmanship

gastronomics * the signature cooking style or cuisine of a given culture or country

gastrophysics * the application of experimental scientific methodologies to cooking

gastroporn * dishy dishes; the representation of food in an exaggeratedly sensual manner, from luxurious images of plated food to luscious cookbook or menu prose

geremumble * to gut seafood, or garbage fish

glacier * a chef who prepares frozen and cold desserts in a large professional kitchen

gralloch * to disembowel deer; to dress venison for the pot

gratinate * to broil or grill food until it is brown on top; to cook *au gratin*

grillardin * a specialist grill cook within the brigade de cuisine system

grub-spoiler * an older humorous term for a humble cook

hasteler * a roasting cook, in particular one who turns the spit

haute barnyard * high-end cooking which foregrounds the farm origins of the food

haute cuisine * high-quality cooking, especially in the classic refined French style

hippogastronomy * humorously, the art of cooking and consuming horse flesh

home economist * a domestic cook— god, goddess, or otherwise

hooshgod * a hash cook of little skill or sophistication, notably one serving at camp

home-style

of cooking or other culinary preparation, simple and unpretentious

hypercooking * preparing meals in a manner which most economizes on energy and other resource consumption

icer * one skilled in preparing and spreading icing on cakes and pastries

indore * to glaze or make golden, as pie crust with egg yolk

indulciate * to sweeten a dish

infumate * to cure food or dry by smoking

injelly * to enclose food in jelly, as with meat preserved for use in jars

interlardment * in cooking, the mixing of lean meat with layers of bacon or fat

jipper * to baste a dish with gravy, lard, or dripping as it cooks

jugging * the practice of stewing or boiling game for a length of time in a casserole

julienning * a technique for chopping vegetables by way of long, thin knife strokes

juniperate * to flavour food with juniper berries

kippering * preparing fish by splitting butterfly fashion, salting, and smoking

kitchen * to season or give relish to a dish

kitchen-aphorism * the precepts of culinary wisdom; the study of kitchen craft

kitchenary * a rarely encountered synonym for culinary

kitchendom * the world and the ways of cooks and chefs

kitchening * from the humble act of cooking, to the high art of cookery

kitchenist * a comedic term for a cook, or one who labours in the kitchen for a living

kitchenry * kitchen staff considered collectively; also, the fine art of cooking itself

kitchen-vassalage * confinement to the drudgery of the kitchen

kitchen-wallah * a cook's assistant, allocated only inferior kitchen duties

koshering * preparing meals according to the prescriptions and proscriptions of Jewish dietary law, notably drawing the blood from flesh or fowl with water and salt

la sauce est tout! * the secret's in the sauce

laminating * in baking, the process of preparing dough puff-pastry style

leavening * in baking, causing bread or dough to rise through the addition of yeast

legumier * a specially assigned vegetable cook within the brigade kitchen regime

liaison * in culinary speak, the process of thickening sauce with egg yolks and cream

liquor * to glaze pie crust; alternatively, to impregnate or flavour food with alcohol

maceration * in cooking, the softening or breaking of food into pieces using a liquid

mageira * the female sublimation or suppression of libido through cooking

mageirocophobia * a fear and loathing of cooking: "can't cook, won't cook!"

magirics * cooking considered as artistic endeavour or scientific discipline

magirologist * an expert and experienced cook; one well versed in kitchen craft

malkin * a term originally denoting a kitchen skivvy or scullery wench

marination * the soaking or steeping of food in a seasoned liquid prior to cooking

marling * the process of sousing food in vinegar

marmiton * an apprentice cook; alternatively, a pot washer or kitchen porter

matelote * to stew a dish of fish or eels in red wine

mediastine * a kitchen drudge or dogsbody

mellify * to sweeten or saturate with honey

messman * a military cook

microcook * to cook or reheat food in a microwave oven

miscookery * rank bad or otherwise inexpert cooking

mistaste * to spoil the flavour of a dish

mixiria * a procedure for preserving meat and fish, whereby the foodstuff is roasted in its own fat then sealed in a jar with another layer of fat atop

molecular gastronomy * the application of the principles of molecular chemistry to the practical science of cooking

Mrs Beeton * an acknowledged authority on cooking

muriate * to pickle food in brine

nappage * in baking, the process of glazing fruit tart with diluted apricot jam to prevent drying out

nectarize * to sweeten or saturate with nectar

nixtamalization * a culinary treatment wherein maize is rinsed and cooked in limewater; the resulting dough is the basis for corn tortillas, tamales, and suchlike

nostrum * a food recipe

nouvelle cuisine * a modernist culinary aesthetic accentuating freshness of ingredients and elegance of presentation

obdulcorate * to thoroughly sweeten

origanize * to enhance or flavour with marjoram or oregano

overdress * to overcook or overseason a dish

panage * the practice of coating food in breadcrumbs before cooking

panbroiling * the action of cooking meat in a pan with little to no fat

panifice * the craft or artifice of breadmaking

parbaking * partially baking a yeast product before it is rapidly frozen for storage

parboiling * partially boiling food prior to further cooking in another fashion

parbroiling * a method of dry-heating food in the oven until it is mostly cooked

passulate * to sun-dry or otherwise dehydrate grapes to produce raisins

pastrycookery * the preparation of hotcakes and other pastry items

patissier * a master pastry cook within the brigade de cuisine restaurant hierarchy

paunch * to gut the internal organs from a rabbit or hare before putting it in the pot

pearling * in confectionery, a procedure for bringing sugar or syrup to the sweet-spot of stickiness known as "pearl"

petecury * good, honest cooking on a small or simple scale

piquer * to insert garlic or another flavour ingredient when dressing meat or poultry

pistate * to bake, in old coinage

pizzaiolo * a professional pizza maker, notably in the traditional Neapolitan style

plongeur * a restaurant kitchen's resident dish washer

poisoner * jocularly, a cook feeding a team of sheep shearers in the Outback

poissonnier * a specialist fish and shellfish cook in the restaurant brigade system

ponasking * the act of roasting game or fish on a spit or stick by an open fire

popinary * a lunchroom cook; by one learned account, a mere "egg scrambler"

porcupine * a former method of preparing beef or veal for the table

porger * one who renders meat kosher by removing the forbidden fats, veins, and sinews from a slaughtered animal's hindquarters

pottinger * a maker of thick soups, stocks, or stews; alternatively, a vegetable cook

pot-wrassler * a term applied over the years to chefs, cooks and kitchen maids alike

pudding-wright * a person skilled in making puddings

purée * to blend or strain fruit or vegetables to the consistency of smooth cream

quaddle * to parboil, or heat food in water or stock at just below boiling point

quadriller * to score the surface of grilled or broiled food in a criss-cross pattern

quinse * to carve up game birds such as plover or quail for the pot

rander * one who prepares meat by cutting the flesh into "rands" or long strips

razzle * to singe meat on the outside, leaving the inside not thoroughly cooked

receipt * the original English-language word for recipe, before the French alternative became the established vogue

recessipe * a cost-saving "recession recipe" that helps stretch one's food budget

recipe * a structured set of written notes detailing how to cook a given dish

recoct * to rehash food for a second or further time

red-cooking * a variant Asian braising technique also known as Chinese stewing

refreshing * the action of plunging cooked vegetables or herbs into cold water

regeneration * the action of heating and preparing food from frozen

remouillage * in cooking, the "rewetting" or reusing of bones from a previous stock

robatayaki * Japanese "fireside cooking," somewhat similar to western barbecuing

rôtisseur * a senior roast cook in the brigade restaurant regime

roundsman * a swing cook who fills in as required for all stations in the kitchen

saccharinize * to sweeten by the addition of saccharin rather than sugar

salamandering * the act of browning or broiling food under a red-hot metal plate

saliture * the process of preserving or perking up food with salt or pickle

saucier * a professional cook whose *métier* is preparing sauces; a sauté chef

sauté * to shallow-fry food quickly in a modest amount of hot fat, tossing as one goes

scollop * to bake oysters in a scallop shell or similarly shaped small pan

scrape-trencher * a college kitchen servant who cleans scholars' plates after use

scullion * a kitchen boy

scullionize * to perform menial kitchen tasks

scullionry * common kitchen service

seasonage * the addition of salt, herbs, spices, and the like to impart extra flavour to a made dish

shallow-fry * to pan-cook cutlets, fillets, or suchlike portions of food in a little hot oil

shirr * to poach eggs in cream rather than water

shucking * the act of deshelling oysters or clams prior to draining and cooking

slushy * a ship's cook

soupify * to make or convert into soup

sous-chef * the second in overall command within a large professional kitchen

sousing * the act of pickling victuals, usually vegetables, in vinegar

sous-vide * a cooking technique whereby food is first vacuum-sealed in a plastic pouch, then steamed low and slow

spalder * to split a fish open in order to cure it preparatory to cooking

spatchcock * to grill or "dispatch" fowl without fanfare or frills

spatulate * to scrape cake mixture from a bowl with the aid of a slice

spherification * in culinary science, shaping liquid food into balls resembling fish-roe

spitchcock * to cut up and cook eel

spit-roast * to cook meat skewered on a spit suspended over an open fire

spoil-broth * disparagingly, a cook

spud-barber * one who peels potatoes, an ancestral art known as spud-bashing

squiller * anciently, a kitchen servant placed in charge of all scullery work

sugarcoat * to sweeten an item of prepared food by blanketing it in sugar

sugarcraft * the art of embellishing cakes and cookies with icing sugar

superchill * to chill food to a moderate subzero temperature

stir-frying

a means of cooking mixed chopped food rapidly on a high heat, stirring the items in the wok or pan briskly all the while

suprêming * the process of making a rich cream sauce, such as a *suprême* or *velouté*

sweal * to roast a sheep whole in its own skin

swenge * an obsolete term meaning to beat eggs

symbolize * to blend ingredients in cooking

techno-cuisine * a synonym for molecular gastronomy

tenderization * a mode of softening meat using a special culinary hammer

teppanyaki * a form of Japanese cooking using a griddle built into the diner's table

throating * the action of heading and gutting a fish from gills to vent before cooking

tournant * a swing cook, one fulfilling largely auxiliary duties

trancheur * a large commercial kitchen's expert meat carver

turnbroach * formerly, a person who operates a roasting spit; a turnspit

twecipe * a micro-recipe for the social media era

über-chef * a head chef or top cook

undercook * to fail to heat a dish through sufficiently

undertranch * to carve up a porpoise for the table

vandyking * a manner of food-slicing deploying distinctive decorative zigzag cuts

velveting * a food-coating technique commonly used in Chinese stir-fry cuisine

waynpain * the lowest of lowly medieval kitchen servants or scullions

whig * to make or turn sour; to cause to curdle

CHAPTER 8

Tasting Notes: Flavour, Freshness (and So Forth)

> *"I like a cook who smiles out loud when he tastes his own work."*
> —**Robert Farrar Capon**

acerbitude * sourness or sharpness of taste, as with unripe fruit

acescency * tartness or asperity of taste

acetarious * denoting vegetables or plants used raw in salad, such as lettuce or cress

acetosity * the quality of being sour-tasting or vinegarish

acidulousness * a degree of sharpness or bitterness in flavour

ackerspritted * said of gathered potatoes that have sprouted prematurely

acridity * an uncomfortably corrosive bitterness of taste

acrimonious * extremely pungent to taste

acritude * an astringency in food that is irritating to the organs of taste

addleness * the degree of putrefaction or rottenness of eggs

agerdows * an early anglicization of agrodolce or aigredoux— "bittersweet"

al dente * of pasta, cooked firmer to the bite, not soggy or soft

173

alimonious * nourishing, full of goodness

alliaceous * tasting of garlic, leeks, or onions; garlicky

amarulence * bitterness of taste

ambrosiate * exceptionally sweet and pleasing to savour

ampery * a regional descriptor for cheese that is starting to reek and decay

amygdalaceous * having the flavour of almonds

amylaceous * starchy; applies to non-nitrogenous foods

apiaceous * savouring of parsley or similar herbs

appetizing * mouth-wateringly tasty

areastiness * rankness or rancidity in food.

argute * sharp of taste

aromatical * emitting an agreeable and appetizing odour

asparaginous * having shoots or stalks eaten in the fashion of asparagus spears

asperity * roughness or tartness of taste

assertive * denoting a cheese with a strong taste or aroma

astringency * sourness or similar harshness of taste

aurantiaceous * redolent of sour oranges

austereness * bitterness of taste

avenaceous * oaty

azymous * of bread, unleavened

bacon-farced * stuffed with bacon, as with pheasant and other game birds

barfsome * foul-tasting; nauseating

barnyardy * describes the musty flavour and aroma found in certain cheeses

battlesome * rich, filling, and nutritious

bedevilled * grilled or broiled with hot, spicy condiments

bismarcked * denotes herring that has been marinated prior to cooking

bitterness * one of the four core acknowledged flavour principles, along with sweetness, sourness, and saltiness

bittersweet * of food, imparting sweetness initially, with bitter notes to follow

blandness * the condition of being unseasoned or wanting in taste

bletted * of certain fruits, become soft and sweet to eat only after thorough ripening

blue-vinnied * of food in general, mouldy; more particularly, veined in the characteristic manner of blue cheeses

boisterous * formerly, coarse-tasting or tough to eat; unpalatable

borized * concerning meat cuts from animals infused with borax prior to slaughter

brackish * having an overpoweringly salty or briny taste

bread-combed * of honey, candied or sugary

brinage * the quality of brackishness or saltiness

brineless * of a dish, lacking in salt

briskness * an agreeable piquance or sharpness of taste

bromated * of baked goods, treated with a flour improver to strengthen the dough

butyrousness * butteriness, with regard to taste or texture

calorie-laden * of a prepared dish or item of food, overly rich or luxurious

caricous * figgy

carneous * meaty

caseous * cheesy

cathalic * briny; heavy on the salt

causticity * a biting or burning pungency of taste

cayenned * seasoned with cayenne peppers

cepaceous * smelling or tasting of garlic or onion

cerealious * pertaining to the qualities or characteristics of corn or edible grain

charchaunt * a medieval cookery term meaning thick or rich in consistency

charqued * a variant rendition of jerked, or dry-preserved

chewery * sour and on the point of going bad; not fresh

chickenability * humorously, that property that makes food as popular as chicken

chicoried * flavoured with chicory or endive, a bitter-tasting leafy vegetable

chocolatesque * reminiscent of or intended to resemble chocolate

chokely * denoting food that is dry and gritty in texture

churnability * the churning quality of butter, fat, cream, and the like

cibarious * fit to be eaten, edible; pertaining to food

cinnamonic * redolent or tasting of cinnamon

citrusy * having the flavour or aroma of lemons or some other citrus fruit; lemony

clupeoid * concerning or of the nature of the herring, anchovy, or sardine

cnisa * the characteristic fumes of cooking fat

coctible * cookable

coctile * baked or bakeable

compoted * coated in syrup

concoquent * of a set of ingredients, boiled together thoroughly

conditaneous * fit for pickling or preserving

confyte * seasoned or preserved

congustable * having a comparable flavour or taste

consumptible * edible, consumable

cookability * suitability or fitness for cooking

crabbedness * marked acridity or asperity of taste

creatic * pertaining to meat or animal food more broadly

crinkle-cut * of potato crisps or chips, shaped by slicing with a corrugated blade

croceate * of the colour or spice-nature of saffron

cucurbitaceous * having the bitterness of squashes, pumpkins, and the like

dainteous * delicious; pleasing to the palate

decoctible * capable of having flavour extracted through seething or boiling

decadent

a gastronomical cliché denoting a rich and luxuriant dessert

defiable * edible, as in digestible in the stomach

degerminated * of cornmeal, having shed most of its bran and germ during milling

deglutible * edible, as in capable of being swallowed

degustatory * highly flavoursome

dehydrated * in the form of instant or powdered food, such as soup mix or pot noodle

delectable * delicious; savoury to taste

delicative * dainty of taste; of the nature of delicacy foods

deliciosity * the quality of being highly pleasing to the palate

delish * informally, delicious

desiccated * of food, dried or powdered for preservation

devorative * capable of being or intended to be consumed in a single bite

devourable * that may be effortlessly and enjoyably scoffed

digestibility * the susceptibility of being well digested, as with wholesome food

disgustful * literally, offensive to taste; disgusting

distastable * quite unpleasant to the taste or unappealing to the palate

distasted * bland; devoid of flavour

doneness * the extent to which a dish has been sufficiently cooked for consumption

double-breasted * of turkeys, commercially bred to produce copious breast meat, though arguably at the expense of flavour

dough-baken * slack-baked, so remaining doughy

dulcitude * sweetness of taste

dulcoamare * bittersweet

dulcorous * sweet tasting

eager-dulce * simultaneously sweet and sour to taste

eatableness * the quality of being edible, or fit and proper for consumption

eatworthy * deserving of consumption; palatable

edibility * safeness and suitability for eating

edulious * edible, consumable

empyreumatized * of food, burnt or charred

enriched * with nutrients lost in the food-processing cycle restored or replaced

escal * eminently fit to be eaten

escalloped * of oysters, dressed with breadcrumbs, cream and condiments

esculency * edibility

eubrotic * good to eat

exalted * pungent or otherwise intense in flavour

excrementitious * shit—full of empty calories or ingredients of no nutritional value

explosive * a taste descriptor indicating a cheese bursting with flavour

exquisite * highly savoury; choice of flavour

extra-virgin * of olive oil, made from the first pressing of the finest-quality fruits

fabaceous * bean-like; having the property of beans

famelic * serving to stimulate the appetite, as with the smell of freshly cooked meat

farinaceous * being mealy in texture, or having the odour of milled wheat flour

fatuous * insipid; weak tasting

fieriness * a quality of food producing a sensation of heat when consumed

fillupy * of a food item or meal, satisfying

finger-lickin' good * supremely tasty

fire-fanged * of cheese, having acquired a scorched appearance or burnt taste

flavido * zestiness

flavour * that property of food or drink that excites the sense of taste

flavouriferous * "bearing flavour"—a poetical nonce word

flavourlessness * blandness or an outright absence of taste

flavourousness * the quality of being packed with flavour

flavoursome * full of flavour or relish; flavoury

food-grade * in respect of ingredients, of a quality suitable for human consumption

forfried * overfried

fortified * of an article or class of food, strengthened with added nutrients

foul-tasting * offensive to the palate

fracid * of fruit, overripe; decayed or in the process of decaying

free-range * of eggs, produced by poultry allowed to roam on open ground

freeze-dried * dehydrated at low temperature to preserve and extend shelf-life

frosted * decorated with icing or dusted with powdered sugar

frowy * musty, fusty, or stale

fructaceous * fruity

frumentarious * made of wheat or similar grain; corn-like

full-flavoured * intense in taste

fulsome * of food, cloying, highly filling, and hard to digest

fumette * the high scent or stench of meat or game when kept long

fusiony * characteristic of blending diverse food elements and cooking techniques from different cuisines

gadoid * concerning or of the nature of the cod, pollock, whiting, haddock, or hake

gallinaceous * pertaining to the qualities of domestic poultry or game birds

gaminess * the quality of being rank or pungent in flavour and aroma

gelatinous * possessing a jelly-like texture or consistency

geusioleptic * packed with flavour

gluten-free * of a dish or diet, containing strictly no gluten, a family of proteins commonly found in cereal grains

gobbity * pleasing to the palate

goloptious * wickedly delicious

gorgeable * that can be eagerly savoured and swallowed

graminaceous * wheaten or oaten

granulated * crushed or powdered, as of sugar

graveolent * having a heavy, fetid odour, as with rancid butter or putrid eggs

greenness * sourness or unripeness; alternatively, a want of season or spice

grossularious * of the nature of grapefruit or gooseberry

gruellous * resembling oatmeal pap in taste or texture

gustable * tasteable, indeed tasting of something pleasant; relishsome

gustatious * tasty, delicious

gustativeness * the quality of possessing flavour

gusto * good savour

halimous * suggestive of common or table salt

haut-gout * the intense gaminess of meat on the turn, once a highly prized taste

high-fibre * heavy in dietary fibre, supporting good digestive function

highly seasoned * richly flavoured with spices or condiments

honeysome * crammed with honey or similar sweetness

hordeaceous * of or like barley with regard to nuttiness and chewiness

horror * an outdated expression for coarseness or loathsomeness of taste

hungrifying * whetting the appetite for food

hyperoxide * extremely pungent to taste

hyperpalatable * addictively tasty—hitting the proverbial "sweet spot"

iblaunched * blanched or boiled

ill-flavoured * insapory; unsavoury

impalatable * positively distasteful

impoignant * of a dish, insipid and uninspiring; devoid of pep or piquancy

inalimental * not affording nourishment; innutritious

incocted * raw, uncooked

incontunded * with regard to fruit and spices, neither bruised nor pounded

indigerable * indigestible

indigestibleness * the quality of being heavy on the stomach or harsh on the palate

inedible * unsafe or unsuitable for human consumption, as with toadstools, say

inesculent * inedible; unpalatable

ingustible * wholly lacking in any detectable flavour; tasteless

innutritiousness * a want in food of nutrients or other positive alimentary properties

insapory * ill-tasting

insipidness * blandness, tastelessness

instantized * of formula milk or powdered foods, easily reconstituted or prepared

instimulating * not exactly tickling the old taste buds

insuave * of no delicate taste

insulsed * unsalted; hence, left devoid of flavour

intastable * incapable of being perceived or appreciated by the palate

irrelishable * unappetizing

juglandaceous * walnutty

jumbo * a commercial descriptor for a certain, very large class of shrimp

jussulent * rich in broth; soup-like in consistency

kebabable * of processed meat, suitable for being cooked on a spit or skewer

keestless * an old Scots expression meaning tasteless

kitchenable * fit for cooking and serving at table

kitchenless * lacking relish or seasoning

kokumi * a posited sixth flavour: "rich taste" with long finish and fatty mouthfeel

kosherness * of food, a fitness to be consumed in accordance with Jewish dietary law

lamiaceous * minty, take one

lampante * of olive oil, inferior; graded unfit for consumption without further refining

leguminous * having the character of legumes, such as peas and beans

lemony * made from lemons or tasting sharply of them

licious * highly pleasing to the palate

liquorsome * tempting to the palate; appetizing

lite * low in either fat or calories

livered * of bread, heavy, having failed to rise during baking

long-life * treated so as not to perish or go off quickly

loppered * of milk, in some degree clotted, curdled, or coagulated

low-cal * of naturally restricted or artificially reduced calorific value

lumpshious * finger-licking good

lusciousness * a rich and indulgent sweetness of taste

malossol * a taste descriptor for high-grade caviar preserved in a low-salt brine

mandible * eatable; fit to be eaten

manducable * chewable in preparation for swallowing; edible

marilled * marinated, or pickled in brine

marmaladed * spread or smeared with fruit preserve

marzipanned * coated in a thick paste of ground almonds, egg whites, and sugar

masticability * the textural quality of chewiness in food

meatable * fit and proper to be consumed as a foodstuff

medium-rare * describes meat cooked to leave a warm red centre

mellaginous * honey-like

mellite * sweet to taste

melt-in-the-mouth * of cake, pastry and so forth, delectably light and soft

menthaceous * minty, take two

mi-chèvre * of cheese, denoting that it is composed of majority goat's milk

microwaveable * suitable for or capable of cooking in a microwave oven

miliaceous * of the nature of millet or millet-seed

mistrum * of fare, either execrable in quality or exiguous in quantity

monofloral * of honey, varietal; composed chiefly of nectar from one plant species

monounsaturated * describes a healthy option vegetable oil or fat such as canola

mordicancy * the pungent or biting quality of relishes such as mustard

moreish * rich, delicious and filling

mortified * in respect of meat, made tender by hanging

mouldy * decaying from age or damp, as of neglected bread or cheese

mouth-watering * highly gratifying to the sense of taste

multigrained * of bread, with two or more types of grain in the bake

mundified * of seeds or grains, hulled, or unhusked

muriatic * briny or salty

musaceous * of the nature of bananas or edible plantains

mustiness * the spoiled, disagreeable condition of food gone fusty or stale

muttoniness * the quality of mutton, being the meat of an adult sheep

nauseative * of such as fatty foods, causing the stomach to revolt or the gorge to rise

nectareous * heavenly sweet

nidor * the tang of cooked meat

nidorulent * imparting an overpowering bouquet of greasy or fatty meat

no-bake * of cakes, desserts, and similar treats, not requiring to be baked

nondairy * containing no milk or derived produce such as cream

nonfattening * of a foodstuff, not causing weight gain when eaten in moderation

nonsaporific * failing to impart flavour

noshable * well tasty

nucamentaceous * nutty; having the properties or qualities of nuts

nuttiness * the condition of being redolent of or tasting like nuts

nutmeggy * spiced with nutmeg

nutrimentive * nutritious; efficient and nourishing as a food

off-taste * an unwelcome twang in food that has been tainted or turned

oleraceous * having the nature of a potherb for kitchen use

omphacine * expressed from unripe fruit, typically olives or grapes, or crab apples

onkus * Antipodean slang· for food considered stale or of inferior quality

open-meated * juicy; said of certain cheeses

orchard-fresh * of fruit, as if picked straight off the tree

orexigenic * serving to whet the appetite for food—be it through taste, smell, or look

oven-ready * of poultry, plucked and prepared prior to sale for instant oven-cooking

over easy * of an egg, lightly fried and flipped to leave the yolk unbroken yet runny

overcooked * dish-wise, overheated during preparation and so somewhat spoiled

overluscious * overly rich or sweet to taste

oystered * served or eaten with oysters

pabulous * nourishing, alimental; full of the goodness of food

palatableness * agreeability of flavour; savouriness

palate-tickling * titillating to the taste buds

palative * acceptable to the palate

paneity * the property or particularity of being bread

panifiable * of flour, fit for use in breadmaking

pantagruelian * of a meal, of prodigious proportions

parsleyed * describes veined blue cheeses, with mould resembling sprigs of parsley

pastinaceous * full of the properties or qualities of parsnips

peppercorny * spicy after the fashion of dried black pepper berries

pepperiness * the pungent or fiery quality of a given ingredient or dish; "spice"

percoct * well-cooked, perhaps slightly overdone

perished * rotten or decayed; gone off, bad, mouldy, or such

pertish * somewhat pungent or sharp-tasting

pickle-cured * of vegetables, preserved in vinegar or brine

pinguescent * of meat, fatty or greasy; fattening

piperitious * hot, peppery, and pungent

piquancy * invigorating tang or zest

piscose * fishy to taste

planked * in regard to fish, notably shad, cooked attached to a small wooden board

pobby * of food, pulpy or mushy; resembling porridge or similar

poignance * pungency or sharpness of taste

pomacious * consisting of apples

ponticity * sourness or tartness in food and drink

pourover * denotes a sauce poured over prepared food immediately prior to serving

pancakish

in the style or nature of a pancake or toastie

pressure-cooked * prepared for eating in an airtight vessel under steam pressure

proteinaceous * rich in protein

pulmentarious * made with gruel, or resembling pottage

pungitive * biting or bitter to taste

quailed * curdled or coagulated, as milk; also, wilted by heating, as banana-leaf

quarred * soured or clotted

raciness * piquancy or sharpness of taste—"bite"

radiopasteurized * partially sterilized by means of exposure to ionizing radiation

raftiness * a foul-smelling rancidness often found with bacon

ragouted * of meat, stewed with vegetables in a highly flavoured seasoning

rammishness * an overpowering rankness of odour or taste

rancidity * the sour taint of fatty or oily foods gone stale

ranciduous * having a disagreeable buttery taste, as with decomposing meat

ratheripe * of fruit or grain, tending to ripen precociously

ravelled * of bread, made from wholemeal flour, or flour with the bran left in

ready-to-serve * of a main dish, pre-cooked and requiring no further preparation

réchauffé * of food, reheated; alternatively, cooked using leftovers

reconstituted * of powdered and concentrated milk, rehydrated for consumption

reduced-sodium * of a foodstuff, serving or meal, low in salt

rehydratable * easily prepared from powdered form; a NASA space food category

relishsome * savoury, appetizing

rendered * of fat, melted and clarified for cooking purposes

restiness * a spoiled food aroma suggestive of rancidity

restringent * harsh or sour to taste

revoltingness * that negative quality of food or drink eliciting nausea and disgust

rhubarb * sour or acrid to taste; "bitterness"

rizzared * of fish, especially haddock, sun-dried

robust * strong-tasting

rosselled * of apples, decayed or overripe

rumpled * of eggs, scrambled

saccharaceous * sweet; containing sugar

saccharineish * somewhat saccharine or sweet tasting

saccharinity * cloying sweetness

saignant * of meat, served bloody or rare; purposefully underdone

salinous * tasting of salt

salsamentarious * salty, or salted

salsitude * saltiness or brackishness

salso-acid * both bitter and sour to taste

salsuginous * impregnated with salt; well-salted

saltiness * the condition of being salty to taste

saltness * piquancy of taste or flavour

sam-sodden * half-cooked

sapidness * the quality of having a strong and agreeable taste

sapient * possessing flavour

sapor * taste or savour

saporific * yielding taste; savoury

saporine * pertaining to taste or flavour

satiating * of food, satisfyingly filling

sauceless * devoid of seasoning, or indeed any flavour whatsoever

savouriness * that property of food which imparts a rich and salty flavour

savourlessness * a complete want of taste or tang

savoursome * stimulating or tempting to the palate

scrumdiddlyumptious * most tasty indeed

scrumptiousness * plain deliciousness

scrumpy * an archaic regionalism that variously meant overbaked or undercooked

seasonable * saporous, savorous

seasonedness * the condition of being well-seasoned or otherwise relishsome

semese * half-eaten

semiskimmed * containing less animal fat and fewer calories than full-cream milk

sentiment * taste, flavour—a term from a more poetical, bygone era

sesamine * suggestive of or suffused with sesame oil

sialogenous * of food, mouth-watering

sickliness * a nauseating oversweetness in prepared food or drink

sinapistic * consisting or redolent of mustard

sin-free * indicates foods which slimmers may consume without concern for quantity or calories

sipidity * savour or flavour; sapidness

sirupiness * sugariness

sivedy * full of bran

skippery * of cheese, alive with maggots

smatchless * devoid of "smack" or flavour

smokiness * the distinctive taste or aroma of smoked food

snappiness * liveliness of flavour; tang

soddenness * the unpalatable condition of food which has been improperly boiled

soft-centred * of sweets or chocolates containing a soft filling such as cream or jelly

sourcroutish * tasting like or at least hinting of sauerkraut

sourhead * sourness or over-acidity in food

Southern-fried * especially regarding chicken, coated and fried Southern-style

spendsavour * that has lost its savour

speustic * baked or cooked in haste

spewsome * in Antipodean vernacular, so disgusting to taste as to make one retch

spiceful

prepared with spices aplenty; hot and tangy to taste

spiciness * a fiery pepperiness of flavour

spinaceous * spinach-like

staleness * loss of palatability or edibility, as with bread gone hard

stomach-whetting * highly appetizing

stone-ground * denotes flour that has been milled so as to retain both bran and germ

stoved * a Scotticism meaning stewed

stretched-curd * in relation to cheese, manufactured using the pasta filata technique

stypticalness * asperity or austerity of taste

suaveolent * yielding a delicate, sweet cooking odour

subacidulous * in some degree sour to taste

subacted * of food, digested

subastringent * somewhat harsh or acidic to the palate

sublimed * of olive oil, refined

succulent * especially said of meat cuts, perfectly tender and juicy

sugar-candyish * very sweet, having the character of clarified or crystallized sugar

sugar-free * with sugar removed, or at least substituted by a surrogate sweetener

sugariness * intense sweetness

sugarsweet * exceptionally but not cloyingly sweet to taste

sugrative * honeyed, sugary, and sweet

sunnyside up * of an egg, fried on one side leaving a soft and unbroken yolk on top

superacidity * extreme sourness in food

superfine * of sugar or flour, inter alia, denoting a foodstuff of the highest grade

suppable * pleasant to eat

sweet & sour * prepared in a sauce containing sugar and vinegar or lemon juice

sweetishness * the quality of being subtly sweet

syrupical * syrupy, treacly

tad-larruping * simply darned delicious

tanginess * penetrating spiciness or savour

tarage * to possess flavour; to taste of something rather than nothing

tartarousness * tartness, sourness; the quality of acidity in food

tartish * somewhat pungent in flavour

tasteable * perceptible to the palate

tastelessness * absence of relish

tastesome * toothsome; agreeable to the palate

taste-tested * having passed the taste test by popular approval

tastive * tasty; imparting welcome flavour

teeth-rife * a now obsolete dialectal expression meaning palatable

tenellous * with regard to the quality of meat, somewhat tender

tharfling * of bread, unleavened

191

thermostabilized * of packaged food in the main, preserved by heating

thundered * of milk, soured by the discharge of atmospheric electricity

tincture * a subtle taste or flavour

titillating * appetizing or attractive to the palate

toothsomeness * savouriness; a tempting tastiness

tooth-tempting * tasty; mouth-watering

toppingly * of milk skimmings, cheesy

tremblant * of beef, boiled; a reference from medieval cookery

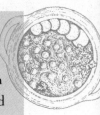

twice-laid

nautical slang for a serving that has been recooked or rehashed

trufflesque * tasting of, or with a texture similar to, truffles

twang * a pronounced and persistent ill-taste

umami * the proposed fifth taste element—the savouriness of broth and cooked meat

umbelliferous * of the nature of the carrot family and like herbaceous food plants

unappetizing * off-putting by virtue of poor flavour, aroma or presentation

unconcocted * consumed but not digested

uncondited * of an article of food or a prepared dish, plain; not seasoned in any way

unconfected * neither pickled nor preserved

uncoqued * raw; uncooked

unctuous * an older term for meat deemed to be greasy, fat or rich

undelectable * a quaint euphemism for tasteless, or worse— positively distasteful

underdone * of meat, still slightly raw after cooking

underseasoned * deficient in spice or relish, hence lacking in flavour

uneatableness * sheer inedibility

ungarbished * of a fish seized at sea, yet to be gutted or filleted for cooking

unlaced * of an animal slaughtered for the pot, yet to be dressed for cooking

unleavened * of bread, made without yeast or any other raising agent

unmatured * denotes a food that has still to acquire maximum flavour

unpalatability * in matters culinary, an unpleasantness or poverty of taste

unrepulsive * reasonably savoury; "not bad" taste-wise

unsavoury * wanting in savouriness or downright disagreeable to taste

unstomachable * unappetizing, unpalatable

unsweetened * containing no added sugar or artificial sweeteners

untoothsome * unpleasant to taste

unwhigged * of milk, not soured

vacuum-packed * sealed and sold in airtight wrapping to maintain food freshness

valiant * strong-tasting; assertive in flavour

vappous * flat, flavourless, insipid to taste

vegan-friendly * suitable as a foodstuff for vegans, being devoid of dairy or flesh

venisonized * dressed and cooked so as to resemble and taste of deer-flesh

verdour * an invigorating and agreeable freshness or briskness in fruits

vinegarishness * a synonym for sourness

virose * of food, rancid in aroma and noxious in nature

vitaillous * pertaining to food; nourishing

vituline * relating to or resembling veal

wafern * of bread, baked thin and wafery

wallowish * sickly in flavour; cloying, over-sweet

washed-rind * denotes a class of sweaty and downright stinky cheeses

wearishness * destitution of savour; insipidity

weft * ill-flavour; want of savouriness

well-corned * of beef, satisfactorily cured by salting

wheaten * made from wheat flour or grain

wholegrain * made with unprocessed cereal grains or seeds — germ, bran, and all

wholesomeness * of food, the quality of being nutritious and health-giving

wishy-washiness * an excessive weakness or wateriness in liquid food

yfarced * of poultry, meat, or game, stuffed

yuckiness * the negative quality of being disagreeable or disgusting to the palate

yumminess * a simply scrumptious deliciousness

zestiness * an agreeable pungency or piquancy of taste

zinginess * a pleasant sharpness, sparkle, or spice in food

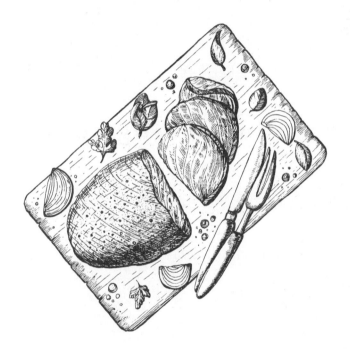

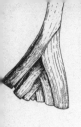

Something to Digest

CHAPTER 9

The Physiology of Consumption

> *"To eat is to appropriate by destruction."*
> **— Jean-Paul Sartre**

achlorhydria * a deficiency of acid in the gastric juices

acholia * a failure to secrete chole or bile, thereby compromising the digestion of fats

achylia * an absence or paucity of gastric fluid in the digestive tract

acor * stomach acidity

aerogastria * bloating of the stomach with swallowed air

agastronomia * "butterflies," lowered or lost nervous control of the stomach

agita * acid indigestion, or heartburn

aglossia * lacking a tongue to taste food with

aglutition * an inability to swallow

agomphious * lacking teeth to chew food with

alactasia * lactase deficiency in the small intestine, leading to lactose intolerance

amasesis * the physical inability to chew

aminopeptidase * a gut compound central to the digestive breakdown of proteins

amylase * a salivary enzyme initiating the entire bodily process of food digestion

amylodyspepsia * discomfort in digesting foods with a high starch content

analepsy * erroneously, epilepsy as deemed to be rooted in gastric dysfunction

anenterous * lacking in the organs of digestion

antacid * a remedy to counteract excessive, erosive stomach acid

antiperistalsis * an upward motion in the gullet causing food to "repeat"

apepsinia * a lack of protein-splitting digestive enzymes in the gastric juices

apepsy * imperfect digestion; mild alimentary impairment

aphagopraxia * the loss of the capacity to swallow food

aphagosis * an inability to eat

aptyalism * an absence or deficiency of salivary juice

autopepsia * the digestion or ulceration of the stomach's lining by its own secretions

bathygastria * downward displacement of the stomach, causing digestive discomfort

biliousness * an outdated term for dyspepsia with queasiness and wind; liverishness

borborygmus * the rumbling of a tummy that is empty or otherwise angry

bradiopepsy * sluggish or difficult digestion

bradymasesis * slowness or struggle in chewing

bradyphagia * abnormal lethargy in eating or swallowing

bromatoeccrisis * the egestion, or rectal evacuation, of undigested food

cackle-stomached * "kecklish" or nauseous with regard to food, and inclined to vomit

cacogastria * impaired or improper digestive function; dyspepsia

cacophagia * any functional derangement of the organs of digestion and nutrition

cacosplanchnia * emaciation through indigestion

calyculus gustatorius * a gustatory corpuscle, or taste bud in common currency

carbohydrase * a key enzyme in helping the body to digest and synthesize carbs

cardialgia * heartburn; mild indigestion

cardiospasm * an obstructive contraction in the oesophagus, causing regurgitation

chalasia * relaxation of the lower oesophageal sphincter, causing gastric reflux

cholestasis * suppression of the flow of bile into the small gut, or duodenum

cholorrhoea * an excessive secretion of digestive bile into the duodenum

chyle * a milky nutrient fluid absorbed by the intestinal mucosa during digestion

chylogaster * the "chyle-chamber," or duodenum

chylopoietics * the ecosystem of glands and organs forming the body's gastric juices

chylosis * the formation of chyle from the semifluid food mass fed into the small gut

chyme * the partially digested pulpy residue of food as first processed in the stomach; it is then converted into chyle when passed into the duodenum

chymification * the transformation of food in the stomach into chyme

chymoplania * any abnormal metastasis or "wandering" of chyme

chymosepsis * the putrefactive fermentation of chyme within the stomach

chymozemia * a morbid increase in intestinal secretions

coeliac passion * a gouty digestive disease of the small gut, wherein nutrients fail to be fully absorbed; it is caused by an adverse congenital reaction to gluten foods

collatitious viscera * collectively, the digestive tract organs; the belly and the bowels

collywobbles * nervous stomach or bellyache; gastrointestinal distress more broadly

colodyspepsia * reflex indigestion caused by a constipated colon

commanducate * to chew with attentive thoroughness

cricopharyngeus * a swallowing muscle, a.k.a. the upper oesophageal sphincter

cuspids * the "canine" teeth of adult humans, evolved to grip, rip, and rend meat

deglutate * to swallow down

denticate * to go munch-crunch-crush when eating

digerate * to digest food

digerent * any preparation promoting good digestion

digestation * the act of taking food into the body to make it fit to become part thereof

digestment * the physiological action of digestion

digestory * an archaic term for the digestive organs or apparatus of the body

digesture * the faculty, principle, or physical power of digestion

dilative * serving to digest or diffuse food

dolichogastry * having a distended or extended stomach

dumpling-depot * humorously, the stomach

duodenum * the first, short section of the small gut, processing chyme into chyle

dyscatabrosis * difficulty in swallowing food

dysmasesis * difficulty in mastication, or chewing food

dyspepsia * chronic indigestion

dyspepsodynia * chronic indigestion with much pain

dysphagia nervosa * a spasm of the food-pipe making swallowing difficult

dysthelasia * difficulty in sucking, or indeed in giving suck

dystrypsia * impaired secretion of the digestive juices of the pancreas

enterogastritis * inflammation or infection of the digestive system; "stomach flu"

enterokinesia * peristalsis; the muscular contraction of the lower alimentary canal

enteropeptidase * a substance produced in the duodenum activating the pancreatic zymogens, thereby facilitating the digestion and absorption of dietary proteins

enzymolysis * the breakdown of foods through digestive fermentation in the gut

eructate * to belch or burp

erygmatic * given to belching

euchlorhydria * good acidity of the gastric juices

eupepticity * a state of agreeableness arising from healthy digestion

euphagia * any normal and proper pattern of eating or processing of food

flatingness * an archaic word meaning nausea arising from digestive disorder

fletcherize * to chew food to a pulp before swallowing

fundoplication * a surgical procedure to treat gastroesophageal reflux

gasterataxia * a disarrangement of, or disturbance in, stomach digestion

gastrelcobrosis * ulceration of the stomach

gastrerethismus * an irritation or upsetting of the stomach

gastricism * the ascription of all disease to the afflictions and infirmities of the belly

gastricity * a condition of chronic stomach complaint

gastrocoeliac * any substance acting directly on the organs of digestion

gastroenterology * the medical science of the digestive organs and their disorders

gastroenteropathy * any disease or derangement of the alimentary canal

gastroesthesia * the state of having a sensitive—weak or easily upset—stomach

gastrohyponervia * the defective activity of the nerves of the stomach

gastroparesis * paralysis of the stomach, with food going largely undigested

gastrorrhoea * the hypersecretion or regurgitant flow of the stomach's juices

gastrostomy * the introduction of a feeding device into the stomach via the abdomen to deliver supplemental nutritional support

gastrotympanites * gaseous distension of the stomach; bloating

gastroxynsis * abnormal acidity of the stomach

glossophagine * feeding with the tongue

glossopyrosis * a burning sensation on the tongue caused by hot and spicy food

glutition * the act of swallowing

gnathodynamics * the study of masticatory force and efficiency

gnathology * the study of the full masticatory apparatus—jaws, teeth, and tongue

gormy-ruddles * the guts, or gastrointestinal tract, in old vernacular coin

gurgullion * the oesophagus, a.k.a. the gullet, gorge, or food-pipe

hypergastritis * severe alimentary ailment

hyperpepsia * excessive rapidity of digestion

hyperprochoresis * the abnormally swift passage of food through the full GI tract

hypersialosis * excessive salivation; hydrostomia

hypopepsinia * a deficiency of pepsin, a key digestive enzyme, in the stomach

incisors * front teeth adapted for cutting and shearing food into chewable morsels

incoction * an absolute failure or absence of digestive activity

indigestion * dyspepsia or heartburn; difficulty or discomfort in digesting food

indignation * the revolt of the stomach against unwelcome or unwholesome food

ingestion * the action of taking food and drink into the body

inglutition * the action of swallowing

insuction * the action of consuming food and other sustenance by sucking

inviscation * the admixing of food with saliva and mucus in the act of chewing

ischochymia * the suppression of gastric juices with retention of food in the stomach

juxtapyloric * adjacent to the pylorus, or "gate" connecting stomach and duodenum

lactose-intolerant * unable to consume milk-based food or drink without digestive discomfort

lemoparalysis * paresis of the gorge or food-pipe

lemostenosis * contraction or constriction of the gullet

lientery * alimentary diarrhoea; the discharge of food that is only partially digested

lipase * a pancreatic enzyme serving to digest fats and catalyze them into fatty acids

lipostomosis * a lack of a mouth to feed with

malacogastrosis * the softening or perforation of the coats of the stomach

maldigestion * poor digestion with diminished uptake of nutrients

manducation * the action of chewing food

masseter * the major muscle of mastication in the human animal

masticate * to chew; to reduce food to a pulp prior to swallowing

masticators * humorously, the teeth or the jaws

megalogastria * gross distension or dilatation of the stomach

megaoesophagus * abnormal enlargement of the gullet due to failure of peristalsis

melitoptyalism * the secretion of sweet-tasting saliva

merycism * regurgitation or repeating of food, often followed by its reswallowing

merycology * the study of rumination and regurgitation

microflora * the gut's own friendly bacteria, important for digestive tract health

molars * the large, flat crushing and grinding teeth found at the back of the mouth

Montezuma's revenge * food poisoning abroad with unpleasant "colonsequences"

morsitation * the action of repeated biting or gnawing

mulligrubs * gastrointestinal distress of any fashion, or depression therefrom

myenteric plexus * a bundle of nerve cells serving to detect the presence of food in the alimentary canal and instructing the intestines to pass it along once processed

myzesis * the action of taking in sustenance by sucking or suckling, as at the breast

narcopepsia * slowness or stalling of the process of digestion

nasogastric * of the nose and stomach, as in a tube for passing food down the gullet

newington butts * rhyming slang for "guts," can refer to either stomach or entrails

nidorosity * a forthright meaty belch

odontamblyogmus * tooth-edge; oral sensitivity to cold foods such as ice cream

odontosphacelismus * tooth decay from bacteria in plaque feeding on sugary foods

odynophagia * painful swallowing; may be a symptom of oesophageal disease

oesophagectasis * dilation or distension of the oesophagus

oesophagectomy * total or partial surgical removal of the food-pipe

oesophagitis * inflammation of the food-pipe—a common symptom is heartburn

oesophagodynia * pain in the gullet

oesophagogastroplasty * plastic repair of the oesophagus and stomach; cardioplasty

oesophagoplegy * paralysis of the gullet

oesophagostomy * the creation of an artificial opening in the food-pipe to allow emergency feeding

olfactory epithelium * the nasal smell pad, distinguishing food and drink aromas

oligochylia * incompetent secretion of the gastric juices

oligopepsia * insufficient or enfeebled digestion

opisthogastric * behind or back of the stomach

oxyregmia * acid eructation, or reflux

oxysitia * an unpleasant acidity of the stomach; literally "sharp food"

palatoglossus * a muscle of the tongue and soft palate initiating the swallow reflex

palirrhoea * the regurgitation or repetition of food from the stomach

pancreas * the "sweetbread," a gland with an exocrine function that aids digestion

parbreaking * the act of belching, or bringing up gas from the stomach's contents

pepsia * digestion, in medical parlance

pepsiniferous * secreting pepsin, one of the principal digestive enzymes

peptics * the scientific study of digestion; also, the digestive organs themselves

peptogaster * the alimentary canal, or digestive tract

peristalsis * the series of propulsive rhythmic contractions that process food through firstly the oesophagus and latterly the intestines

phagodynamometer * an apparatus for measuring the force exerted in chewing food

pharyngemphraxis * blockage or obstruction of the pharynx

pharyngocace * gangrene of the uppermost part of the digestive tract

pharyngocynanche * inflammation or angina of the pharynx

pharyngoxerosis * abnormal dryness of the pharynx

pharynx * the portion of the alimentary canal found at the top of the throat, before the oesophagus

pneumophagia * the neurotic gulping or swallowing of air

pnigerophobia * a fear of choking, as manifested by avoidance of swallowing food or fluid

poltophagy * the prolonged chewing of food until it resembles a squishy pulp

polygastria * the excessive secretion of gastric juices

polysialia * the excessive production of salivary juices

porus gustatorius * a small pore or opening in the taste buds of the tongue

prebiotics * non-digestible food ingredients promoting a healthy GI tract microbiota

premastication * the prior chewing of food, for example in order to feed it to babies

presbyoesophagus * degeneration of the motor function of the food-pipe later in life

presbyphagia * frailty in swallowing associated with the elderly

probiotics * live bacteria or yeasts taken to bolster or balance one's gut microflora

protogaster * the embryonic foregut, becoming in time the full digestive tract

pseudodyspepsia * nervous rather than organic indigestion; gastric neurasthenia

pseudodysphagia * a psychogenic phobia of swallowing solids for fear of choking

pseudoptyalism * the drooling of accumulated saliva due to dysphagia

psomophagy * swallowing food without first thoroughly chewing

ptyalin * salivary amylase, assisting in the predigestion of starch into sugar

ptyalorrhoea * an abundant secretion and flow of salivary fluid

ptysmagogue * any agent promoting the secretion of saliva

pylorospasm * spastic closure of the pylorus, slowing the evacuation of digested food from the stomach and leading to projectile vomiting

pyrosis * highly acidic gastric reflux, or "sour stomach" as it was once known

reboke * to burp or belch following feeding

regurgitation * the involuntary return or reflux of food following its ingestion

rejumble * to "rejolt" or rise again in the stomach; to repeat through indigestibility

remastication * rumination; the chewing of food, or in animals—cud, yet again

ructuosity * a pattern of frequent or excessive belching

rugitus * "tummy rumbles," or borborygmus

ruminate * to chew and chew once more

rumination * an eating disorder in which food is regurgitated and reswallowed

salivals * the salivary glands of the mouth

salpingopharyngeus * a muscle responsible for raising the pharynx during glutition

siagonology * the study of the physiology and functioning of the jawbones

sialadenotropic * exerting an influence on the operation of the salivary glands

sialaporia * a destitution or deficiency of saliva

sialoaerophagy * the habitual drawing in and swallowing over of spit and air

sialodochium * a salivary gland duct

sialogastrone * a putative saliva protein inhibiting the secretion of stomach acid

sialoschesis * the suppression of the normal flow of saliva

sialozemia * the overstimulation and overflow of saliva

soda * an obsolete term for indigestion or heartburn

sorbillate * to sip liquid food such as soup, sauce, or gravy

sordes gastricae * foul deposits of undigested food and mucus lying in the stomach

steatolysis * the emulsification of fat during digestion, preparatory to absorption

steatorrhoea * the production of fatty stools as a result of digestive incompetence

stomachic * a drug to stimulate a sluggish stomach into action

stomatogastric * pertaining to the mouth and stomach

stylopharyngeus * a muscle serving to facilitate swallowing through dilation of the upper portion of the alimentary canal

subruminative * digesting

succorrhoea * an abnormal increase in the volume and flow of digestive fluids

succus entericus * the watery digestive secretions of the small intestine

sugescent * pertaining to the act of sucking

swallow-pipe * the gorge or oesophagus, in layperson's language

synbiotics * combination prebiotic and probiotic dietary cum digestive supplements

taste-goblet * an older, more poetic name for the humble taste bud

temporalis * a chewing muscle responsible for grinding food between the molars

tooth-work * the action of mastication

tormina * gastrointestinal distress; colic, gripes

transglutting * the action of swallowing over food

trypsin * a digestive enzyme serving to break down proteins in the small intestine

unmeltung * Old English indigestion

upbraiding * eructation, reflux, and regurgitation

uraniscus * the roof of the mouth, or palate—whence the faculty of "taste"

ventriculus * the stomach, or similar digestive cavity

vermiculation * the peristaltic undulation of food along the digestive tract

victualling-office * the stomach, as affectionately known in former times

wambliness * the motion of a queasy or subverted stomach

wiffle-woffles * alimentary distress, be it bellyache or bowel complaint

ysophage * the swallow-pipe

Food Science and Nutrition

> *"Let food be thy medicine and medicine be thy food."*
> **— Hippocrates**

acesulphames * a class of low-calorie artificial food sweeteners

acetoglycerides * fats used in shortenings and spreads and to coat food with film

acidophiline * a synthetic potable fermented yogurt taken to treat intestinal disease

acidulants * additives used to confer a sharp—tart, sour, or acidic—flavour to foods

acrylamide * a chemical found in burnt toast and roast potatoes—is it carcinogenic?

adulteration * the illicit bulking out of foodstuffs with inferior or ersatz substances

aequum * the amount of food required to maintain a healthy body weight

aeromonas * a genus of enteric pathogens that commonly cause food poisoning

aflatoxins * liver-toxic metabolites found in stored peanuts and cereals

agenization * the earlier use of a food improver, agene, to age flour in breadmaking

aleuronat * a flour substitute used to bake breadstuffs for diabetics

alkalization * in the chocolate industry, the neutralization of cocoa's natural acidity by the use of potassium carbonate

allantiasis * food poisoning caused by the inadequate preservation of sausage meat

allicin * a chemical compound responsible for giving garlic its telltale smell and taste

allotrophic * relating to food with lowered and potentially negative nutritive value

alphatocopherol * a variant vitamin E antioxidant found in high concentrations in almonds and spinach

alphenic * condensed white barley sugar, formerly taken for its medicinal properties

alveograph * a tool for measuring the rheological or stretching properties of dough

ammonium carbonate * baker's ammonia—a popular leavening agent

amylometer * a device used to test the quality and quantity of starch in potatoes

amylopectin * a starch responsible for the gelatinous nature of cooked sticky rice

animalization * the process of nutrient absorption in digestion

anisakiasis * a gut infection from eating certain raw or undercooked fish or squid

anthoxanthins * a family of plant compounds responsible for the white, cream, and yellow pigmentation of many foods; found, inter alia, in ripe bananas

antihuff * a substance once widely used to adulterate cheese

antioxidants * molecules with marked anti-inflammatory properties concentrated in fresh fruit and vegetables; they also help inhibit the deterioration of stored food

appertization * the process of ridding perishable foods of microorganisms to create "commercial sterility"

appestat * a physiological mechanism purportedly located in the hypothalamus from where it regulates appetite and our response to hunger

arabinose * a sugar isolated from gum arabic with use as a food additive across Asia

ariboflavinosis * a dietary deficiency of vitamin B2

aspartame * a powerful artificial sweetener, subject to ongoing health controversy

aspergillus niger * a fungal food contaminant causing black mould to grow on such as grapes, onions, and peanuts

astaxanthin * a carotenoid pigment that gives salmon flesh its appealing pink colour

atriplicism * poisoning by spinach or other spinach-like green vegetable

aurantiamarin * a glucoside responsible for the bitter flavour of oranges

autolysis * the partial digestion of food by the action of its own enzymes such as occurs when meat is hung

avenin * a glutinous protein found in oats; certain individuals have a sensitivity to it

azorubine * a synthetic food supplement widely used in the confectionery industry; it is subject to concern over potential side-effects relating to childhood hyperactivity

bactofugation * the elimination of bacteria from milk via high-speed centrifuging

bactometer * an instrument for estimating the degree of bacterial contamination of the nutrients in food and drink

beeturia * the production of pink-red urine consequent upon eating beetroot

bioflavonoids * a diverse group of phytonutrients widely available in fresh raw fruit and vegetables

biopreservation * a method of preserving food using natural antimicrobial agents

botulism * neurotoxic paralysis arising from improperly canned or preserved food

bradytrophia * the sluggish action of the nutritive processes

brevibacterium * a mould responsible for the telltale "smelly feet" odour of cheese

bridgmanization * a means of sterilizing food using high hydrostatic pressure

bromatography * a learned treatise on food and nutrition

bromatology * food science; the study of foodstuffs in relation to health and diet

bromatometry * calculation of the daily intake of food required by an individual

bromatotoxicon * any agent active in the spoiling or poisoning of food

bromatotoxism * food poisoning

bromelain * a widely employed meat tenderizing protease, derived from pineapples

bromophenol * a compound responsible for the "seacoast" odour of certain fresh fish

brucellosis * a disease contracted by consuming raw minced meat or milk

butylated hydroxytoluene * an antioxidizing additive used in processed fatty foods

butyroscope * an instrument for determining the percentage of butterfat in milk

calorie * a unit of food energy

calorifacient * creating body heat or causing sweat, as with such as hot chilli peppers

cambium * along with gluten and ros, one of the three "alimentary humours" anciently posited to nourish the body

campylobacter jejuni * a germ group commonly causing food poisoning

canthaxanthin * a reddish pigment that richly colours the yolks of duck eggs

capsaicin * a compound found in the placental ribs of chilli peppers, producing their notoriously pungent "heat"

capsorubin * a peppery flavouring and pink food colouring derived from paprika

carbohydrates * one of the basic food groups, including sugars, starches and fibres; carbs are the principal source of energy for most of the world's population

carbonatation * a chemical purification process used to refine sugar from sugar beet

carboxymethylcellulose * a food stabilizer and thickener, plus appetite suppressant

cardioprotective * describes food healthy for the heart, such as dark chocolate

cariogenicity * the degree to which a given processed food causes tooth decay

carnosine * a naturally occurring molecule used as a sports and dietary supplement

carotenoids * a class of organic pigments giving rise to the bright red, yellow and orange hues found in many fruits and vegetables, including such as ripe tomatoes

carrageenans * seaweed extracts used in food manufacturing as thickening agents

caseation * the process by which milk becomes cheese via coagulation or curdling

caseinogen * the principal protein found in fresh cow's milk

castoreum * the exudate of a beaver's butt, valued as a substitute vanilla flavouring

catabolism * that part of the metabolic process that releases energy from food

cathepsins * proteolytic enzymes responsible for cell-digestion when game is "hung"

chavicine * an alkaloid imparting the pungent notes found in ground black pepper

chitosan * a sugar obtained from shellfish exoskeletons, used as a dietary supplement to reduce cholesterol and promote weight loss

cholecalciferol * vitamin D3; taken supplementarily from fish liver oil and egg yolks

cholesterol * a lipid molecule found in concentration in foods high in saturated fats

chymopapain * an enzyme occurring in papayas, efficacious as a meat tenderizer

ciguatera * food poisoning from consuming the toxic flesh of contaminated reef-fish

clarifixation * a technique employed in the dairy industry to produce homogenized milk

clonorchiasis * a severe infection of the biliary tract caused by flukes in raw fish

clostridium perfringens * a foodborne bacterial pathogen known as the "café germ"

coacervation * a process ostensibly causing bread to go stale

coagulum * rennet, an enzyme complex used in cheesemaking to curdle milk

Codex Alimentarius * the "Food Code," a set of harmonized global food production and food safety standards

colostrum * the trophic proto-breastmilk produced after delivery; "baby superfood"

concorporate * to assimilate nutrients into the body by digestive action

creamometer * an instrument for determining the fraction of cream in milk

cyanocobalamin * a synthetic form of vitamin B12, suitable for vegans

cyclamate * an artificial sweetener widely banned due to fears it may be carcinogenic

cyclosporiasis * a GI tract infection picked up from soft fruits and salad vegetables

cynarine * a property of artichokes responsible for making subsequently consumed food or drink taste sweeter

deglutinate * to make foods such as cereals, especially wheat flour, gluten-free

dehydrofreezing * a technique for drying out and preserving fruit and vegetables

depectinization * the removal of pectin from fruit pulp to produce a clear thin juice

deutoplasm * the nonliving nutritive matter stored in egg yolk

dextrinization * the browning of starch as occurs in toasting bread and baking cakes

diethylpropione * an appetite suppressant indicated for the treatment of obesity

diphyllobothriasis * a tapeworm infestation transmitted by way of raw or undercooked freshwater fish

dysvitaminosis * a nutritional disorder caused by imbalanced vitamin intake

enterohaemorrhagic E. coli * a pathogen responsible for the bloody flux; it is usually acquired through eating undercooked or unpasteurized food

equicaloric * yielding equal amounts of food energy through metabolic action

ergocalciferol * vitamin D2; found in food, it is available as a dietary supplement in cases of vitamin D deficiency, malabsorption of calcium, and rickets

ergotism * a form of bread poisoning owing to a fungal disease of cereals such as rye

erythorbate * a chemical additive found in many factory-produced foods today

ethoxyquin * a compound approved for use to prevent colour loss in certain spices

extensograph * a device for determining the elasticity of dough as an indicator of its baking quality

farinometry * measurement of the gluten content of flour

favism * an extreme hereditary allergic reaction to eating broad beans

fermentogens * substances that convert food into its nutritional constituents

flash-pasteurization * a variant mode of food sterilization whereby perishable beverages are held at a higher temperature for a shorter period of time

flatulogenic * of a particular foodstuff, tending to produce copious intestinal gas

flavonols * a class of compounds, abundant in cocoa, thought to enhance cognitive functioning

folate * a B vitamin widely added to grain products to combat folic acid deficiency

foodborne * transmitted by way of oral ingestion, as in instances of food poisoning

foodomics * an emergent multi-disciplinary approach to human nutrition embracing food chemistry, the biological sciences, and data analysis

freezerburn * the telltale uneven texture and discolouration found in frozen food that has been improperly packaged, allowing the ice to sublimate

frigi-canning * a commercial-scale food preservation technique using controlled heating followed by aseptic sealing and storing at a low temperature

fructokinase * an important enzyme in metabolizing fruit sugar in the body

fucoidan * a claimed anticarcinogenic seaweed extract included in certain dietary supplements

furcellaran * a polysaccharide used in the food industry as a gelling agent

galactosaemia * congenital lactose intolerance

gelatin * a water-soluble peptide and protein mix used to prepare jellies

genetotrophic * of genes and nutrition, with special reference to inherited metabolic defects inhibiting the assimilation of essential food elements

geosmin * a compound responsible for the earthy taint in foods such as beets

ghrelin * the "hunger hormone," a peptide stimulating appetite and food intake

gliadins * a class of gluten proteins allowing bread to rise properly during baking

glucagon * a pancreatic polypeptide involved in suppressing hunger pangs

glucokinase * a liver enzyme with a key role in carbohydrate metabolism

gluside * a zero-calorie, super-saccharine sweetening agent

glutenins * a group of cereal proteins lending strength and elasticity to dough

glycerol * a syrupy liquid with some use as a sweetener and food preservative

glycogen * the main form in which carbohydrate is stored in body tissue and muscle

glycolysis * the metabolic breakdown of glucose or blood sugar, obtained from food, to release energy for the body

glyconutrients * a loose group of plant carbohydrates of dubious nutritional merit

glycosuria * the presence of extra sugar in the urine after heavy carbohydrate intake

grayanotoxins * responsible for a rare condition known as "mad honey intoxication"

haemotroph * nutrition supplied to the embryo through the maternal bloodstream

halite * rock salt; it is generally pinkish and a healthier dietary option than sea salt

helicobacter pylori * a stomach germ causing chronic gastritis and peptic ulcers

hemicellulose * a polysaccharide carbohydrate found in fruit and vegetables, and source of dietary fibre in human nutrition

histotroph * nutrient material supplied to the embryo through the maternal tissue

homeosis * a redundant term for the bodily absorption of nutrients from food

homogenization * a means of treating milk so that the cream does not separate

hordein * a simple protein found in barley; some people may be food-sensitive to it

humanization * the addition of water and sugar to cow's milk to make it potable for infants

humectants * food additives with efficacy in reducing moisture loss

hydrocooling * a method of chilling fruit and vegetables to arrest further ripening

hydrogenation * a reaction process rendering all the fats in vegetable oils saturated

hyfoma * an ecosystem of hygienic food production and processing methods

hypercholesterolaemia * the presence of excess cholesterol in the blood stream; foods high in saturated fats should be avoided or their consumption limited

hyperingestation * the supra-optimal intake of those nutrients required for health

ichthulin * a rich substance present in the yolk of fish eggs, notably salmon roe

ichthyoallyeinotoxism * hallucinatory poisoning from the consumption of fish flesh

ichthyonosia * a fish allergy

ichthysmus * poisoning by fish or shellfish

inassimilation * malabsorption; the failure to properly incorporate food constituents

incretin * a gastrointestinal factor stimulating insulin secretion in response to meals

intolerance * an inability to ingest particular food groups without adverse reaction

inulins * helpful prebiotic dietary fibres widely found in fruits, vegetables, and herbs

invertase * an enzyme used in confectionery production to hydrolyze table sugar

irradiation * the exposure of food to gamma rays to destroy bacteria and parasites

isocaloric * in terms of contrasting dietary food portions, of similar calorific value

isoflavone * a cardioprotective phytochemical present in legumes, such as soya beans

isoglucose * food science shorthand for high-fructose corn syrup

isomalt * a sugar substitute notable for not promoting tooth decay

ispaghula * a dietary fibre infrequently used as a food thickening agent and laxative

kilocalory * in nutritional science, a unit of food energy equal to one large calorie

kreotoxism * a form of food poisoning from the consumption of tainted meat

kuru * a fatal brain disease transmitted through acts of ritual cannibalism

lactalbumin * a highly nutritious protein abundantly present in milk whey

lactobutyrometry * a means of calculating the percentage of cream in milk

lactoserum * whey; contains most of the lactose and minerals found in milk

laevulose * a.k.a. fructose, a simple sugar found especially in fruit and honey

lathyrism * a state of spastic paralysis brought about by eating chickpeas or dhal

lecithin * a soya bean product used as an emulsifier in chocolate manufacturing

leptin * a hormone regulating appetite and body fat, telling you when you are full

listeriosis * poisoning through ingestion of listerella, a foodborne bacterium

lycopene * an antioxidant phytonutrient particularly abundant in tomatoes

lye-peeling * the removal of skins from fruit and veg via hot caustic soda solution

lyophilization * cryodesiccation; freeze-drying perishable foods for ease of transport

macrominerals * those minerals required by the body in amounts over 100 mg a day

macronutrients * the three major food groups—fats, proteins, and carbs—required in large amounts to maintain the body's energy economy and sustain a healthy diet

malabsorption * the impaired assimilation of nutrients across the GI tract

mallorizing * the exposure of food to very high temperatures during pasteurization

maltitol * a synthetic bulk sweetener used in the production of sugar-free chocolates

maltodextrin * a powder used to stabilize, sweeten and thicken packaged foods

mannotetrose * a non-digestible carbohydrate found in beans, causing flatulence

medicina dietetica * nutrition considered as a discreet body of medical learning

melitismus * the use of honey as a sweetener in pharmaceutical preparations

metabolization * the chemical transformation of food into energy within the body

methionine * a dietary-essential protein-builder, obtainable in the highest concentrations through eating chicken and fish

microaerophiles * a group of bacteria capable of spoiling even sealed food

micronization * a method of rapidly warming food using infrared radiation

micronutrients * dietary trace minerals, vitamins, and phytochemicals, collectively

mixograph * a chart providing baking data on the dough mixes of different wheats

monosaccharides * the simplest forms of sugar and most basic units of carbohydrates

monosodium glutamate * a popular flavour enhancer in Asian cookery

multivitamins * dietary supplements containing several vitamin boosters

muscarine * a deadly alkaloid poison found on certain fungi as well as rotten fish

mycetism * mushroom poisoning

mycotoxicology * the study of fungi and mushrooms in relation to food poisoning

natamycin * an antifungal agent used in the food industry as a natural preservative

niacin * vitamin B3; its paucity in the human diet is the major cause of pellagra

nitrosomyoglobin * a compound producing the signature red colour of cured meat

norbixin * a golden-yellow food colouring

nutraceuticals * dietary supplements or designer foods promising medicinal benefits

nutratives * the organs of metabolic action, supplying nourishment to the body

nutricosmetics * food supplements alleged to enhance skin tone and delay ageing

nutrification * enrichment with micronutrients—trace minerals and vitamins

nutrigenomics * the study of the impact of food and diet on gene expression

nutriology * the science of nutritional therapy

nutriomics * a new discipline where biochemistry meets food science meets genetics

nutritorium * the nutritive apparatus of the body considered in its holistic entirety

nutriture * the body's nutritional status

ochratoxins * a class of hazardous food contaminants found in commodities from cereal grains to dried fruits

oenocyanin * a grape skin extract used as a strawberry-red food colouring agent

olfactronics * the scientific assessment and analysis of vapours and smells; applied within the food preparation industry as an adjunct quality control measure

oligofructose * a calorie-reduced alternative commercial sweetener

oligotrophic * relating to food that is deficient in nutritional content and value

ophthalamin * an obsolete name for vitamin A, found inter alia in carrots

opisthorchiasis * a severe infection of the biliary tract caused by flukes in raw fish

orectic * a substance, compound, or drug serving to stimulate the appetite

orexin * hypocretin; a neuropeptide activating the brain's feed behaviour receptors

orthophenylphenol * an antimicrobial agent used to keep fruit and vegetables fresh

oryzenin * the principal protein found in rice, concentrated in the seeds

osmazome * pure juice extract of meat, lending its characteristic flavour and smell

ovalbumin * the chief protein present in egg white

oxicalorimetry * assessment of the calorific value of food via combustion chamber

oxystearin * a sequestering agent used in the production of salad creams

paciferin * an infection-resistant factor found in unprocessed food

pancreatization * the treatment of food with an enzyme mixture to aid digestion

paragonimiasis * an infection from eating raw or uncooked shellfish and crustaceans

pasteurization * the heating of food to kill unhealthy or unwanted microorganisms

pectinization * in food processing, the treatment of extracted fruit juice with the enzyme pectinase to achieve further clarification or more intense concentration

penicillium * a mould used commercially to produce the veins in blue cheeses

peptonizing * the process of treating food to make it artificially pre-digested

perillartine * a non-nutritive synthetic sweetener, two thousand times as sweet as sucrose

phaeophytin * a compound causing cooked vegetables to lose their vivid green colour

phaseolamin * a dietary aid helping to prevent carbohydrates from being digested

phenylpropanolamine * a once popular under-the-counter appetite suppressant

phosphatase * a milk enzyme whose presence indicates inadequate pasteurization

phosphatation * a procedure for clarifying melt syrup in sugar refineries

phylloquinone * the principal dietary form of vitamin K, obtained especially from leafy greens and brassica vegetables and with some use as a food supplement

phytonutrients * healthy chemical compounds found in plant food

phytosterol * a food additive with potential cholesterol-lowing properties

picowave * to expose food to radiation to destroy insects, worms, and bacteria

pigbel * a lethal food poisoning associated with the ritual consumption of pork

pioscope * an apparatus for determining the purity of milk by its opacity and colour

plasmon * powdered infant formula milk, being an extract of soluble milk proteins

polyavitaminosis * nutritional imbalance owing to the deficient intake of more than one vitamin group

polydextrose * a bulking agent used to improve the taste and texture of low-calorie foods

polyunsaturates * fatty acids, typically found in vegetables and fish oil

ponderocrescive * with regard to food, tending to stimulate weight gain

ponderoperditive * with regard to food, tending to stimulate weight loss

potassium bicarbonate * a food additive, specifically a leavening agent in baking

predigestion * the controlled enzymatic digestion of food prior to human ingestion

proanthocyanins * a group of powerful antioxidant bioflavonoids present in berries

prolamins * a group of plant storage proteins concentrated in the seeds of cereal grains including wheat, barley, rye, and corn

proteinology * the science of proteins and the protein-nutrient balance of the body

proteolysis *
the enzymatic
degradation of
proteins into peptides
and amino acids

ptomaine poisoning *
an incorrect and now
discarded synonym
for food poisoning

propionibacterium

a starter culture
used to cause
holes to form
in Swiss cheese

pyridoxine * vitamin
B6, found in many foods as well as in supplementary form; it is required by the body to allow it to utilize the energy stored in the foods one eats

quercetin * a plant pigment touted as a superfood supplement

radicidation * the destruction of food pathogens by way of ionizing radiation

radurization * the application of low-dose irradiation to eliminate insect eggs and larvae as well as targeted spoilage microorganisms in perishable foods

raffinose * a non-digestible sugar found in beans and sprouts, creating flatus

raphania * a delirium formerly attributed to infection from eating wild radish

refrigeration * the preservation of foodstuffs through a process of cooling or chilling

retinol * a potent form of vitamin A in food, essential for maintaining good eyesight

retrogradation * a change in starch structure causing baked produce to go stale

rhizopus * a pathogenic fungus or plant spoilage genus, including bread mould

riboflavin * a B-complex vitamin added to cereal to enhance its nutritional value

saccharifier * an apparatus for converting starch in sugar production

saccharimeter * a device used in the food trade for determining the purity of sugar

saccharin * the world's first artificial sweetener

saccharum officinarum * sugarcane; the chief source of sucrose, or table sugar

saleratus * sodium bicarbonate, or baking soda—the main element in baking powder

salmonellosis * a form of food poisoning mainly transmitted through the consumption of raw or undercooked eggs

saltpetre * sodium nitrate; one of the oldest meat curing agents available

scombrotoxin * a poison transmitted via ingestion of decaying mackerel or tuna flesh

Scoville scale * an organoleptic test of the pungency of chilli peppers and spicy food

secalin * a form of gluten found in rye, rendering it intolerable to coeliac patients

sequestrants * a group of additives used to help preserve and stabilize food

shigellosis * bacillary dysentery, a foodborne infection of the digestive system

siderosis * a bone marrow disease caused by iron leached from cooking utensils into food

sitogen * a yeast product once advanced as a vegetarian alternative to meat extract

sitosterol * a corn oil extract used as a dietary supplement to reduce cholesterol

sitotoxism * food poisoning in general; in particular, poisoning by mouldy grain

sodium alginate * a substance of some versatility in modern molecular gastronomy

solanine * a toxic alkaloid present in potatoes that have sprouted or turned green

sorbitol * a low-calorie alternative to cane sugar, used widely by diabetics

sotolon * an aroma compound smelling of fenugreek or curry in high concentration

stabilizers * any natural ingredients or synthetic additives used to stabilize food

stackburn * a deterioration in the quality of factory canned food improperly cooled

sterigmatocystin * a moderately toxic black mould naturally found in certain cheeses

stiparogenic * with regard to food, tending to promote constipation

stiparolytic * with regard to food, tending to prevent or relieve constipation

staphylococcus aureus

a salad vegetable pathogen and common cause of food poisoning

sucralose * a zero-calorie artificial sweetener with 650 times the intensity of sugar

sucroglycerides * a group of compounds used as food emulsifiers and stabilizers

sulphoraphane * a component of leafy green vegetables serving to neutralize free radicals

supervitaminosis * the toxic effects of too high an intake of supplementary vitamins

supplementation * the practice of enriching foodstuffs with nutritional supplements

tachyalimentation * the accelerated passage of glucose into the bloodstream

tartrazine * a food colouring agent alleged to cause hyperactivity in children

tempering * a stabilization process imparting luscious gloss and texture to chocolate

tenderometer * a device for measuring the tenderness of raw peas during processing

tetrodotoxin * the active agent in fugu or puffer fish poisoning

texturizers * a set of additives used to improve the texture of processed food

theobromine * the key central nervous system stimulant present in chocolate

thermization * a low-heat treatment for milk, less severe than pasteurization

thermogenic * with regard to food supplements, acting to raise one's metabolic rate

thermopeeling * in food processing, a method of exfoliating tough-skinned fruits

thiabendazole * a fungicide used to protect bananas from mould, rot, blight, or stain

thiamine * vitamin B1, used as a supplement to fortify rice, cereal, bread, and pasta

threonine * best obtained through lean meat and soybeans, an amino acid vital to the synthesis of protein in the human body

threpsis * a dated synonym for trophism, or nutrition

threpsology * the science or doctrine of nutrition; alternatively, a treatise on such

tocopherols * a class of vitamin E antioxidants typically derived from vegetable oils

torula * a yeast cultured as a flavouring substitute for monosodium glutamate

tragacanth * a natural gum and effective food emulsifier enjoying a long shelf life

transglutaminase * "meat glue," a protein-bonding enzyme used in food processing

trichinelliasis * a disease caused by eating raw or undercooked pork or wild game

trichinoscope * an instrument used to examine meat for signs of trichinae infection

trimethylamine * a compound noted for causing unpleasantly fishy seafood aromas

trophodynamics * the bodily energies governing nourishment and metabolism

trophopathy * any disease negatively affecting or serving to disorder nutrition

trophoplasm * nutrative protoplasm, or the nutritional element of an organic cell

tryptophan * an "essential" amino acid, available in most protein-based foods

tsiology * a learned treatise on tea and its health-enhancing properties

tyramine * a compound known to elevate blood pressure in those eating aged cheese

tyrosinase * an enzyme responsible for turning peeled or sliced fruit and veg brown

tyrotoxism * poisoning from cheese, milk, or other dairy product

ultrapasteurization * the process of milk sterilization conducted at high temperature

uperization * a means of sterilizing milk by injecting pressurized steam

vacreation * the removal of disagreeable aromas from cream by steam distillation

vanillin * essence of vanilla, the world's most popular flavour compound

vaporose * of food, tending to cause overweight people to perspire

vaporous * of food in the gut, tending to cause flatulence

ventosity * the "windiness" or flatulent quality of food, vegetable matter in particular

verocytotoxin * an enteric pathogen transmitted through ingestion of undercooked beef, unpasteurized milk, soft cheeses, or raw vegetables such as sprouts

vibriosis * an infection acquired by eating raw oysters or undercooked seafood

viscogen * a thickening agent used for whipping cream

vitamers * any close chemical compounds able to fulfil a common vitamin function

vitaminization * the practice of fortifying foodstuffs with nutrients and vitamins

vittelin * the chief protein present in egg yolk

xanthophylls * pigments lending egg yolks and chicken flesh their yellow colouring

xylitol * a natural alternative to sugar, used to sweeten both food and chewing gum

yersiniosis * a gut infection contracted by ingesting raw pork or unpasteurized milk

yusho * a skin-staining disease caused by consuming contaminated rice oil

zeaxanthin * a carotenoid pigment used in the food industry as a colouring agent

zeismus * a skin disease produced by the immoderate consumption of corn

zoopherin * vitamin B12, a.k.a. folate, widely present in meat, fish, and dairy produce; vegans are thereby at especial risk of folic acid deficiency anaemia

zyminized * partially predigested by enzymatic action, as with meat suppositories

zymotachygraph * an apparatus measuring the gas produced in a fermenting dough

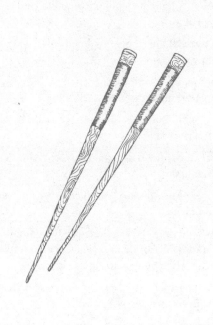

PART TWO

All the Trimmings

You Are What
You Eat

CHAPTER 11

Dietary Regimes and Feeding Routines

> *"Tell me what you eat, and I will tell you what you are."*
> — **Jean Anthelme Brillat-Savarin**

acreophagy * commitment to a meatless diet

acridophagy * the consumption of grasshoppers, locusts, or crickets — protein-rich staples in certain austere climes

adipate * to eat fat, indeed to wax fat; beefing oneself up with fatty foods

aglycositosis * enjoying a diet that is free of sugary or sweet-tasting foods

alimentology * the science or study of human feeding and nutrition

alimentotherapy * any regulated system of healthy feeding and eating

alliaphagy * to consume garlic within one's regular diet

ampelotherapy * grape-cure; the medico-dietetic recommendation of the nourishing properties of grapes

amphivorous * happily eating both animal and vegetable products

anopsology * a raw-food doctrine guided by modern theories of primitive nutrition

anticarnivorous * ethically opposed to eating meat; crusadingly vegetarian or vegan

apogalactismus * weaning a child off the mother's breast and onto a diet of solids

aristophagy * a vanishingly rare synonym for vegetarianism, as in "best eating"

artophagous * consuming bread or similar baked products

baccivorous * given to eating berries

Bantingism * a slimming regime popular in the nineteenth century; its guiding principles were the avoidance of fats, starches, oils, and sugars in favour of proteins

batrachophagous * characterized by eating frogs, or at least the leggy parts thereof

botryotherapeutics * feeding on grapes or berries to assist in recovery from illness

bovivorous * enjoying a hearty appetite and hefty capacity for beef

bromatotherapy * food-cure; treating illness by way of a specially chosen diet

calorie-controlled * of a diet, restricted and regulated in nutritional consumption

carbo-loading * the crash-consumption of carbohydrate-rich foods, especially by endurance sports participants ahead of a particularly gruelling physical challenge

cancrivorous

feeding on crabmeat or other crustaceans such as lobsters and crayfish

carbophobia * the shunning of carbohydrates; obsessively pursuing a low-carb diet

carnism * a pro-meat false consciousness alleged to have been inculcated in Western consumers by a dark alliance of commercial and ideological interests

carnivory * the consumption of animal tissue or flesh—though not exclusively so

carnophobia * a powerful aversion to feeding on the flesh of slaughtered animals

carpophagous * enjoying the fruits of fruit-eating, along with seeds

carpophobia * the avoidance of fruit; a consequence of poor dietary history or habits

cepivorous * keen on onions

cerealism * advocacy of or adherence to a cereal diet; more loosely, vegetarianism

concarnivorous * only eating meals that contain at least one portion of meat

creophagism * carnivory; meat or flesh eating

cyotrophy * the in utero nourishment of the developing fetus

demitarianism * a commitment to cutting one's meat consumption in half

dieta juscula * a broth diet, once widely promoted to restore convalescents to health

dietary * a regulated diet or prescribed course of feeding; also, a diet book

dietetics * the science of human nutrition as a practical guide to healthy eating

dietotherapeutics * the application of a medically informed dietary regime

dietotoxicity * the capacity of some foodstuffs to be harmful when consumed as components of a poor or unbalanced diet

disdiet * an eating regime that is in some measure disordered or irregular

embryotrophy * the in utero nourishment of the developing child

entomophagy * the human consumption of creepy-crawlies

equivorous * devouring horse meat

euryphagy * partaking of a varied diet, encompassing a broad sweep of foodstuffs

eutrophy * normal healthy nutrition and feeding; enjoying a good, balanced diet

flesh-diet * carnivorism; the heavy consumption of meat

flexitarianism * a soft vegetarianism that takes a relaxed position with regard to the occasional eating of meat

freeganism * an ethico-eco movement which subsists on the surplus vegetarian food discarded by mainstream consumer society

fruitarianism * a form of veganism restricting consumption to fruit, nuts, and seeds

frugivorous

eating fruit as a dietary staple

fucivorous * subsisting on edible seaweed

fungivorous * pursuing a diet rich in mushrooms

galactodieta * a dairy-based dietary regime

galactophagous * milk-consuming

galactotherapy * a milk remedy for mothers or wet-nurses to assist infants at suck

gallinivorous * a nonce word for feeding on poultry or fowls

gastrogavage * artificial or forced feeding by means of stomach tube

glycositosis * the heavy consumption of sweet or sugary foods

Grahamism * a historical vegetarian dietary system championed eponymously by the Reverend Sylvester Graham

graminivorous * thriving on a diet rich in cereals

granivorous * thriving on a diet rich in grains

herbicarnivorous * cheerfully eating both flora and fauna as sources of food

herbivory * humorously in respect of humans, vegetarianism — "eat up your greens!"

holozoic * describes obtaining food by consuming other complex, organic matter — a mode of nutrition pursued by the human animal

hyperalimentation * the intravenous drip-feeding of nutrients in solution; alternatively, the parenteral administration of nutrients in cases of GI tract dysfunction

ichthyophagous * feeding on fish

insectarianism * the practice of eating assorted bugs and grubs

instincto * a fringe feeding philosophy where only single raw or ripe foods, selected according to immediate sensory stimulus, are consumed

kynophagy * the consumption of dog flesh; culturally accepted in numerous nations

lachanophobia * scrupulously shunning vegetables; colloquially, "salad-dodging"

lactipotous * milk-fed

lactivory * consuming milk or, more broadly, dairy as a major source of nutrition

lactovegetarianism * the consumption of dairy products, excluding eggs, within the framework of a meat and fish-free diet

leguminivorous * eating a diet rich in beans, peas, and other legumes

leptotrophia * subsisting on a meagre diet, featuring mostly light and frugal meals

lessetarianism * a semi-vegetarian dietary posture that allows for modest meat consumption

lestobiosis * survival by opportunistically pilfering others' food stocks; parasitism

liquidarianism * a health fad strictly limiting nutritional intake to fruit juices

macrophagous * feeding on pieces of relatively large particulate matter, as humans and the higher animals do

meiobutyric * in reference to diet, one economical in the consumption of butter

melliphagous * given to eating honey

metatrophia * a change of diet

microtrapezia * a very light diet, consisting of easily digestible foods

monodiet * a diet confined to a single type of food or food group

monophagism * the practice of eating just one square meal per day

monophagy * a strong desire or preference for one type of food; a restricted palate

monotrophic * surviving on a single source of nutrition

nucivorous * nut-devouring

nutricatia * wet-nursing; the practice of feeding an infant at the breast

offivorous * literally "offal-eating," said disparagingly of someone with a poor diet

oligoallergenic * describes an "elemental" diet undertaken to isolate the toxic effects of particular nutrients in cases of suspected food allergy

oligophagous * consuming only a restricted range of foods

omnivory * the practice of eating a little bit of this and a little bit of that; a mixed diet

omositia * eating raw, uncooked food

oophagy * the consumption of a diet rich in eggs

ophiophagy * the consumption of snake-meat

opsophagy * extreme fussiness of diet, refusing to eat all but the choicest delicacies

orrhotherapy * whey-cure; the commitment to a diet prescriptively heavy on gruel

oryzivorous * subsisting on a diet heavily dependent on rice

ovivorous * dining regularly on lamb, hogget or mutton

ovolactovegetarianism * the consumption of dairy products, including eggs, within the framework of a meat and fish free diet

paleo * a modern attempt to revive the putatively pristine diet of the Pleistocene era

pamphagous * widely plundering the animal and plant kingdoms alike for food; omnivorous

panivorous * given to eating lots of bread

pantophagy * omnivorousness; the consumption of a great variety of foods

parasitism * a strategy of, literally, feeding at another's expense

phagology * the study of, or a learned dissertation on, feeding and eating habits

phagotherapy * consuming extra-rich food to boost recovery or restore strength

phagotrophy * broadly, obtaining bodily nourishment and energy by ingesting food

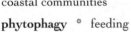

pescetarianism

the restriction of one's flesh consumption to fish or seafood

phycophagy * feeding on algae or seaweed, staples among certain food-poor coastal communities

phytophagy * feeding on vegetables or the products of the plant kingdom

piscivorous * fish-eating

pleobutyric * in reference to diet, one generous in the consumption of butter

pollo-pescetarianism * a semi-vegetarian diet allowing for the occasional consumption of chicken and fish

pollotarianism * an otherwise vegetarian diet supplemented by poultry

polyphagy * eating a varied diet

pomivorous * devouring apples

porcipophagic * pig-eating

prasophagy * having a diet heavy in leeks, or with leeks as the local staple

proteinophobia * a pronounced dislike and avoidance of protein-rich foods

Pythagorean * pertaining to a vegetarian diet free of beans as well as meat

radicivorous * pursuing a diet rich in root vegetables

rawfoodism * a health fad for uncooked, unprocessed food

rectal alimentation * the therapeutic administration of food via nutrient enemas

reducetarianism * the practice of gradually eliminating meat from one's diet

regimen * a disciplined style of feeding such as prescribed by a special health diet

sarcophagy * the practice of carnivory; feeding on either raw flesh or cooked meat

saurophagous * substantially subsisting on lizard-flesh or the meat of other reptiles

seminivorous * given to snacking on seeds; a practice evidently not just for the birds

sitiology * the science of food and nutrition, with special reference to dietetics

sitotherapy * the therapeutic use of food or similar dietetic treatment for illness

skipitarianism * urban scavenging or foraging for freegan leftovers

stenophagy * pursuing a diet tolerating only a narrow or limited range of foods

sycophagous * enjoying a diet rich in figs

teuthophagy * jocularly, the consumption of squid as a staple from the sea's bounty

thalerophagous * having a predilection for eating fresh vegetables above all else

theriotrophical * wet-nursed by wild beasts, as in the legend of Romulus and Remus

thermophagy * a strong preference for cooked, if not piping hot, food

trophology * the practice of combining specific food groups within meals in pursuit of optimal healthy eating results

trophotherapy * the treatment of a medical complaint by way of the best efforts of modern nutritional and dietary science

tuddorfoster * the action of breastfeeding or nourishing offspring

tyrophagous * cheese-eating

uberate * to breastfeed; to give suck

veganism * abstention from animal flesh, foods, or products in their entirety

vegetarianism * the elimination of meat, fish, and so forth from one's diet

vegecurious

trying out a vegetarian diet before fully committing to the lifestyle

vegetivorous * given to eating and enjoying vegetables

venisonivorous * keen to consume the flesh of wild or hunted animals

vitarianism * a dietary subset of veganism limiting nutritional intake to raw fruit and vegetables only, with no concession to grain foods

vitellophagy * the consumption of egg yolk

xenophagy * a radical or categorical change in diet

xerophagy * eating dry food; the proverbial punishment diet of bread and water

yo-yo dieting * constantly bouncing from one slimming or food fad to the next

zen macrobiotics * a strict dietary regime endorsing "harmonic" whole pure foods, notably brown rice, while shunning processed foods in an attempt to prolong life

zomotherapeutics * a regime of raw meat or expressed meat juice formerly offered to those in convalescence from tuberculosis

zoophagy * carnivorousness; the consumption of animal flesh

zootrophy * in evolutionary strategy, a dietary mode dependent on material derived from other living organisms, especially animals, as a source of nutrition and energy

CHAPTER 12

Picas, Phagias, and Other Perverted Appetites

> *"Vegetarians are cool. All I eat are vegetarians."*
> —Ted Nugent

acuphagia * a craze for ingesting sharp objects

allocoprophagia * eating someone else's shit; indicative of psychological disturbance

allotriophagia * the craving for non-standard foods or non-nutritive substances

amylophagia * excessive consumption of corn-starch; a disposition developed most frequently during pregnancy

androphagy * "man-eating" or cannibalism; the practice of devouring human flesh

anthropophagism * another synonym for cannibalism—who knew it was so popular?

arachnivory * feeding on spiders: think of the lunatic Renfield in *Dracula*

argillophagia * the heavy consumption of white clay to augment low mineral intake; widely resorted to as late as the recent past in some dirt-poor farming communities

autocoprophagia * feeding on one's own faeces

autosarcophagy * self-cannibalism, from chewing on one's fingernails to feeding on one's own skin or body parts

brephophagy * the cannibalism of young children

cannibality * devouring the flesh of your fellow creatures

cautopyreiophagia * ingesting burnt matchheads or ashes, a passion that can result in renal failure

cerophagia * eating wax, human or otherwise

cheilophagia * the chronic biting of the lips

chthonophagia * the eager consumption of dirt or other earthy matter

cissa * the craving for unusual or unwholesome substances in pregnancy

cittosis * an abnormal desire for strange foods or noxious substances

coniophagia * a compulsion to ingest dust

coprophagia * the eating of excrement

cryptotrichotillomania * a mania for swallowing one's plucked-out hair

dermatophagia * a compulsion to bite, gnaw on, or eat one's own skin, most commonly at the fingers around the nails

dysorexia * any depraved or unnatural appetite; more loosely, an eating disorder

emetophagia * a pica for digesting vomit

encephalophagy * the consumption of neural matter as a source of nutrition

endophagy * cannibalism as customarily practised within a tribe or social group

exophagy * eating one's enemies for breakfast; the cannibalism of outgroup captives

feminivorous * devouring the flesh of women

ferrivorous * feeding on iron; coined in the clinical literature after the "Idiot of Ostend," who addictively swallowed such objects as nails, screws, and knives

formiphagia * a depravity of diet involving the devouring of ants

geomelophagia * the compulsive excessive consumption of raw potatoes

geophagism * a dirt-pica for earth, soil, or clay; a depraved appetite found within deprived communities

gooberphagia * a nonce word meaning the chronic consumption of peanuts

gynophagia * the psychotic killing, cooking, and consumption of a female victim

haematophagia * vampiric blood-sucking

haliphagia * the ingestion of unhealthy quantities of table salt or other salts

heterorexia * the derangement of the appetite, as evidenced by cravings for inedible or indigestible foods

hominivorous * devouring man-flesh

hyalophagia * the pathological consumption of glass

hyperorality * the compulsive stuffing of inedible objects into the mouth

kaolinophagia * a form of geophagism in which kaolin minerals are the dominant earthy material consumed

kreatophagia * eating raw flesh

lactaphilia * an adult fetish for consuming breast milk

limosis * depravity or degeneracy in appetite as a product of disease

lithophagia * a stone-pica for such as rocks and pebbles

metallophagia * a mania for swallowing metal objects

mucophagia * the habit of eating boogies, nasal mucus being entirely non-nutritional

necrophagia * the sexual cannibalism of corpses

necrophagism * the eating of carrion, being the decaying flesh of dead animals

omophagia * the consumption of raw flesh; the roots of the term lie in the feasts of antiquity for the wine-god Bacchus, at which goat entrails were frenziedly devoured

onychophagia * the practice of biting one's fingernails compulsively

paedophagy * child-eating, in legend or in life

pagophagia * the excessive consumption of ice, driven by iron deficiency anaemia

paratrophy * a pattern of disordered, defective, or otherwise depraved feeding

pica

a generic term for eating disorders centring around non-nutritive substances

parorexia * any perversion of a healthy and natural human appetite

parthenophagia * the lust murder cum cannibalism of virgins or young children

phthirophagous * given to consuming body lice

placentophagia * feeding on conserved and cooked womb-cake

plumbophagia * a craving to consume lead

pyophagia * a predilection for swallowing pus

reingestion * the consumption of one's own voided faecal pellets or piss

rhypophagy * the eating of filth, refuse, or even excrement

sanguinivory * the consumption of uncooked blood, direct from source

scatophagia * the eating of excrement as a paraphilic or psychotic practice

scolecophagia * as the old ditty goes, "I think I'll go and eat worms"

seminophagia * the consumption of semen during the act of fellatio

sexual autophagy * flaying one's own skin and eating it for sexual gratification

teknophagy * eating babies for breakfast

248

theanthropophagy * the sacrificial devourment of a godlike person

theophagy * the sacramental consumption of a deity or divinity

thyestean * possessing marked cannibalistic proclivities and appetites

toxicophagous * addicted to eating poisonous substances

transumption * in anthropology, the ritualistic consumption of deceased kin

trichophagia * the compulsive chewing and swallowing of hair

urophagia * the practice of consuming urine, largely for misguided health reasons

vorarephilia * a cannibalistic sex fantasy re eating another or being eaten in turn

Wendigo psychosis * a terror that one must be a cannibal for being curious to taste human flesh

xenorexia * pica; the craving to eat matter regarded as unfit for human consumption

xylophagia * a craze for ingesting paper or wood products

CHAPTER 13

Eat or Be Eaten: Nature's Food Chain

"Nature, red in tooth and claw."
—Alfred, Lord Tennyson

acariphagous * feeding on mites; said of amphibians, inter alia

adelphophagy * the in utero cannibalization of a sibling fetus, as practised by some species of sharks

algivorous * subsisting on algae, as many aquatic organisms commonly do

ambivory * the herbivorous consumption of both grasses and broad-leafed plants

anthophagous * feeding on flowers, as with insect grubs

aphidivory * the eating of aphids, a prized ladybird meal

apivory * the act of feeding on bees, a specialized dietary strategy of some bird species

araneophagy * the eating of spiders, notably by predatory fellow arachnids

avivory * preying on birds—or indeed other birds, in the case of certain hawks and falcons

biophagery * the practice of devouring organisms while they are still alive and kicking

bryophagy * the consumption of mosses, chiefly a dietary item among insect species

ceratophagy * the consumption of cornified animal tissue or hair by insects

coccidophagy * the predation of scale insects by rival insect orders

colacobiosis * settled social parasitism, whereby one community of insects lives permanently within and off another

copromycetophagy * the consumption of fungal pathogens found growing within animal faeces

dendrophagous * devouring trees or bark, as porcupines in winter

detritivory * the practice of feeding on the waste or remains of various flora and fauna

durophagy * the specialized eating of hard-shelled or exoskeletal organisms, such as crabs by saki monkeys

ectoophagy * the feeding on nearby eggs by newly hatched insect larvae

embryophagy * the intrauterine devourment of another member of a developing brood

endoophagy * the feeding on nearby host eggs by newly hatched parasitic insect larvae

entomonecrophagous * in relation to insects, gorging on dead arthropods

erucivorous * habitually feeding on caterpillars

fimivorous * dung-devouring, in the manner of coprophagans such as the dung beetle

florisugent * as the hummingbird, that feeds by sucking nectar from flowers

florivorous * primarily eating flowers

folivorous * subsisting on leaves or foliage

forbivorous * greedy for sunflowers, as notoriously is the grasshopper

formivorous * having a taste for ants

frondivorous * feeding on fronds, the large leaves of palms, ferns, or similar

fructivorous * consuming mainly fruit

gallivorous * as with certain insect larvae, feeding on abnormal plant growths, or galls

gumnivorous * supping on tree sap

haemophagous * devouring blood

harpactophagy * insect-on-insect predation

helminthophagy * feeding on helminths, or parasitic worms

holophytic * obtaining nutrition by way of photosynthesis, as with green plants

hyperparasitism * a macabre food-chain relationship wherein a parasite, usually an insect, feeds off another parasitic organism, whose host in turn may itself be yet another parasite

hypocarnivory * in zoology, the consumption of flesh as a minority component of the animal's overall diet

insectivorous * given to devouring insects — may refer to carnivorous plants and animals alike

isophagous * feeding on a similar or allied species, as fungi

keratophagy * the practice of snakes consuming their own skin after it is shed

kleptoparasitism * a strategy of surreptitiously stealing other animals' prey or plundering their food hoards

larvivorous * grubbing on grubs

lepidophagy * the consumption of the scales of fellow fishes

lichenivory * living off lichens

lignivory * of critters, feeding on wood

lignophagia * an equine pica for chewing or consuming wood matter

limivorous * eating mud, in the manner of certain earthworms

macrophytophagy * a marine diet based on higher, more complex plant material

malacophagy * the eating of molluscs, a meal variously enjoyed by certain fish and spiders

mallophagous * consuming wool or fleece, as per biting lice

matriphagy * an arachnid interaction whereby spiderlings consume their own mother

mellisugous * that feeds by sucking honey

merdivorous * feeding on faecal matter or more substantial dung deposits

microbivorous * subsisting on microorganisms or microbial life forms, notably bacteria

microphagous * of invertebrates, consuming chiefly or only very small plants or prey

mixomycetophagy * the consumption of slime mould, a delicacy among some insect orders

molluscivory * more consumption of molluscs, in this case by higher animal species only

mucivorous * feeding on plant exudate or mucilage

mycoparasitism * a form of fungus-on-fungus feeding behaviour

mycophagy * a diet consisting principally if not exclusively of fungi

myristicivorous * thriving on nutmeg as a key item within a broader avian diet

myrmecophagy * the eating of ants, notably by specialist feeders such as the aardvark

necrophytophagous * habitually feeding on dead plant material

nectarivorous * subsisting on, or given to substantially eating, nectar

neustophagy * the consumption of neustons, organisms found on the surface film of water

osmotrophic * acquiring nutrition by the process of absorption, as fungi do

ossivorous * given to feeding on animal bones

osteophagy

a perverted cattle appetite for bones

ovophagy * more intrauterine cannibal feeding, whereby an embryo devours sibling eggs

palmivorous * deriving nourishment from palm leaves or trees, mealybug-style

palynophagy * feeding on pollen, a practice found within a number of beetle families

panphytophagy * the consumption of a diverse range of plant species

parasitoidism * the gruesome slow devouring from within of a host body by insect grubs

paratrophic * parasitic; feeding off a host organism

phagophily * feeding on parasites, after the fashion of pseudoscorpions

phloeophagy * the consumption of bark, as by weevils

phyllophagous * leaf-eating

phytivory * the use of plants or herbage as a significant food source by animals

phytosuccivorous * devouring plant sap or juice

pinivorous * feeding on pine nuts; birds and animals are wont to eat the seeds, while insects prefer the needles

piperivorous * keen on peppers, as birds such as the toucan

planktotrophy * the action of deriving nourishment from plankton

plantivorous * herbivorous; feeding on plants and vegetable matter

plasmophagous * consuming plasma, a term used with regard to protozoans

pleophagous * capable of eating an abundance of food sources, substances, or species

plurivorous * of parasites or fungi, feeding on host organisms of many different kinds

poephagous * eating grass or herbage, in the manner of the kangaroo

predation * the act and evolutionary strategy of feeding on prey

pupivorous * devouring the pupae of other insects

quercivorous * feeding on the leaves of oak trees

reptilivorous * partial to eating reptiles, as per a number of specialist bird predators

rhizophagy * the consumption of roots or rhizomes, chiefly in the context of insect nutrition

sanguisugent * as per the vampire bat, blood-sucking

saprophagy * the practice of insects feeding on decomposing organic material

saproxylophagy * the consumption of dead or decaying wood matter

sarconecrophagy * the practice of insects feeding on the carcasses of vertebrates

sarcophilous * flesh-loving; said of the Tasmanian devil, nature's largest carnivorous marsupial

scavenging * foraging for and feeding on any dead plant or animal material available

scisophagy * insect feeding on the organic debris of the plant and animal kingdoms

serpentivorous * feeding on snake flesh or the meat of other ophidians

solenophagous * with reference to haemophagous insects, drawing nourishment directly from the blood vessels of host organisms

spongivorous * subsisting primarily on sponges, as with sea turtles

sporophagy * the consumption of fungal spores by insects

stercovorous * finding nourishment in excrement; a reference to insect eating habits

telmophagous * with reference to haemophagous insects, feeding on pools of spilled blood

termitophagy * subsisting on a diet rich in termites

trophallaxis * the transfer of solids or fluids regurgitated via mouth or anus; a feeding behaviour observed within certain social insect groups

trophobiosis * the mutual exchange of nutriment within a symbiotic relationship

univorous * of parasites or fungi, feeding exclusively on a single host organism

vermivorous * variously feeding on worms, grubs or insect vermin

xylivory * the consumption of wood on the part of herbivorous termites

zoopharmacognosy * animal self-medication: instinctively eating selective plants, soils, insects, and so forth as a prophylactic measure

zoosaprophagy * surviving on decaying animal matter

zoosuccivory * feeding on animal blood, lymph, or other liquid bodily secretions

Whet Your
Appetite

CHAPTER 14

Feast: Gluttony and Greed

> *"Never eat more than you can lift."*
> — **Miss Piggy**

accloy * to eat to excess, overburdening the stomach to the point of nausea

acoria * having a pathologically great appetite, one that literally cannot be sated

adephagia * a condition characterized by a morbidly large capacity for food

adipomania * putting on extra weight through eating too many fatty junk foods

agroteyed * bloated from overeating

alimentiveness * the instinctual drive for food elevated to the point of gluttony

all-devouring * possessing an unflagging, nay indefatigable, appetite for food

antrectomy * surgical excision of the lower stomach walls, proposed as a radical antiobesity procedure

bariatrics * the branch of medicine dealing with the aetiology and prophylaxis of obesity

batten * to gorge upon a certain foodstuff, or grow fat by feeding

belly-rack * an instance of gormandizing, or feasting ravenously

brozier * to eat someone out of house and home

bulimy * gross gluttony; literally "ox hunger"

caninus appetitus * an animalistic impulse to feed that knows no restraint

carnivoracity * greed for meat

cibomania * a compulsion to eat anything going

comedonious * given to overeating

conarotic * well-fed, and rather plump with it

crapulent * cropsick; physically ill from an excess of food and drink

cravicious * greedy or gluttonous, in West Indies jive-talk

cynorexia * a voracious appetite, like that of a ravening wolf

depascent * eating or feeding greedily

devourment * the rapid and ravenous dispatch of food

diabesity * type 2 diabetes, caused by overeating and subsequent weight gain

edacious * gluttonous; greedy for grub

edacity * an impressive capacity for food, as befits a lusty appetite

enfarce * to eat to excess, literally stuffing one's stomach with food

englutting * gobbling down food without pause or poise

engorgement * the action of devouring a meal beyond the natural point of plenitude

epulosity * feasting to excess

esurine * voracious of appetite

falconish * ravenous; "hawk-hungry" as it were

farcinate * to cram one's belly with food

fat-fed * battened; become corpulent through forced or unconstrained feeding

feederism * the fetishistic overfeeding of one's sexual partner

feeding frenzy * an orgy of face-cramming and stomach-stuffing

food coma * lethargy attendant upon the overconsumption of overly rich food

forage * in earlier usage, to overindulge the demands of the stomach

forsling * to devour utterly, swallowing food down swiftly in large mouthfuls

fress * to eat abundantly—and often

fulsomeness * the state of being surfeited with food to the point of sickness

gastrimargy * clinically pathological gluttony

gastrolatrous * literally, belly-worshipping; figuratively, hedonistically overeating

gastroplasty * stomach-stapling to restrict food intake and control weight

gavage * the force-feeding of maidens ahead of marriage as practised in some traditional cultures where obesity in a prospective bride is aesthetically prized

globesity * the worldwide epidemic of overeating and problematic weight gain

gloterie * good, Old English gluttery or gluttony

glutterous * insatiable in appetite

gluttonishness * persistent immoderation in matters of food consumption

gluttonism * alimentary avarice in action

gluttony * the vice of excessive eating; one of the seven so-called deadly sins

glycopathia * illness caused by excessive consumption of sweets

gorging * filling the gorge or gullet; hence, feeding greedily

gormandize * to eat with great relish and little restraint

gorp * to eat greedily

gulleting * gulping down food in considerable quantity

gulligutted * gluttonous and with a corporation to show for it

gulosity * sheer greediness for food

gurgitation * the heavy consumption of food far beyond simple satiation of bodily needs

guttlesome * vitiated in appetite

guttrell * somewhat gluttonous

gut-worship * inordinate fondness for and intake of food

guzzledom * a state of contented devourment of food and drink

helluation * a reckless, abandoned gluttony

hoggishness * coarse, swinish gluttony

hungrisome * ravening; voracious

hyperalimentosis * illness or disease arising from excessive feeding

hyperorexia * excessive appetite, as medically determined

hyperphagic * given to bouts of insatiable cramming of food

ingluvious * an archaic synonym for gluttonous

ingordigiousness * a consuming passion in affairs of the stomach

ingurgitate * to eat most immoderately

insatiable * incapable of satisfying the appetite; without alimentary limit

intemperance * debauchery of the appetite; the overthrowing of all self-restraint

impinguinate

to grow fat on rich food

jejunoileal bypass * a now discontinued surgical procedure in cases of morbid obesity

lecherous * in old Scots usage, having an overly lusty relationship with food

locust-like * all-devouring; stripping the proverbial cupboard bare

lupine * invincible in appetite; hungry like the wolf

lycorexia * a morbid and limitless appetite, especially for raw meat

mouch * to gobble greedily

multivorous * extreme in appetite

nimis * according to Saint Aquinas on gluttony and excess, the partaking of food in immodest quantity castigated theologically as sinful indulgence

obesity * literally "over-eating"; a medical condition consequent upon the constant intake of empty calories and attendant accumulation of excess body fat

obesogenic * tending to promote toxic levels of obesity within society; a charge made inter alia against the modern convenience food ethos

oferwist * Anglo-Saxon gluttony

omnivorant * possessing the capacity to devour all manner of foods in remarkable quantities

oreximania * inordinate consumption of food from fear or loathing of being thin

overindulgence * regular eating to excess

overnutrition * euphemistically, obesity; resulting in particular from a junk-food diet

over-quat * to glut oneself with food beyond the point of healthy repletion

phagomania * unconquerable alimental avarice

philogastric * inclined to indulge the stomach

piggishness * mannerless greed and overeating

pollakiphagia * abnormal frequency of eating

polyorexia * excessive appetite; bulimy

polyphagia * uncontrollable overeating, indicative of some underlying disease

polysarcia * a superannuated clinical term for obesity

polytrophy * a condition of excessive dietary or nutritional intake

Prader-Willi * a genetic syndrome featuring a compulsion to overeat

provand-prickt * overfed; rendered sick by too much rich food

qualmyish * cropsick or crapulent; having a stomach fit from excess in consumption

rapacity * a ravenous capacity for food

ravenage * devouring gluttony

ravenize * to devour with great haste and hunger

regorge * to swallow food eagerly, or once again

repartake * to return to the table for an extra helping of food

repletiate * to eat so as to satisfy even the heaviest of appetites

rounge * to champ merrily on one's meal, or devour with great vigour

satiety * the condition of feeling beyond full or glutted after eating a hearty meal

saturate * to eat oneself to a standstill

savorous * sensually greedy for the gratifications of the table

scarf * to scoff or eat with great gusto

scorpacciata * binge-eating, especially on locally sourced seasonal food

sitiomania * an abnormal craving for food, in either variety or simple quantity

slummock * to gobble one's dinner up in a greedy or slovenly manner

stodge-ful * crammed, stuffed, or gorged with grub

stomachful * possessing an impressive appetite and belly capacity to match

suffonsified * in Canadian argot, full up and politely refusing more food

supersizing * going for the jumbo portions

suralimentation * a clinical circumlocution for plain old overfeeding

surcharge * to overfill the stomach

surfeiture * gastric greed

tachyphagia * bolting food down in a schizoid fashion

tigerantic * jocularly, having a ferocious appetite

tuburcinate * to eat greedily

vagotomy * resection of the vagus nerve to reduce hunger pangs in the obese

ventripotential * mighty of stomach — hence gluttonous

voracious * ravenous in appetite

voracity * greediness in eating

voraginous * all-devouring; voracious of food

voration * an act or instance of greedy and speedy devourment

vorax * greedy; slave to the demands of the belly

vulturous * opportunistically ravenous for any available pickings

well-nourished * a euphemism for overfed, even obese

wolfishness * a tendency to attack any food going without refinement or restraint

xertz * to gulp one's grub down greedily

yaffling * eating greedily and noisily

yeverness * an older, lost word for gluttony

yevrisome * a Northern dialectal expression meaning ravenously greedy

yollop * to swallow one's food lustily and hastily

CHAPTER 15

Fast:
Denial and
Disgust

*"I've been on a diet for two weeks, and all I've lost is
two weeks."*
—Totie Fields

abrosia * desisting from food for a set period, for example on spiritual grounds

abstemious * fastidious and frugal in the consumption of food

abstinency * abstaining from food or fasting

anorectous * lacking in appetite

anorexia athletica * an eating disorder characterized by excessive exercise to discipline the body and establish dominance over the desire for food

anorexia mirabilis * prodigious fasting on the part of young women from religious piety and a desire to mortify the sinful flesh; a malady noted in the Middle Ages

anorexiant * serving to promote appetite loss

anoreximania * extreme reluctance to eat for fear of becoming fat

anorexy * want of appetite or decreased sensitivity to the demands of the stomach

apastia * refusal to eat as an expression of mental illness

aphagia * a refusal to swallow food, from either physical discomfort or psychological distress

apocarteresis * ritual suicide by self-starvation

apokreo * abstinence from meat for three weeks at Lent, as practised in the Greek Orthodox Church

aposity * loathing for the very sight, or even at the mere thought, of food

appetiteless * marked by want of desire for food

asitia * lack of appetite, extending to an utter aversion to food

bantingized * having dieted to lose weight

bdelygmia * a pathological disgust for food

binge-purge syndrome * the eating disorder known clinically as bulimia nervosa

breatharianism * a doctrine promising a healthy life without the need for food; the body's essential nutrients are purportedly derived instead from prajna and prayer

bulimarexia * disordered eating exhibiting elements of both bulimic and anorexic behaviour, wherein the binge-purge is atoned for immediately by a period of fasting

bulimia nervosa * a disease marked by the alternate bingeing and purging of food

calorie-conscious * anxious to slim and wary of eating beyond the bare minimum

cibophobia * a morbid fear of or distaste for food

crash-dieting * the action of abruptly and austerely curtailing one's calorie intake

degout * disgust: a nauseating physical disinclination to partake of food

dharna * an Indian hunger strike; more precisely, claiming justice by protest fasting

diabulimia * an eating disorder not yet formally recognized in which a type 1 diabetic reduces or refuses insulin in order to shed weight

disgustion * loathing for food and drink; disgust literally means "offensive to taste"

disrelish * a more moderate dislike or distaste for food and drink

distasture * a nauseating revulsion for food

eating-disordered * afflicted by a hostile and dysfunctional relationship to food

embertide * the quarterly period when a three-day Christian vigil of fasting falls

emetomania * a compulsion to vomit as a symptom of bulimia nervosa

esurial * surrendered to fasting

fastidium ciborum * a clinical, psychogenic abhorrence of food

fasting-tide * a season of fast and abstinence from food

forfasted * thoroughly emaciated or exhausted from fasting

gustless * devoid of appetite

Hooverize * to be frugal in one's consumption of food

hunger-cure * the treatment of disease through fasting

hyporexia * diminishment of appetite

inappetency * simple lack of appetite

inedia * the hypothesized ability to survive without food or water during an extended period of religiously observed fasting, perhaps through divine intercession

jejunation * fasting; medically regulated or voluntary ritual abstinence from food

jour maigre * a day of religious fast and abstinence, when all meat is to be shunned

ketosis * a state of carbohydrate insufficiency, commonly sought by slimmers, where the body draws energy from its fat stores instead of glucose, its primary fuel source

Lenten-faced * the mournful visage of a person who has too long desisted from food

macerate * to cause the body to grow thin and the flesh to waste through fasting

manorexia * anorexia nervosa in men; male-pattern disordered eating

nauseate * to reject food with an accompanying sensation of sickness

nesteia * an obsolete medical term for fasting

nestiatry * a form of therapy involving the reduction of food intake or absolute fast

orexifugic * serving to dispel or dampen the appetite

orthorexia * an unhealthy obsession with eating chiefly low-calorie foodstuffs

phagophobia

a fear of eating or swallowing food

pingling * eating without joy or appetite; merely picking at or otherwise playing with the food on one's plate

pregorexia * extreme dieting to counteract or control weight gain during pregnancy

procrescophobia * a dread of putting on weight; hence the urge to stay slim at the expense of calorific intake

pseudoanorexia * loss of appetite attendant upon distress accompanying eating

quadragesimal * a rigorous fast, notably one enduring for the forty days of Lent

refrain * to abstain from, inter alia, food

santhara * in Jainism, the ethical commission of suicide through fasting

sawm * the period of fasting from dawn to dusk during Ramadan

sitapophasis * refusal to eat as revelation of serious mental disturbance

sitieirgia * hysterical anorexia; a clinical term that has long since fallen into disfavour

sitophobia * a morbid repugnance for food

slenderizing * a rarely encountered synonym for slimming or dieting

Spartan regimen * a supremely disciplined regime of restraint in feeding and eating

stammagust * a thrawn, thoroughgoing disgust for food of any kind whatsoever

stomachlessness * acute absence or loss of appetite

thinspiration * the promotion of a dangerously food-averse, female anorexia chic

trichinophobia * a fear of food poisoning, in turn poisoning one's attitude to food

unlust * chronic aversion to food in general or absence of appetite for a given meal

unwhet * to spoil the appetite

weight-watching * limiting one's food intake in an endeavour to shed excess pounds

CHAPTER 16

Famine:
Hunger and
Starvation

> *"Hunger knows no friend but its feeder."*
> —**Aristophanes**

acceleration * starvation, in erstwhile tramp and traveller argot

affamish * to starve or die of hunger

affamishing * the infliction of hunger or starvation

afingered * reduced to a condition of extreme hunger

anshum-scranshum * a famished scramble to grab what meagre fare is available

aporinosis * broadly, any disorder caused by a lack of nutrition or dietary deficit

appetizement * a craving for food stemming from a grievous want of sustenance

asterve * to perish from hunger or starve another out

athrepsy * marasmic debility caused by extreme childhood malnutrition

atrophia * an obsolete expression for wasting away from undernourishment

autophagy * the consumption of the body's own cells and tissues in starvation

avitaminosis * any disease or condition produced by chronic vitamin deprivation

baitless * being without food or means of refreshment

271

barbiers * an early anglicization of beriberi, a thiamine deficiency disorder found in locations where white rice is a staple and access to other sources of food is restricted

belly-pinched * suffering the pangs of hunger

belly-watch * the sensation of hunger, as experienced in the pit of the stomach

bitytite * a humorous term for hunger, artfully playing on "appetite"

bread-and-butterless

lacking even the food basics

cachexia africana * lethargy formerly attributed to eating clay as a means to assuage hunger pangs in food-poor communities scattered across the tropical latitudes

cacotrophy * a superannuated medical term for malnutrition

catabolysis * the most severe stage of malnutrition, wherein the body begins to cannibalize its own muscle and fat reserves

clemmed * pinched with hunger

cruggy * hungry, in historical slang

denourishment * clinical care by way of controlled nutritional deprivation

dine with Duke Humphrey * to go without dinner—and not through choice!

dinnerish * hungry and impatient for mealtime to arrive

dystrophia * an outmoded medical term for broad functional degeneration arising from defective or deprived nutrition

dystrophoneurosis * a neurological disorder caused by a restricted diet and the inadequate nourishment of the nerves

effamished * pushed to the very extremities of starvation

emaciation * severe weight loss due to extended calorific deficit and decline

enfamine * to subdue through, or otherwise purposely cause to suffer, famine

esuriate * to go hungry

esurience * simple hunger; healthy appetite

esurition * the experience of being hungry

faggotless * without food

famelicose * oftentimes hungry

famine * to suffer or expire from a lack of food

famine-pinched * famished; starving unto death

famishment * a state of starvation

famylous * exceedingly hungry

flesh-fallen * emaciated; physically much reduced through hunger

foodlessness * the condition of being devoid of any source of nourishment

forclem * to thoroughly starve

forhungered * caused to die of hunger

gastralgokenosis * the paroxysmal pains of an empty stomach

grubbish * somewhat peckish

gutfoundered * diseased from the effects of malnourishment

hangry * ill-tempered or otherwise irritable as a result of hunger

hunger osteomalacia * vitamin D or calcium deficiency in malnourished adults

hunger-bane * death by hunger

hunger-starve * to go starved oneself or starve another out

hungrify * to cause to be hungry

hungriousness * the experience of not having enough food to fill one's belly

hypoalimentation * insufficient or otherwise inadequate dietary intake

hypovitaminosis * undernourishment caused by deficiency in vitamin intake

ill-nourished * suffering from insufficient nutritional intake

impastuous * famished

inanition * starvation, or the profound exhaustion attendant upon it

jejunity * a rare synonym for hunger; the jejunum was once called the "hungry gut"

kwashiorkor * a tropical childhood protein deficiency disorder widely encountered in areas already afflicted by endemic food poverty

Lang Reed * historically, the period of perennial nutritional scarcity pre-spring, when food stocks were commonly at their lowest

limoctonia * death from or suicide by hunger

limophobia * a consuming terror or horror of hunger, especially starvation

limophoitos * madness due to lack of food

limophthisis * emaciation due to lack of food

limopsora * a scurvy-like skin disease caused by hunger or deficient diet

limoseric * pertaining to "limos," or clinical hunger

luncheonless * going unfed at noon

mal de caribou * alternatively, "rabbit starvation," paradoxical malnutrition caused by the consumption of abundant lean meat in the absence of any other food sources

malnourishment * poor nutrition, be it from eating junk food or calorie insufficiency

malnutrition * popularly understood to mean undernourishment as a consequence of food scarcity; may also, however, refer to poor dietary observance of any kind

marasmus * a severe wasting and weakening occurring in malnourished infants

marcor * a severe wasting and weakening occurring in malnourished adults

meat-stint * a deficiency of food, hence going without

meat-yabble * righteously hungry; having worked up a powerful appetite

meteliest * hunger; want of food in Old English times

microtrophous * underfed

muesli-belt malnutrition * a hypothesized nutritional deficit and imbalance experienced by the offspring of deluded foodies enforcing fad diets on their family

munchies * weed-induced but non-hallucinatory hunger cravings

nutritional melalgia * a burning ache in the limbs or their extremities attributed to prolonged undernourishment; notably, deprivation of protein and B vitamins

oligotrophy * a condition of insufficient or restricted nutrition; lack of nourishment

paedatrophy * chronic childhood undernourishment; a synonym for marasmus

pannam-struck * hungry, but without as much as a crust to eat

peckishness * slight and easily satisfiable hunger

pecksome * moderately hungry; keen to grab a bite to eat

peina * an obsolete medical term for profound hunger short of starvation

peinotherapy * "hunger-cure"; the clinical supervision of a regime of food restriction in an attempt to starve the body of those nutrients suspected of causing illness

pellagra * a niacin deficiency disorder found typically in developing countries where communities are overly reliant on maize crops in the face of wider food scarcity

phrynoderma * "toad skin" disease; caused by multiple nutritional deficiency

pinch-gutted * stomach-achingly hungry

punishment of Tantalus * namely, to starve alone amid food aplenty

rachitis * rickets; bone softening and bowleggedness from childhood malnutrition

rassasay * to satisfy the cravings of one starved of food

ravenousness * sharp, maddening hunger

scorbutus * scurvy; an ascorbic acid deficiency disorder once associated with sailors on long sea voyages, but still found where food aid is required for famine relief

scrannish * somewhat hungry; peckish

sharpsetness * the experience of piercing hunger pangs

starven * famished

stomach-worm * hunger itself gnawing away inside one's guts

stomatonecrosis * oral gangrene as a lifelong stamp of severe infant malnutrition

subalimentation * undernourishment; malnutrition in its popular sense

subsist * to survive on a food-poor, no-frills diet or at an austere nutritional level

supperless * making do without an evening meal

trophonosis * any disease or condition consequent upon marked nutritional deficit

tuckerless * being without food

unbreakfasted * gone to work—or school, or play—without a bite in one's belly

undernourished * semi-starved, or at a minimum unhealthily underfed

undinnered * unfed

unvictualled * not provided with food or anticipated rations

victless * starving, being devoid of all sustenance

yapness * hunger

yawpish * hungry

yerd-hunger * a final, overwhelming desire for food in one knocking at death's door

zygomycosis * a fungal infection, known in its gastrointestinal form to target those already immuno-compromised through starvation or extreme malnutrition

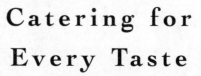

Catering for
Every Taste

CHAPTER 17

Supplying, Selling, and Serving

> *"Laughter is brightest, where food is best."*
> **— Irish proverb**

acatery * a manorial storeroom for purchased foodstuffs — that is, all items with the exception of home baking and brewing products

acatour * a caterer or, more broadly, a quartermaster

accubita * an ancient Roman dining room, where feasters would recline on couches

after-mess * a dining area for crew situated at the rear of a ship in naval service

alimentation * the provision of nourishment; also, a deli or similar store specializing in selling continental foods

aliture * the action of supplying nourishment and refreshment

allspice * a grocer, in the vernacular of a bygone era

annonary * pertaining to the food trade and the transactions of the food market

appellation contrôlée * a certificate guaranteeing the geographical provenance and authenticity of a given foodstuff

appose * to serve dishes at table

archdapifership * in European history, the office of the retainer entrusted with serving a new emperor his first meal, which he presented on horseback

auberge * a swanky restaurant in the French style

automat * a self-service cafeteria, where snacks are dispensed by vending machine

a-vealing * the act of procuring calf meat

baitland * a port where refreshments may be procured to replenish a ship's stores

bakehouse * a place where breadstuffs and other baked products are made and sold

bakerdom

bakers considered collectively or as a community with shared interests

barrow-bunter * a costermonger, one who sells fruit and vegetables from a handcart

battels * a set of college accounts itemizing provisions purchased from the kitchen

baxter * a lady baker

beanery-queen * a waitress serving in a down-market restaurant or diner

billet * a restaurant bill of fare; a menu

bistro * a small restaurant serving moderately priced meals in an informal ambience

bladarius * historically, a dealer in grain

blockman * a butcher's or fishmonger's assistant who cuts the meat and fillets the fish

blumba * a metal certification tag attached to meat passed as kosher

bouch * a meal allowance granted by a nobleman to his retinue or court

bovicide * jocularly, a butcher; literally one who slaughters cattle

brasserie * a relaxed mid-range restaurant in the traditional French style

breadery * an artisanal bakery

bread-wright * an obsolete term for a baker

breastaurant * an eatery staffed by scantily clad hostesses

bustaurant * an eatery set up in a converted bus

butcherdom * the realm, work, or trade of butchers

butcher-row * a shambles, or meat market

butter-factor * a tradesman who buys butter direct from farmers to sell wholesale

buttery * a substantial pantry; also, a college room where meals are sold to scholars

café chantant * a caff gaff where customers are entertained with music and song

cafeteria * a self-service diner offering refreshment to staff, visitors, and so forth

cakery * an establishment making and selling cakes and similar baked treats

cameriere * a waiter in an Italian-themed restaurant

candier * a comfit-maker

cantinier * one who keeps a canteen or similar victualling establishment

carhop * a waitress, often on skates, who serves customers at a drive-in restaurant

carnificial * concerning butchers and their bloody work

carnish-ken * in old criminal argot, a thieves' eatery

carvership * the office and station of meat-carver to the king

carvery * a buffet or establishment where meat is carved for patrons to consume

cashmarie * a hawker or pedlar of fish

caterership * the business of providing or purveying food; purveyorship

catering * the action or trade of supplying and serving food off-site

cenacle * a dining room; especially, the room where the Last Supper was eaten

charcutier * a pork butcher

char-wallah * an Indian boy or man servant who brings tea

chator * an early variant of caterer; nothing more than an etymological curio today

cheesemongering * the business of selling cheese and cheese products

cheesewright * an artisan cheesemaker; one who provisions others with cheese

chicken-butcher * in black humour, a poulterer

chippy * fondly, an establishment selling or serving battered fish with fries

chocolaterie * a shop selling chocolates on the same premises where they are made

chocolatier * a manufacturer or seller of fine craft chocolate confections

chophouse * formerly, a men-only diner specializing in traditional cooked meats

chuck-wagon * a cart or powered vehicle used to convey or purvey food

churrascaria * a restaurant serving barbecued meat dishes South American style

coffeehouse * a café serving coffee with cakes and other sugary baked bites

comfit-maker * a confectioner

commissariat * an army office responsible for providing troops with food and forage

commissary * a workplace cafeteria, notably one supporting a film or TV studio

commons * an American scholastic dining hall or the meal communally taken there

companage * a field labourer or tenant farmer's workday ration of food, to be taken with his own bread

confectionary * the subdepartment of a manorial kitchen responsible for producing desserts and sweetmeats

confectioner * a candier, one who makes and sells comfits, cakes, and candies

confiserie * a sweetie shop

cookshop * a store selling either cooked food or cooking utilities and utensils

corkage * a restaurant charge for serving alcohol bought off-premises

corn-chandler * a retailer or dealer in corn and allied foodstuffs

corn-jobber * a merchant who hoards corn

corrody * a regular charitable allowance of food once supplied by a religious order

coshery * a feudal obligation to provide food and purveyances to a lord and his men

costermongery * the practice of hawking fruit and vegetables street to street

costerwife * a woman who sells apples and other fruit from a stall or handcart

crêperie * an eatery specializing in crêpes, galettes, and suchlike pastries

crustulary * an archaic term for one who earns his crust making pastries and pies

cybercafé * a cafeteria offering internet facilities

dairyman * one engaged in retailing milk and other dairy produce

dapifer * a servant who brings meals of meat to the dinner table

dapinate * to serve meat dishes and other fleshy luxuries at table

deaconing * the practice of putting the freshest looking fare to the fore at market

delicatessen * a shop or counter selling relishes, *bonnes bouches*, and various cold cuts

diet-kitchen * a charitable establishment dispensing healthy fare to the hungry

dinette * a recess set aside for taking meals; alternatively, a small restaurant

disper * a portion or allocation of college victuals

drive-thru * a fast-food facility allowing travelling customers to place their orders to-go from their vehicles

drysaltery * the trade in food preservatives or goods such as pickles and dried meat

duckeasy * a restaurant that furtively serves foie gras, or fattened duck liver, in contravention of local bylaws prohibiting its sale on grounds of animal cruelty

dutching * the irradiation of food gone bad in order to dress it up as good for sale

eatertainment * a vogue within the restaurant trade for combining the meal experience with entertainment based on sporting, musical, or cinematic themes

eatery * informally, a restaurant; a place where meals are cooked and served

eggler * one who hawks eggs and poultry; a poulterer

eighty-sixed * restaurant code meaning service is not available, or "nixed"; it might be that the requested dish is off the menu or that the customer is to be declined

eirmonger * an egg dealer

eschansonnery * a butlery, being a space for storing victuals in an old great house

exceedings * extra provision of college commons allowed on festive days

fish-cadger * a fishmonger

fish-jousting * the practice of going street to street peddling fish

fishmongering * the business of selling or dealing in fish

fleshhewery * a butcher's shop or shambles, where animals are slaughtered, dressed, and sold direct

fleshmonger * a butcher, or vendor of meat cuts

fodderer * a now-obsolete term for a caterer, one who supplies food on a large scale

food-court * an area with multiple self-service units retailing a variety of meals

foodery * an establishment selling prepared food

foodservice * the catering trade, in American English

fraterer * a monk in charge of food in a monastery refectory

fratery * a refectory, or monastical dining room

fromager * a cheesemaker; also, one who deals in cheese, wholesale or retail

fromology * the art and etiquette of serving cheese

fructerist * a broker, dealer, or vendor of fruit

fruitery * a repository or storeroom for fruit

frumentation * a public dole of corn once distributed to the rebellious Roman poor

frubbishing

an old pedlar's ruse of dressing up fruit and vegetables to disguise damage or decay

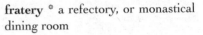

furnitor * a baker, notably one with principal responsibility for the oven

garlicmonger * a trader or retailer of garlic

garner * an outhouse or barn storing supplies of threshed grain; a granary

gastrophilanthropist * one who caters for the appetites of others before himself

gastropreneur * one with some commercial savvy and dash in the restaurant trade

gastropub * a bar serving complementary high-end beer and food

gelateria * an ice cream parlour

granator * a guardian or overseer of a granary or salt store

grasshopper * one who waits or attends on guests at a tea garden or picnic

grease-trough * a lunch counter or snack bar

greengrocer's * a shop stocking and selling a wide range of fruit and vegetables

grillroom * a restaurant offering a choice selection of grilled meat and fish dishes

groceraunt * an establishment combining grocery store and restaurant

grocerdom * the domain of grocers; grocers considered in the collective

groceteria * a self-service grocery store

grubbing-crib * a cheap, no-frills eatery

gustatory * a banqueting spot; any place where patrons gather to enjoy good cooking

habben-kairer * in old canting argot, a baker

half-rations * a reduced meal allowance, if not a more restrictive punishment diet

hashery * a North American chophouse, or inexpensive and rather utilitarian diner

hash-slinger * a waiter or waitress in a down-market dining spot

headwaiter * a senior dining room staffer with supervisory authority on the floor

ichthyopolist * a rather fanciful term for a plain old fishmonger

jerrywag-shop * a coffeeshop

jowter * an itinerant fish pedlar

kashrut * a body of Jewish religious dietary laws and regulations

khansaman * an Indian table servant or butler; the head of the pantry and kitchen

kitchener * an officer charged with overseeing the operation of a monastery kitchen

kitchen-midden * a prehistoric site full of discarded shells and bones indicating where primitive people once congregated to feed

klondyking * the business of exporting fresh herring from Scottish waters to Europe

konditorei * a shop selling cake and coffee; a Mitteleuropean patisserie

lachanopolist * another fanciful term, this time for a plain old greengrocer

lachanopoll * a place where herbs and vegetables are sold

lardary * originally, a storeroom for bacon; latterly, a closet for general foodstuffs

lardiner * an official responsible for preserving meat and fish in a castle or mansion

leguminarius * a medieval dealer in pulses and vegetables; later known as a potager

liverison * a food allowance formerly dispensed to servants and house staff

Lobster Palace * a lavish restaurant located within New York's theatre district

luncheonette * a snack bar purveying light lunches and refreshments

lunchery * colloquially, a cookroom or canteen selling or serving up lunch

luncheteria * North American slang for a cafeteria or lunchroom

macegrief * in old law, one who receives then retails stolen food; rarely, a butcher

macellarious * resembling a meat market, butcher's shop, or abattoir

maître d'hôtel * the headwaiter managing the front of house in an upmarket eatery

mancipleship * the station of one responsible for purchasing victuals for college, court, or monastery

manutention * in certain university colleges, the transgression of supplying another scholar with one's own victuals or provisions

Master of the Rolls * humorously, a baker

McDonaldization * the tendency of consumer culture broadly to adopt the hallmark features of the fast-food industry, viz convenience, efficiency, and homogenization

mealing * the provision of meals at a boarding house; dinner-school catering

meals-on-wheels * a catering service delivering cooked food to the elderly or infirm

meat-corn * a grain allowance once awarded to servants or feudal retainers

meatsman * a caterer

menu * a restaurant's bill of culinary fare

menu gastronomique * a restaurant's set gourmet menu, catering for more expensive tastes or those with more experienced or experimental palates

milk-badger * a person who sells milk door-to-door

milko * a milkman, delivering milk and allied products such as cream on his round

mocteroof * the practice of burnishing blemished or out-of-date food before sale

moira * a professional Bengali sweets-maker, or member of the caste of sugar workers

muffin-puncher * a baker of muffins

mungarly-casa * a baker's shop, in old thieves' argot

mustarder * a manufacturer or dealer in mustard

Naafi * a British military canteen or catering establishment

noshery * a diner or snack bar

nurshment * the act of providing food

oecus * a domestic dining room

omnibus * an assistant or apprentice waiter

oporopolist * a fruitseller

opsonator * a highfalutin term for a high-end caterer

osteria * a simple Italian restaurant, or an eating-house in the Italian style

ox-feller * a retail trader in butchermeat

oyster-callet * a low term for a woman or girl who sells oysters

palingman * a dealer in or seller of eels

panary * a storehouse for bread and similar products

paninoteca * a speciality sandwich bar

pannam-fencer * a street vendor selling pastries

pannierman * a hawker of fish at market

pantler * an officer in charge of bread and cheese supplies in an old manorial home

pastler * one who makes and sells pastries or pies

patronne * a female restaurateur or keeper of an eating-house

penarious * pertaining to victuals and the provision thereof

penny university * an early coffeehouse; the penny refers to the admission fee

pepperer * one who deals in peppers and spices; a grocer

peppier * a suggested comic nomenclature for a waiter at a swanky restaurant whose exclusive function is to furnish diners with freshly ground pepper

pestaurant * an eatery serving up bugs and grubs

piccolo * a waiter's assistant or second in a restaurant

pillory * a baker or breadmaker

piscary * a fish market; alternatively, a fishmonger

pistor * a corn-grinder, or baker

pistorical * pertaining to baking

pistrine * a bakery or bakehouse

pittancer * one who doles out festive food and drink to members of a religious house

pizzeria * a pizza parlour

plateman * a staff member with key responsibility for a restaurant's tableware

plum-duffer * a Victorian-era street vendor of plum duff or Christmas pudding

popinal * concerning eating-houses or the provision of food and drink

popote * a canteen or soldiers' mess; also, a field kitchen used by the catering corps

pop-up * a temporary restaurant venture or event catering point

posho * a field "portion" or ration distributed among East African safari porters

potager * one who sells herbs and vegetables grown in their own kitchen garden

poulterer * a dealer in poultry, eggs, hares, and game

progman * an official appointed to procure or otherwise requisition food, or "prog"

provant * to provide troops with victuals

proveditor * a quartermaster or caterer

provedore * a food larder; alternatively, a business engaged in victualling ships

providence * the provision of food for a special event or entertainment

provisorship * the office or rank of superintendent of food stores

prower * an obsolete term for a caterer

pupuseria * a shop selling or serving Salvadorean-style tortilla dishes

purveyance * the action of either supplying or stocking up on food

purveyoress * a female caterer, or commercial-scale food supplier

qassab * a Muslim caste of professional butchers

refectionary * pertaining to the supply of foodstuffs and refreshments

refectorian * historically, an officer placed in charge of a monastery's food stores

refectuary * an institutional dining room where communal meals are partaken

regratery * the action of a middleman who purchases victuals for local resale at profit

relais * a French restaurant providing accommodation and fine traveller's fare

reservatory * a cupboard, closet or other such space or repository for storing food

restaurateur * a proprietor of a public eating-house

restauration * a restaurant or superior dining establishment

restaurative * providing the functions of a restaurant

revictualment * the action of furnishing fresh food supplies

rippier * a dealer who brings fish from the coast to market inland

roastery * an establishment which prepares and sells roasted meat

robata * a Japanese restaurant featuring a charcoal grill on which food is cooked before diners seated at the counter

salsary-man * an officer of the Queen's Pantry, in charge of the sauces

salt-cadger * one who sells salt door-to-door

saltfat * a salt cellar

salumeria * a delicatessen specializing in retailing Italian cured meats and cold cuts

saucery * a manorial kitchen subdepartment where sauces are prepared and stored

scalco * a banquet manager in medieval or early modern era Italy

scalding-house * a subordinate division and room of a great, medieval kitchen responsible for scalding animal carcasses and washing and cleaning eating utensils

selmelier * an expert in the culinary use of salt, advising diners of the correct choice of condiment to complement their meal

serjeant garbager * an officer of the old royal kitchen in charge of the poultry

service à la française * a restaurant serving style whereby all dishes come at once

service à la russe * a restaurant serving style whereby each dish comes as a discrete course in its own right

sewery * a division of a stately home formerly responsible for preparing the dining table, seating the guests, and tasting and serving the food

shambles * a butcher's shop or district; originally, it denoted a stall selling meat

shisanyama * a barbecue facility provided by a South African butcher, where customers purchase meat which is flame-grilled for them over an open fire, or *braai*

shomer * a Jewish food inspector and dietary law enforcer, charged with passing food as kosher or "fit" to sell, serve, or consume; also known as a *mashgiach*

short-commons * a meagre or otherwise insufficient allowance of communal food

short-order * of a diner, serving to turn easy-to-cook food orders round rapidly

simpsonize * to practise unfair trading whereby milk is diluted with water

slink-butcher * a butcher with a reputation for selling inferior or unfit meat

sloppy joe's * an inexpensive and unpretentious eatery

snackette * a West Indies snack bar

snaedinghus * an early English eating place or cookshop

sommelier * a high-end restaurant's resident specialist wine steward

souperism * the devious historical practice of Irish Protestant clergy seeking to convert Papist paupers via soup kitchen charity

soupy * a US military mess call, summoning servicemen to table

spence * a buttery or pantry; a storeroom for victuals and liquors in general

spice-bazaar * a spice market

spichus * a medieval spice house or repository

steaka-da-oyst * an Italian-styled or themed restaurant in Australia

stolovaya * a basic, no-nonsense canteen or cafeteria

stover * the provision of refreshments for the road

strangle-goose * a disparaging term for a poulterer

suffraggi * a servant who waits at table

sugar-baker * a confectioner

sulphuring * a beauty treatment for fruit and veg that is past its best, creating a uniform colour to hide decay from prospective customers

sushiya * a sushi bar

sustentation * the action of providing food and nourishment

sutlerage * the business of catering to an armed force or garrison

sutlership * the occupation of one who purveys victuals to troops

sutlery * a victualling department for the military

symbelhus * a historical banqueting hall

tabernacle * a company of bakers

table-board * the regular provision of meals to a steady customer

talqual * "just as they come," a term for netted fish sold on landing without sorting

tandoori * a catch-all term for a UK curry restaurant

taqueria * a restaurant specializing in Mexican food

tea-shoppe * a tearoom with a nostalgic aesthetic, complete with faux period décor

thermopolist * one who sells hot food, especially meat cuts

tragematopolist * a confectioner or maker and seller of sweetmeats

traiteur * a caterer or delicatessen proprietor who sells prepared meals

trapeza * a refectory sustaining the clergy of an Eastern Orthodox church

trattoria * a restaurant serving Italian food

treating-house * an eatery offering patrons entertainment with their meal

trenchepain * formerly, a servant who cut bread for diners at table

trencher-fee * a diner's obligation to leave scraps of food from their meal by way of alimentary alms for the hungry

trencherman * a caterer

trencher-squire * a servant with general waiting duties at table

triclinium * a Roman dining room of the classical era

tripe-dresser * a dealer or retailer in tripe, being a ruminant's edible innards

tronc * a system of pooling gratuities among restaurant staff

trophophoric * having the function of supplying food or aliment

tuck-shop * an in-school kiosk selling a range of snacks and confectioneries

twiccere * one formerly with responsibility for apportioning meals in a monastery

vegetate * to furnish with fruit and vegetables

vendification * an aspect of the gentrification of the urban street food scene, whereby hipster food carts displace humble chuck-wagons from their established pitches

viander * historically, one who provided comestibles for a medieval household

victual * to supply with food

victuallership * the office of victualler, the supplier of food to the armed forces

victualling-house * an eatery, inn, or tavern

visceration * the distribution of raw meat shares, such as of a slaughtered hog, among hunters

vitaillement * the act of catering; victualling

vitteler * a victualler; a caterer to the armed forces

vivandier * a camp follower supplying food and drink to soldiers in the field

volxkuche * a "people's kitchen," offering free or at-cost communal food to squatters

waferer * an artisan maker and vendor of dainty cakes and pastries

waiterhood * restaurant staff who attend on table considered as a class

waiterage

the performance of a waiter's duties, notably the serving of food

waitership * the position of a professional waiter or an internship working a restaurant floor

waitressing * in service as a waitress; the occupation of working as such

waitron * a person of no fixed gender who takes food orders and serves meals

whittle-gate * a former custom whereby a visiting clergyman had the right to partake of food at his host's table and expense

yarbmonger * a retailer of herbs

CHAPTER 18

Kitchen and Table

> *"You don't need a silver fork to eat good food."*
> — **Paul Prudhomme**

Aga * a heavy cast-iron heat storage stove and range used for cooking

alfoil * kitchen tinfoil for cooking or wrapping food

ambry * a small recessed kitchen pantry; a meat-safe

antigriddle * a cooktop with a negative 30 degree Fahrenheit surface capable of flash-freezing food

argyll * a metal, usually silver, gravy dish

ashet * a large flat plate or dish; from the French, *assiette*

autoclave * a large pressure cooker used to sterilize meat products

auto-defrost * a facility commonly found in microwaves, freezers, and refrigerators

babracot * an early barbecue featuring a grate supported over an open wood or charcoal fire for smoking or broiling joints of meat

bait-poke * a workman's provision bag; a packed lunch bag

bakeware * the class of cooking vessels—trays and dishes— used in oven baking

bakstone * a slab formerly heated beside the hearth to make home oatcakes

ballotin * a decorative rectangular cardboard box holding chocolates or candies

balneum * a bain-marie, or heated bath for gently warming or cooking delicate foods

bashron * an old kettle, or basting ladle for applying hot cooking liquids to the pot

baster * a tube for sucking up and squirting gravy to moisten meat on the roast

batterie de cuisine * the aggregate apparatus used for preparing and serving meals

belagot * a large iron pot for cooking cow-tripes or "belly-guts" after butchering

bento * a box containing small food items for a Japanese picnic or packed lunch

biggin * a coffeepot with separate compartments for heating the water and grounds

bonbonnière * a small fancy box or jar containing sweetmeats

bottlejack * an old vertical chimney spit or mechanism for roasting meat

brandreth * a three-legged gridiron used to stand pots in front of the kitchen fire

brazier * a North American barbecue apparatus

bread-barge * an oval mess tub used as a container for bread

breakfast-equipage * any set of crockery in use at breakfast time

broacher * a spit or skewer for holding food, especially meat, steady

broiler * an integrated hot grill unit found within an American oven

buccan * a metal or wooden frame over which meat was formerly dried, smoked, or roasted; a proto-barbecue

bummaree * former slang for a bain-marie, or double boiler

burette * a cruet for oil or vinegar

butterknife * a blunt or curved-tipped table knife for cutting and spreading butter

caboose * not so much a galley kitchen as a galleon kitchen; an on-deck cookroom

cafetière * a traditional tall, cylindrical device for making filtered coffee

canaree * a large earthenware or iron pot used to prepare or preserve food

canteen * a chest or case outfitted with cooking utensils and cutlery

caquelon * a fondue pot

carborundum stone * a silicon carbide grindstone used to sharpen kitchen knives

cartouche * greaseproof paper used to cover sauces

casserole * variously, stewpot or saucepan

cassolette * a mini-casserole or vessel for cooking and serving individual dishes

castor * a revolving cruet stand bearing condiment containers and seasoning shakers

cataplana * an item of seafood cookware resembling two hinged clamshells

catmalison * a "cat's curse"—a kitchen cupboard near the ceiling it can't reach to raid

cauldron * a large kettle or boiler

chaffern * a saucepan or chafing dish, suitable for meals that require gentle heating

charbroiler * an appliance on which meat is grilled with the use of charcoal

chargeour * a former platter or "charger," a large dish used to convey cuts of meat

chatty-feeder * old street slang for a spoon

cheeseheck * a rack or frame for drying and storing freshly made cheese

cheesemelter * a powered device for topping off dishes with shredded cheese

chesford * a cheese vat

chinaware * crockery and other tableware made from either china or porcelain

chinois * a finely meshed conical sieve for straining custard, purée, soup, or sauce

chocolatera * a metal pitcher used in South America to prepare hot chocolate

chopsticks * the essential cooking and eating utensils of the Asian kitchen and table

chorkor * a traditional West African oven used to smoke-dry fish

cleaver * a large kitchen knife cum butcher's hatchet for chopping through bone

clingfilm * transparent plastic food wrap

clinker * a silver dinner plate

cocotte * a heat-proof dish used for cooking and serving individual small portions

colander * a perforated metal utensil ideal for rinsing veg or draining pasta and rice

comal * a tortilla griddle, widely used across Mexico and South America

comporteer * a dish with a stemmed base designed to serve dessert or stewed fruits

conjuror * an old device for cooking meat rapidly, burning paper as its fuel source

cookhouse * a military or expeditionary camp kitchen; or, an outdoors galley

cookroom * a simple kitchen or galley

cookshack * a makeshift building or structure where food is cooked and prepared

cookstove * a cooker heated by burning wood or charcoal; popular in rural locales

cooktop * a stove with hotplates integrated into the cabinet top

cookware * the utensils in toto used in cooking—pots, pans, dishes et al.

coolamon * an Australian Aboriginal container cum conveyance for bush tucker

coquille * a serving dish or casserole in the shape of a scallop shell

cordwood * a rough toothpick

couscoussier * a food steamer used in traditional Arabic and North African cuisine

couvert * a spread of table requisites, such as plate, napkin, knife, fork, and spoon

coverslut * a kitchen apron

craggan * a rudimentary earthenware cooking pot unique to the Hebrides of yore

crapaudine * a grill or gridiron specially for cooking game birds

craticula * a classical Roman stove with cooking frame, whence the modern "griddle"

crêpier * a hotplate reserved for making French pancakes and similar pastries

cutlery

the set of tableware utensils used for cutting and eating food

cresser * a small ladle or scoop

crib-box * a container for a schoolchild's packed lunch

crisper * a fridge compartment for keeping fruit and vegetables crisp and fresh

crockery * plates, dishes, cups, saucers, and such made typically of earthenware

crockpot * a countertop, slow-cooking appliance

cruet * a stoppered container holding condiments for use at the dining table

curate's delight * a layered cake stand

daubière * an old copper cooking vessel curiosity

decalcoware * a style of inexpensive dinner plates decorated with printed decals

deepfreeze * a cabinet for rapidly freezing and storing perishable foodstuffs

déjeuner * a breakfast set; the crockery appropriate for early morning dining

dentiscalp * a toothpick

dessert-service * the crockery and similar utensils used to serve dessert

diable * an unglazed earthenware stewpot

diaper * a baby's napkin or feeding bib

dinner-wagon * a wheeled and shelved table for service around the dining room

dinnerware * a synonym for tableware

dipper * a ladle or scoop

dish-bink * a plate rack

dishware * collectively, the dishes and plates used in setting table and serving meals

dixie * a military cooking pot cum mess tin used to brew tea or prepare stew

dormant * a centrepiece dish or ornament which remains on the table during a meal

drageoir * an ornamental receptacle for choice items of confectionery

dredger * a cook's perforated container for sprinkling flour, herbs, or sugar over food

dressel * a dresser or kitchen sideboard

dumb-waiter * a dish-lift, delivering meals from a kitchen to diners on another floor

eating irons * cutlery; handheld implements used to consume food

ecuelle * a double-handled soup bowl, also functioning to serve vegetables

eggbeater * a handheld utensil or appliance for beating eggs or whipping cream

epergne * a decorative table centrepiece, branched with saucers holding relishes, stewed fruits, and so forth

eviscerator * a kitchen utensil used for coring purposes

feast-bed * a special couch for reclining on at meals

firebox * a compartment in a stove or range in which fuel for cooking is burnt

flameware * cooking equipment, often made of glass or clay, designed to withstand the heat of a naked flame

flatware * any flat items of metal crockery; alternatively, domestic cutlery

flesh-crook * a fork or hook designed to remove meat from a cooking pot

food-safe * of containers and suchlike, suitable for use or contact with food

footman * a metal stand positioned by a fireplace to keep food and plates warm

forkchops * a set of chopsticks featuring a small knife and fork on the blunt ends

fridge-freezer * a kitchen unit combining the functions of cooler and chiller

Frigidaire * a once-generic though proprietary name for a refrigerator

frixory * an archaic term for a frying pan

fruggan * an oven rake or poker

fruit-trencher * a wooden tray formerly used as a dessert plate

fry-cooker * an appliance for frying food oil-free, using hot air and infrared heat

furcifer * the original word for fork in English, first appearing in the early 1600s

galley * a ship's kitchen or cooking range

gallows-balk * an iron chimney bar from which pothooks may be suspended

gamasot * a customary Korean cooking cauldron

gardeviance * a ventilated meat-safe or cupboard

garlic press * a device for crushing cloves of garlic to extract the pulp, oils, and juice

gastronorm * denoting the standardized food container sizes used in the catering trade

gelatiera * a device for making ice cream at home

gemellion * a finger bowl or small basin for rinsing one's hands at the table

girdle * a Scottish griddle

glassine * a greaseproof paper used to wrap or separate individual blocks of food

go-ashore * a three-legged iron pot used as a boiler for cooking purposes

gravy-boat * an elongated pitcher for pouring gravy or sauce over one's meal

gridiron * an often hinged or cross-hatched grill for cooking meat, fish, or vegetables

guéridon * an ornamental table or trolley equipped to prepare, cook, and serve food

gyuvech * a Bulgarian earthenware casserole dish

hachoir * a curved-blade food-chopping tool, also known as a *mezzaluna*

handi * a traditional Indo-Pak vessel for cooking and serving curried dishes

hangi * a traditional New Zealand earth oven or firepit

hashi * Japanese-style chopsticks, featuring pointed rather than blunt ends

haybox * a fireless cooker that works off the heat captured in its insulated container

hearth * a cooker hotplate

hibachi * a Japanese "fire bowl"; cooking stove or charcoal brazier with grill atop

holloware * articles of metal or china tableware used to serve food

hotplate * a heated surface or portable heating appliance on which food is cooked

icebox * a refrigerator's integrated ice compartment, or indeed the refrigerator itself

imu * a Hawaiian cooking-pit in which meat and vegetables are baked

jack-flyer * a flywheel for turning a spit-roast

jaffle-iron * a kitchen gadget for making toasted sandwiches

jagger * a pastry cutter, used for crimping pies and similar baked comestibles

jonathan * a stand or rack for holding slices of toasted bread

juicer * an electrical appliance for quickly extracting juice from fruit and vegetables

kamado * a Japanese wood or charcoal fired cookstove, often used as a BBQ grill

karahi * a double-handled, bowl-shaped pan similar to a wok, used to cook curries

kazan * a Central Asian cooking pot cum cauldron

kitchenalia * multiple or miscellaneous items of kitchenware

kitchenette * a modest kitchen cum pantry

kitchen-trade * a collection or comprehensive set of cooking tools and utensils

kitchenware * an assortment of articles and appliances for use in the kitchen

lame * a device for scoring the surface of a loaf before it is placed in the oven

laprobe * a diner's napkin or serviette

lazy Susan * a revolving tabletop stand for ease of distributing food among diners

liquidizer * a food mixer, or machine purposed for making purées and such

mahogany * a dining table

maidenhead * an antiquarian silver spoon featuring a bust of the Virgin Mary on the handle's end

mandoline * a razor-sharp vegetable slicer with adjustable blade

marabout * a large and often ornate antique *cafetière*

marmite * a pot-bellied metal or earthenware stockpot or casserole

mazarine * a pierced oval plate nestled within a deeper dish to drain or serve fish

meal-bowie * a flour-bin or crate containing oatmeal

meal-pock * a beggar's grub-bag

meatfettle * a kitchen chest or cupboard for storing assorted edibles

melangeur * a device, in either domestic or industrial use, for mixing chocolate

mensal * pertaining to, or used at, the dinner table

mezzaluna * a "half-moon" kitchen utensil for chopping herbs and vegetables

microplane * an implement for zesting citrus fruit or finely grating hard cheese

microwave * an oven for heating food by means of EHF electromagnetic radiation

milk-boyne * a shallow tub for holding milk poured from the pail

mixmaster * an electric food mixer

molinet * a whisk or beater; alternatively, a stick for stirring chocolate into hot milk

molinillo * a wooden whisk used in Aztec times for the purpose of making "xocolatl"

mommocky-pan * a vessel in which fragments of broken victuals may be kept

muckinger * a diner's bib or serviette tucked into the collar to protect clothes from food spillage or to wipe the fingers and mouth

muffineer * a table vessel with a perforated cap for sprinkling sugar over muffins

multicooker * a programmable appliance for automated cooking using a timer

muzzling-cheat * a table napkin or serviette

myour * a vintage food grater, used especially for crumbling bread

napery * table linen

necromancer * an early modern era device for rapidly cooking meat

nef * an elaborate ship-shape stand bearing such as cutlery, condiments and napkins

non-stick * of a cooking utensil, coated so as to prevent food adhering to the surface

obelisk * a small spit or skewer

obley-iron * a contrivance for cooking wafers or waffles

obsttortenform * a traditional continental flan pan

olivetta * a vessel for holding olives

Osterizer * a brand of food liquidizer, once used as a generic term for such blenders

ovenette * a small, secondary, or subsidiary oven

ovenproof * in respect of kitchenware, resistant to intense heat

oven-stopliss * an old, wooden oven lid

ovenware * heat-resistant dishes designed for baking and serving oven-cooked food

paellera

a shallow Valencian frying pan which lends the dish of paella its name

overslop * a kitchen pinafore or protective apron

pancheon * a shallow earthenware pan or bowl for making bread or standing milk

pannery * a joke word for cooking pans in their infinite variety and collective glory

pantalettes * decorative paper frills festooning chops served at the dinner table

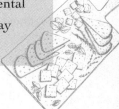

plateau

an ornamental serving tray or platter

papilotte * a greased paper wrapper in which foodstuffs may be cooked and served

pap-warmer * a contraption for keeping food and drink warm overnight

parrilla * a large portable Argentinian barbecue

patella * in classical times, a small shallow dish used to hold solid food items

pattypan * a little fluted tin for baking patties

pennybred * a moulding board for baking penny loaves

pepperbox * a condiment pot with perforated top for sprinkling black pepper

peppermill * a handheld device for grinding peppercorns over pot or plate

percolator * a special pot for brewing ground coffee

pewtery * tableware and such articles made from pewter

pinakion * an antique painted fish plate, or saucer for oils and relishes

pipkinet * a small three-legged earthenware pot used for cooking over direct heat

pizza wheel * a utensil for cutting pizza into slices for ease of consumption

poacher * a special pan for cooking eggs without their shells

porringer * a double saucepan used to cook porridge; also, a bowl for soup or stew

port-pain * a cloth for carrying bread fresh to the table without it touching the hands

possynet * a small metal pot for either cooking or boiling

pothangles * a set or pair of pot-hangers

primus * a portable pressurized burner stove; ideal for cooking at camp or outdoors

prog-box * a student's lunchbox; in particular a receptacle for cake

punnet * a shallow basket for holding fruits, berries, mushrooms and such

Pyrex * a long-established proprietary range of borosilicate glass ovenware

quern * a spice mill or similar condiment grinder

ramekin * a small, glazed ceramic or glass bowl for cooking and serving dishes

range-proof * of pots and pans, suitable for use on a hotplate or ring-burner

rangette * a small gas or electric cooker

rantle-tree * a fixed chimney bar used to suspend hooks holding cooking pots

rastrello * a sharp spoon for gouging the pulp from halved citrus fruits

rawning-knife * a meat cleaver

rax * an extended bar support for roasting spits or other cooking utensils

reamer * an implement for extracting juice from citrus fruits

rechaud * a food warmer consisting of a dish heated from below by naked flame

reckon-crook * a pothook for hanging cooking equipment over a fire

refrigerator * a sturdy upright appliance for chilling perishable food and drink

remoska * an electric mini-oven where the cooking element is housed in the lid

rotimatic * an automatic kitchen appliance for making rotis or unleavened flatbread

rotisserie * an apparatus with a rotating spit for roasting skewered meat

rudicle * an early kitchen spatula or stirring stick

Rumfordized * in the style of a kitchen with a modernized stove or range

runcible spoon * a triple-pronged pickle fork curved like a spoon

saibashi * specially elongated cooking chopsticks

salver * a silver tray reserved for the formal serving of meals at table

samovar * a traditional Russian tea-urn

sangrail * the platter Christ is purported to have used at the Last Supper

sauceboat * a modest pitcher for pouring gravy; a *saucière*

sauteuse * a dedicated sauté pan

savernapron * a table napkin or serviette

scullery * a small kitchen; also, a service room for the care and cleaning of dishes

serveware * an inclusive term for any and all vessels used to serve food at table

shichirin * a portable, lightweight Japanese charcoal grill

silverware * items of silver-alloyed tableware, from dishes to containers to cutlery

simmerstat * a thermostatic control for the grill or hotplate on an electric cooker

skillet * variously, a boiler-pot or frying pan

skimmer * a slotted spoon with some resemblance to a sieve

sklyse * a historical cookery spatula or slice

smokebox * an oven designed specially for food best smoked

sorbetière * a domestic ice cream making machine or device used to prepare sorbet

soupspoon * a large-bowled spoon specially designed for supping from

splashback * a panel fixed behind a cooker to protect the wall from cooking stains

splatter guard * a fry-pan shield preventing hot oil from spattering all and sundry

split-level * of a cooker, housing oven and hob in separately installed units

sporf * a hybrid eating utensil; the spoon is on one end and the fork on the other, with tines for cutting found on the outer edge of the fork

springform * in the style of a round, latched baking tin featuring detachable sides and base

spurtle * a thin, wooden potstick used traditionally to stir such as porridge or broth

steamer * a special type of saucepan in which food can be steam-cooked

sterling * a set of table utensils or general tableware made from sterling silver

stewpan * a deep pot used for stewing or boiling food

stibadium * a semicircular dining bench found in ancient Roman eating rooms

stockpot * a sizeable cooking vessel designed for preparing soup stock or broth

stovetop * a kitchen hob or hotplate

stupnet * a stewpot or saucepan of a bygone era

sucrier * a sugar bowl

sufuria * a large metal cooking pot commonly found throughout East Africa

sukey * an old vernacular term for a teakettle

suribachi * a giant Japanese mortar for grinding roasted sesame seeds

surnape * a cloth laid over any main table cover; also, a napkin for washing at meals

surtout * an archaic term for a tureen

tableclothing * linen for the dinner table

tableware * articles of crockery, cutlery, and glass for serving or taking meals at table

taboon * a clay oven used in Middle Eastern cooking since Biblical times

tagine * a distinctive conical earthenware pot widely used in North African cuisine

tamis * a drum-sieve used to strain sauces, sift flour, or purée various ingredients

tandoor * a cylindrical Indo-Pak oven widely used in cooking and baking

tawa * a circular griddle or frying pan for cooking chapatis and similar breads

teaspoon * a small spoon for adding sugar to hot drinks or taking certain soft foods

terrine * a tightly lidded earthenware vessel used to cook foods such as pâté

thermos * a generic vacuum flask for keeping tea, coffee, soup, and so on warm

thivel * a potstick or spatula for stirring porridge and similar stodgy foodstuffs

tian * a traditional Provençal earthenware casserole or cooking pot

timballo * a traditional baking pan; from the French word for "kettledrum"

tiremoelle * a silver marrow spoon

toaster * an electrical appliance for toasting bread

toque blanche * the traditional tall white hat worn by chefs at work in the kitchen

tormentors * a large forked implement used for toasting bannocks

tourtière * a tart tin, or round baking sheet

trammel * a contrivance hung in a chimney to hold pots and pans in place over a fire

traymobile * a tea-trolley, or small table on castors used to transport food

treenware * cups, dishes, and other items of domestic tableware made from wood

trencherbread * a platter made itself from stale bread — once poor people's cutlery

trendle * a flat, usually circular, tub or trough formerly used in baking

trifid * an antique style of spoon with a wide stem double-notched at the base

tryvette * a tripod used to safely suspend a cooking vessel or kettle over a fire

tupperware * a range of plastic containers used to store or convey food products

tureen * a deep, covered serving vessel handy for soups, stews, sauces or gravies

turpin * a highly stylized vintage teapot

twyfler * a medium dish twixt dessert plate and dinner plate in size

urokotori * an implement used to remove the scales from fish skin prior to cooking

veilleuse * a small decorative burner for heating a bowl or teapot; a food warmer

voider * a large serving plate for distributing sweetmeats at the conclusion of a meal

wafer-tongs * an instrument for handling and baking wafers or waffles over a fire

waffle-iron

a hinged and honeycombed metal press used to toast waffles

wardnape * a mat placed underneath dishes at table to protect the tablecloth

whippit * a whisk for beating eggs or cream by hand

wok * a deep-bowled traditional Chinese stir-fry pan

yabba * a large wooden or earthenware vessel used in cookery and food storage

yetling * a skillet or boiler set on three legs; alternatively, a griddle

zester * a kitchen utensil for expressing the zest from lemons and other citrus fruits

Come Dine
with Me

CHAPTER 19

Dinners:
Making a Meal
of It

> *"Eat breakfast like a king, lunch like a prince, and dinner like a pauper."*
> **—Adelle Davis**

à la carte * of a restaurant meal, denoting that the component dish for each course may be selected from the full menu at the individual price shown

accompaniment * a modest side order of food served with the main dish

after-course * the final dessert course concluding a formal meal

agape * a "love feast" or communal religious meal

ambigu * a banquet featuring various courses or a medley of dishes served together

amuse-bouche * a bite-sized savoury served as an appetizer

anders-meat * a light luncheon or afternoon meal

antepast * a first or pre-course served to whet the appetite for the full meal to come

ante-supper * a course displayed for aesthetic effect before being eaten

antipastic * pertaining to appetizers and hors d'oeuvres

appetizer * an article of food or first course taken to stimulate the appetite

ariston * the classical Greek brunch; it broke the fast, but was taken nearer to noon

arrière-supper * a retiring meal or late supper

arval-feast * a spread formerly laid on during a wake or following a funeral

asado * a meat roast or BBQ: both a national dish and social institution in Argentina

assiette * a mixed taster plate of cold meats or mini-desserts

bait * a light repast taken between meals; specifically, a snack eaten on the road

banchan * a set of small side dishes, shared among diners at a Korean main meal

banquet * originally, a dessert; now, a lavish and often ceremonial dinner occasion

Banyan day * today, a culinary blowout for sailors; formerly, a day when meat was withheld from a ship's crew

baon * a Philippine packed lunch

barbecue * an outdoors social gathering at which meat is roasted and served hot

Barmecide feast * a buffet of chimerical abundance or downright frugality

beanfeast * an annual works dinner, or budget wayzgoose

beever * a between-meals afternoon snack

belly-sacrifice * a gluttonous feast; alternatively, something of which a meal is made

blithemeat * a feast thrown to celebrate the birth of a child

blowout * a stomach-bursting meal enjoyed in hearty and hungry company

blue-plate special * a keenly priced diner meal or mains offer, changing by the day

bonne-bouche * a sweet morsel eaten at the end of a meal to refresh the palate

boodle fight * a regimental table buffet taken standing, without cutlery or dishware

bouffage * a most filling or satisfying meal

braaivleis * a South African "grilled meat" picnic or barbecue get-together

breakstuff * breakfast, first meal of the day, when the overnight fast is broken

bromation * a light refection

bruncheon * a late-morning meal taken in place of breakfast and lunch

brydealo * a bride-ale, or old wedding feast

buffet * a self-service food spread available at an eatery or a social get-together

bunfight * a formal tea party marking a special occasion

burgoo * a fundraising public picnic, named after a famous Kentucky frontier stew

business lunch * a midday meal with trade customers or clients, invariably charged to an expense account

café complet * a light breakfast of coffee and croissants or similar

canapés * buffet finger food, especially decorative bite-sized puff pastries

cenatory * pertaining to dinner or supper

chanoyu * a Japanese green tea ceremony, including full meal

chittery-bite * a snack to warm the spirits of someone shaking from the cold

chota hazri * an Anglo-Indian light repast eaten very early in the morning; dawn tea

chowder-party * a seaside picnic where fish, clams, and suchlike are consumed

churn-getting * an old harvest-home supper for agricultural labourers

clambake * a picnic featuring a heap of clams and potatoes baked over hot stones

collation * a light meal, notably one permitted on fast days

comessation * a shared meal

continental breakfast * a light morning repast, chiefly featuring coffee with breads

convivium * a banquet or feast

cookeyshine * an afternoon social centring on the consumption of cakes or cookies

cookout * an al fresco roast in good company; an American barbecue

cream-kitte * a harvest feast of yesteryear

crudités * traditional French appetizers of raw mixed vegetables with dipping sauce

deipnetic * relating to or appropriate to mealtime

dejune * a Scots breakfast

deskfast * a workplace or otherwise working breakfast

dessert * a confectionery course closing out a meal

dew-bit * a breakfast snack

deximon * a Byzantine banquet or state reception

diet-time * time to eat

dim sum * an assortment of Chinese savoury dumpling bites served as a tea brunch

dinner party * a private soirée and supper at home, with select guests

dinnerette * a modest dinner or one held for a small party

dinner-while * mealtime, dinnertime, or suppertime

dishling * a meagre main course or otherwise scant serving of food at mealtime

doggy bag * leftovers from a restaurant meal bagged as a takeaway for later eating

down-dinner * an afternoon meal

elevenses * a late morning tea or coffee break with biscuits or cake—a term coined by J.R.R. Tolkien

entrée * in North America, a main dish or course; elsewhere, a smaller opening bite or one following the soup course

entremets * a light, sweet side dish, served between the main courses at a supper

epidorpion * a Greek dessert course, or a bite taken after dinner

epulary * akin to or pertaining to a feast

epulation * a grand banquet or feast

extraordinary * an extra dish or food course, most often a dainty morsel

festical * a feast or other festival of food

fish-fry * an open-air supper where fish is fried and consumed

flesh-funeral * an old burial service accompanied by feasting with meat aplenty

foodfest * an event in celebration of food or occasion of extended eating

fork-luncheon * a standing buffet eatable with fingers or forks alone

full English * a traditional hearty British cooked breakfast or brunch

gaudy * a great feast, such as an annual college supper

glorious sinner * rhyming slang for dinner

gramaungere * a sumptuous meal; an expression from the late Middle Ages

grubbery * a public meal

helping * a discrete share or quantity of food served to a single diner at a meal

hesperisma * an ancient Greek evening meal

high tea * a late afternoon or early evening meal accompanied by cake and tea

319

hors d'oeuvre ⁕ a tongue-teasing appetizer presented before a main meal

hunger-bedrip ⁕ an old harvest rite at which the lord furnished his tenants with food

iftar ⁕ the breaking of the day's fast, or the meal taken, after sunset during Ramadan

infare ⁕ a house-warming party cum food spread presented by a newlywed couple

interferculum ⁕ an intervening course or portion of food

intermealiary ⁕ taken between meals

intermess ⁕ an item of food served between courses at a banquet

iron rations ⁕ a pre-packed battlefield, expeditionary, or other emergency meal

jackbite ⁕ an Appalachian snack

jentacular ⁕ pertaining to breakfast or breakfast time

jentation ⁕ breakfast

junkery ⁕ an extravagantly expensive feast or picnic

kaffeeklatsch ⁕ an informal afternoon gathering for coffee and gossip

kaiseki ⁕ a series of tasting-course bites enjoyed at a Japanese tea ceremony

kettledrum ⁕ a large afternoon tea party

kletorion ⁕ a Byzantine feast held in the imperial palace itself

knick-knack ⁕ a social meal where each guest contributes a dish or share of food

lectisternium ⁕ a classical Roman sacrificial feast, where representations of various deities were proffered a propitiatory meal

luncheon ⁕ a formal midday meal

maundy ⁕ a children's feast; with initial capital the term refers to the Last Supper

mealtide ⁕ dinnertime; also, the dinner itself

mell-supper * a feast to celebrate the gathering of the harvest

merenda * a light afternoon repast

mess * a communal meal, or food for a common table in a military canteen

mezze * a selection of light bites to accompany drinks, or as starters to a main meal

midnight feast * a children's surreptitious late-night blowout

mignardise * a small dessert bite or fancy cake reserved for the end of a meal

mixtum * a snack or light bite

mould-meat * a person's final meal before their demise

muffin-worry * an old ladies' bunfight or tea party, popular in Victorian times

nacket * a snack or light lunch, consisting chiefly of bread

nibblies * North American savoury snacks, eaten between meals or with drinks

noonmeat * a farmhand's lunch eaten in the field

nosh-up * a plentiful, improvised meal

nuncheon * a single-plate refreshment taken between meals

okashi * a spread of light confectionery laid on to conclude a formal Japanese meal

omakase * meaning "I'll leave it to you," a multiple course sushi extravaganza where each individual dish in the meal is selected by the chef

opsonation * a sumptuous and sensuous feast, replete with epicurean delights

ordinary * a communal meal; also, a set meal served daily at a fixed price

pannam-time * lunchtime; time to break bread

parrillada * an outdoors mixed-meat grill or barbecue

Passoverish * resembling the traditional meal of the Feast of Unleavened Bread

perpendicular * a finger buffet or stand-up supper

petits fours * a selection of bite-sized cakes or biscuits often offered with coffee at the conclusion of a formal meal

Phagiphany * a Lenten festival commemorating the feeding of the five thousand

picnickish * of the nature of an informal open-air meal enjoyed at a scenic location

pièce de résistance * the chief dish or most remarkable culinary feature of a meal

pigout * a gut-buster of a meal, where an excessive amount of food is tucked away

plat du jour * the "dish of the day" or chef's special recommended by a restaurant

plat principal * the main course or central dish of a formal meal

playpiece * a schoolchild's tasty playtime treat

ploughman's * a faux traditional British pub lunch

poggle-khana * an Anglo-Indian picnic, or "fool's dinner"

post-cenal * occurring or taken after dinner

postlude * the concluding dish of a multiple-course meal

postpast * a modest portion of food consumed following a main meal

potlach * an Alaskan social gathering over a communal meal, where guests contribute home-made dishes and take their "pot luck" in turn

power breakfast * an occasion for heads of state to broker the ultimate "meal deal"

prandicle * a light meal or breakfast snack

prandium * an ancient Roman lunch

pregustation * an appetizer or taster dish eaten before the main offering

preprandial * before dinner

prix fixe * a restaurant meal with restricted course options served at a set price

pudding * a dessert course, either sweet or savoury, coming after the principal dish

pulmenta * classical Roman savoury appetizers

pulpamenta * classical Roman fleshy titbits, either fish or meat, served as starters

pyx-feast * historically, a dinner celebrated by the jury of the Goldsmiths' Company

quaresimal * having the exiguity of meals traditionally eaten during Lent

refection * a light meal, particularly one taken communally in a religious house

regalement * a banquet with entertainment

relevé * a "relief" dish or course to replace one that has been removed from the table

relisher * an appetizer or hors d'oeuvre

repast * a dinner or feast

rere-banquet * a subsequent or secondary banquet enjoyed late into the evening

réveillon * a feast following Midnight Mass or eaten early on Christmas morning

rijsttafel * an elaborate spread featuring a wide selection of Indonesian rice dishes

safari supper * a veritable "moveable feast," with diners consuming different courses at different residences

saulee * a satisfying meal or substantial quantity of food

savoury * a non-sweet course served pre or post main as appetizer or digestive

scambling * a makeshift, haphazard, or otherwise irregular meal

sausage-sizzle

an outdoor civic fundraiser featuring the cooking of sausages

scoobie snax * improvised bites to assuage one's hunger after smoking cannabis

seconds * a subsequent helping of food after the first serving has been polished off

Seder * a Jewish ceremonial feast, held after nightfall at the start of Passover

shore dinner * a multi-course seafood meal

shoulder-feast * a free dinner awarded to pallbearers at a funeral

side-order * an accompaniment, typically veg or fries, to a main, typically meat, dish

slatko * a courtesy offering of some sweet food upon the arrival of house guests

smorgasbord * a Scandinavian cold buffet of appetizers and open sandwiches

solein * a single portion of food or meal for one person

sotelty * a highly elaborate, ornamental entremets popular in centuries past

souper intime * a quiet, private meal for two

spécialité de la maison * a restaurant's signature dish

spreadation * a banquet or other lavish meal

squantum * a clambake or fish-fry

starter * a British first course; else an antipastic appetizer to stimulate the palate

stay-stomach * a snack to dampen the appetite and keep hunger pangs at bay

subaltern's luncheon * humorously, a glass of water—being the sum total of a junior's meal

subcharge * an old Scots term for a second or additional course

substantialities * a main course or central dish

supper * the final meal of the day, taken shortly before retiring

supra * a traditional Georgian feast

surf & turf * a main course or full meal itself featuring seafood served with beefsteak

symbol * one's contribution or share to a picnic or feast

syssition * a communal meal, or mess

table d'hôte * a set, fixed-price meal eaten at a shared table and often at a set time

tabnab * in the naval service, a midmorning savoury snack

taffy-join * a social get-together for the purpose of enjoying treacle or toffee

takeaway * a meal to-go

tanstaafl * a fun acronym—"There ain't no such thing as a free lunch."

tea & eating * a high tea featuring a selection of food items

thali * a dinner of several spiced dishlets, or a set meal at an Indo-Pak curry house

Thyestean feast * a bloody banquet where human flesh is served

tiddlywinks * a selection of gourmet titbits enjoyed after dinner

tapas

a round of bites to accompany a round of drinks, or as a light repast in itself

tiffin * an Anglo-Indian tea or lunch

tightener * a heavy or hearty meal

toffee-scramble * a bunfight or muffin-worry

trifles * formerly a second-course dish featuring cakes, biscuits, jams, and suchlike

trimalchion * resembling a banquet for dissolute gourmands

trimmings * the set of traditional extras and garnishes complementing a central dish

tuck-in * a large informal meal or inviting spread of no-nonsense food

turtle-frolic * a feast of turtle meat

325

Ulster fry * a traditional Irish full-fried breakfast or brunch

undern * a light post-prandial repast; alternatively, a breakfast taken around nine in the morning

viaticum * a snack or ration for the road; also, a communion wafer administered at one's dying hour

voidee * a late snack or dish eaten at leave-taking

wanton-meat * a party or feast to celebrate the birth of a child

warner * a stunt cake presented to "warn" of the arrival of the next course at dinner

wayzgoose * an annual employees' dinner outing

wheatkin * an end-of-harvest rural supper

whets * in the language of early English cooking, appetizers or starters

zakuski * Russian hors d'oeuvres, or bites to accompany shots of vodka

zensai * snacks or starters in Japanese cuisine

CHAPTER 20

Dining: Gastronomy and Gustation

> *"To eat is a necessity, but to eat intelligently is an art."*
> **—François de la Rochefoucauld**

abirging * the Anglo-Saxon faculty of taste

abligurition * sumptuous spending on and lavish serving of food and drink

abrodietical * given to eating daintily or fastidiously

accubation * the action of reclining at table, as per classical Roman dining style

acerbophobia * an extreme aversion to sour or bitter foods

acoustic tribology * a means of measuring "mouthfeel" by recording the acoustic signals emitted by vibrations of the papillae of the tongue rubbing against the palate

after-treat * a lingering, and often unwelcome, aftertaste

ageusia * total loss of or severe impairment to the sense of taste

agitoalimentation * humorously, eating on the go

aleuromancy * divination by way of flour—as in the tradition of fortune cookies

alliumphily * an intense love of garlic—"the stinking rose"—and garlicky foods

alliumphobia * a great distaste for garlic; similarly leeks, chives, shallots, or onions

allotriogeusia * perversion of the sense of taste toward unnatural substances

alomania * a craving for salt, sprinkling it liberally over one's food

ambageusia * concurrent loss of taste on either side of the tongue

amblygeusia * a marked blunting or diminution in the sensitivity of one's palate

anosmia gustatoria * lack or loss of the sense of smell in regard to food appreciation

apician * epicurean, or dainty in food; given to sensuous, indeed indulgent, dining

appetite * the psychological desire for food, as opposed to physiological hunger

arachibutyrophobia * a disgust for peanut butter sticking to the roof of one's mouth

aristology * the art and science of fine dining

artolatry

an excessive love of bread

arugulance * a spoof word coined to mock the snobbery and hauteur of the foodie elite

assavour * to thoroughly relish or enjoy the taste of food

assumption * the taking of food into the body; ingestion, eating

at victuals * at table; engaged in eating

attaste * to taste so as to appreciate; to savour

autophagophobia * a fear of being devoured by cannibals or carnivores

banqueting * laying into or laying on a spread of food

bedinner * to treat to a meal

belly-cheer * to feast lavishly or extravagantly

belly-devout * devoted to good eating

belly-proud * fastidious with regard to food

bistronomy * casual fine dining, enjoying good honest food in an informal ambience

bon appétit! * a near-universally acknowledged enjoinder to enjoy one's fare

bratophobia * an impatience with the presence of young children in a restaurant (question: which one here is the spoiled brat—the adult diner or the child?)

breakfast * literally, to break one's overnight fast with a light morning repast

brychophobia * disgust for the sound of others ripping at and rending their meat

burgerization * the homogenization of modern feeding habits and tastes in favour of fast, cheap, convenient, and protein-rich food

butyrophilic * liking the taste of butter and buttery foods

cacogeusia * the presence of a foul taste in the mouth

carnomania * the profoundly enthusiastic consumption of meat

carpomania * the profoundly enthusiastic consumption of fruit

catillate * to lick a dish of delicious food clean

cenation * the partaking of a meal

chalcenterous * having the proverbial bowels of brass—game for eating anything

chickle * to chew gum

cibation * the action of ingesting food; feeding

cobitis * in prison slang, a loathing of institutional catering

Cockayne * a mythical land of ease and above all bountiful good food

coenaculous * fond of supping or dining

collationing * the act of feasting

comestion * eating, pure and simple

comfort-eating * compensatory consumption; feeding as solace from suffering

commensality * boon companionship at the dining table

connoisseurship * respected critical knowledge of high-quality cuisine

consecotaleophobia * a dread of eating with chopsticks

convivial * keen on eating well in good company

coshering * the historical feasting of Irish nobles and their retainers

coup de graisse * jocularly, death by chocolate or other rich and fatty food

credence * the precautionary foretasting of food for fitness, flavour and safety

cuppedous * decadently fond of delicacies

curryology * the appreciative study of the true food of the gods

dapatical * given to extravagance in feasting

decafathon * a gruelling, extended period of time consuming only healthy food

degulate * to thoroughly enjoy one's grub

degust * to take the time and thought to taste good food with due care and attention

degustation *
the attentive and appreciative savouring of food in small portions

deipnophobia * extreme discomfort at and aversion for dinner parties

delibation * a slight or sneaky foretaste

desucration * the act of reducing or restraining one's sugar intake

dinner-doctrine * witty table-talk

deipnosophism

mastery of the art of dining and dinner party small talk

dinnering * the formal eating of a main, multiple-course meal

discumb * to recline at the table while dining

discussion * colloquially, the action of taking or tasting food

disjune * to break one's fast in the morning

dispatch * to consume food appreciatively

dysgeusia * degradation or disturbance of the sense of taste

eatymology * humorously, the study of eating and the language of food

edibilatory * pertaining to eating

electrogustometry * a method of determining the acuity of a person's sense of taste by passing a current through the surface of the tongue

engulfment * the act of eating or swallowing food whole

epicureanism * the cultivation of a refined taste for the choicest of foods

epicureanize * to impart keen gastronomic judgement in matters of taste

epicurious * interested in dainty fare and the education of the palate

epicurity * devotion to sensuous or sumptuous feasting

epulonic * indulging in the finest of fare

esure * the process of eating

esuriency * a gastronome's fondness for eating

eusitia * having a healthy appetite and appreciation for food

extreme cuisine * adventurous eating—from deep-fried spiders to flame-roasted dog

fare-well * a distinct aftertaste to something one has earlier dispatched

feastful * occupied in the joys of luxurious feeding

foodism * an exaggerated interest in food, especially for the minutiae of preparing, presenting, and partaking of meals

foodoir * a memoir of a life in food, recording prized recipes and memorable dishes

foodscape * a food scene or culinary culture

foodways * the how and why of what we eat; our local eating habits and traditions

foretaste * to savour slightly prior to eating, or to taste before another does

friandise * a weakness for delicacies and other such light bites and delights

gastro-anomie * chronic food-fatigue anent the pretensions of hipster gourmandism

gastrogasm * an intense taste explosion on the tongue

gastrogrotesquerie * eating disgusting food by way of competition or challenge

gastrolatry * the worship of food and indulgence of the whims of the stomach

gastrology * a critically informed appreciation of good cooking

gastronomical * pertaining to matters of the plate and the palate

gastronomy * the study, science, and practice of fine dining

gastrophilism * a passion for delicate eating; epicureanism

gastrophilite * devoted to gastronomy; skilled in the art of superior eating

gastrosophy * wisdom and sensibility in matters of the table and the palate

gelatoology * a nonce word for the nonsense study of the taste and texture of ice cream

geumatophobia * a fear of trying unfamiliar foods and tasting unfamiliar flavours

gewistfullian * to feast and eat one's fill in days of yore

glycobrosis * having a soft spot for sweetmeats and sweet-tasting foods

glycogeusia * a spontaneous, subjective taste of sweetness in the mouth

glycolimia * a craving for sweets or other sugar-rich foods

glycophily * having a terrible liking for cakes, candies, and confectionery

glycophobia * a marked distaste for overly sweet or sugary substances

gourmanderie * a synonym for gastronomy; the love of refined eating

gourmandism * the passions, principles, and practices of the food critic

gourmetise * the expertise of the epicure

gourmetism * yet another synonym for gastronomy; daintiness at the dinner table

goût * the higher faculty of good taste

grubstake * sufficient funds to treat oneself to a meal

gurgulio * an archaic term for the appetite and desire for food

gustation * the action or faculty of tasting

gustatism * a taste hallucination or any synaesthetic experience of flavour

gustatorial * pertaining to the act of tasting and the sensation of taste

gustatorius * post-positively pertaining to taste; as calyculus gustatorius, or taste bud

gustometry * measurement of the taste threshold and sensory response to flavour

hedonic hyperphagia * eating for pure pleasure, rather than the relief of hunger

hemiageusia * loss of taste on one side of the tongue only

heterogeusis * distortion or degeneration of the taste sensorium in its entirety

hippophagism * a passed epicurean craze for horse flesh as an exotic foodstuff

hunchery-munchery * eating at any time of the day instead of taking set meals

hypergeusaesthesia * being left with a bad taste in the mouth due to increased sensitivity to gustatory stimuli

hypogeusia * diminished acuteness in the sense of taste

interdine * to come together over a meal, putting rank or other rivalry aside

jenticulate * to take breakfast

junketaceous * given to ostentatious feasting and conspicuous consumption

kamayan * a Philippine tradition of eating with one's hands only

keep commons * to eat communal meals or share refectory rations

knife-gaty * generous in providing free food and hospitality

lautitious * sumptuous and refined, especially in the consumption of meat

lean cuisine syndrome * the tendency to inform such as doctors or researchers that one enjoys a healthier and less indulgent diet than is strictly true

lexical-gustatory synaesthesia * a rare condition whereby the written or spoken word paradoxically activates the sense of taste

libant * tasting

lickeroushead * a lusty fondness for good fare

licky-licky * in Jamaican patois, being conceited and choosy about the food one eats

liquorish * fussy or fastidious about food

Lucullan * lavish or luxurious with food; sumptuous of banquet

malacia * a weakness or "softness" for sensuous, especially highly spiced, food

mangery * gourmandizing; feasting or banqueting

meatship * good fellowship at the table

meltith-hale * having a wholesome appetite for food

meatmare

a vegetarian or vegan's horror of eating meat

metegift * liberal or lavish with food

missavour * to have a defective sense of taste

monophagize * to dine alone

motching * the unhurried yet surreptitious delectation of dainty foods

munchion * to munch quite audibly, in eager enjoyment of one's meal

mycetophagy * taking an epicurean delight in eating fungi and mushrooms, especially those foraged in the wild

mycophilia * a connoisseur's enthusiasm for edible mushrooms

neurogastronomy * the study of how the brain processes taste and perceives flavour

nibbling * eating with a dainty appetite

nutrication * the action of feeding or eating

nyotaimori * the erotic eating of sushi or sashimi from the body of a naked female

omositiaphobia * a loathing for raw meat fare, such as steak tartare

oneration * the work of eating and dispatching food to the stomach

onionate * to overcome with post-dining belches and breath

opsomania * a pathological pickiness for certain delicacies

opsophagize * to enjoy delicacies, especially fish-based sauces or relishes

orexis * the appetite for food

organolepsis * the full sensory appreciation and experience of food

ornithivorous * wont to consume small game birds as a dainty delight

orthonasal * pertaining to the perception of flavour and aroma within the olfactory epithelium of the nasal cavity, the molecules being drawn through the nose

ostraconophobia * disgust for the taste or texture of shellfish and oysters

ostreophagous * taking an epicurean pleasure in oyster-eating

oxygeusy * heightened sharpness or acuteness in the sense of taste

oysterous * gastronomically gratified and satisfied with oysters

pabulation * the action of taking in sustenance

palate * sophistication or discrimination in taste; the faculty of taste itself

palate-pleasure * the joy of savouring and consuming food

parageusia * a perverted or illusory perception of taste

parosmia * a disorder of the sense of smell and olfactory perception of flavour

partake * to consume food or drink; also, to share a meal

phomance * jocularly, having a deep love for Vietnamese cuisine

picnickery * the practice of eating packaged meals at leisure in the open air

picrogeusia * extreme bitterness in the sense of taste

plutophagy * humorously, consuming only the richest—as in most exclusive and expensive—food

pre-assume * to eat just prior to or further in advance of one's meal

pregust * to taste beforehand, or to sample a dish to confirm its flavour and fitness

prelibate * to savour the first fruits of the harvest

pseudogeusaesthesia * a faux sense of taste triggered by, for example, the aroma of food

pseudogeusia * the subjective sensation of taste, not produced by gustatory stimulus

psychogeusic * pertaining to the facultative perception and interpretation of taste

ranivorousness * having an epicurean passion for bullfrog legs

recreation * restoration of full vigour and faculties through eating

recubation * a posture of relaxed reclining while enjoying one's meal

refect * to refresh—oneself or another—with food and drink; to entertain at table

relish * to thoroughly enjoy a tasty morsel or meal

repetition * the reflux of a taste sensation owing to eructation or indigestion

restaurate * to dine in fine company

restaurometry * a spoof word for the calculation of restaurant service quality

retronasal * pertaining to the perception of flavour and aroma within the olfactory epithelium of the nasal cavity, the molecules being drawn through the mouth

salivate * to literally or figuratively produce spittle in anticipation of tasty food

saporosity * the physical or facultative property by which taste is experienced

savour * to concentrate on fully appreciating each subtle flavour of one's food

scaffing * scrounging for food without showing a shred of self-respect

scranning * the act of begging for food scraps or leftovers

sinne-eating * ceremonial feeding beside the body of one recently deceased

sitophilia * sex play centred on the use or consumption of food

slabbering * swallowing one's meal in rude haste and without refinement

sloffing * coarseness in eating or carelessness in table manners

slottering * crudely emitting animalistic sounds while feeding

smackering * smacking the lips in pleasure while eating, or in anticipation thereof

smatching * the sense of taste

smouster * to consume food in a clandestine manner

snackification * the trend in eating culture toward light bites and eating on the go

snackwave

a movement in dining-out favouring a high-calorie, fast-food aesthetic

sploshing * the act of throwing a food-fight cum sex-party

spoonage * the practice of supping with a spoon

spoon-hale * able to enjoy one's food; consequently, in rude health

squakett * the disagreeable snorting or guttural gobbling of a slovenly feeder

sumptuary laws * regulations imposing restrictions on consumption, most notably in restraint of extravagant, hedonistic expenditure on food and drink

suppering * entertaining guests at supper

swallow * palate or "tooth," discernment in matters of taste

sweet-toothed * having a weakness for dainties or delicacies

swope * to take liquid food with the aid of a spoon; to sup at mealtimes

symbelwynn * ye Olde English joy of feasting

syssitia ＊ in ancient Crete and Sparta, the custom whereby men and youths partook of the day's main meal in their own exclusive company

tallage ＊ the faculty of taste; palate

taste-blindness ＊ the congenital inability to discern certain flavours from others

teeth-watering ＊ the reminiscence of a particularly tasty meal

thig ＊ to partake of a meal on charity

tiffing ＊ the practice of snacking between meals

tooth-music ＊ the sound of someone chomping contentedly on their chow

toothsome ＊ possessing the proverbial sweet tooth

trenchering ＊ the satisfaction of feasting lustily at the table

trencher-philosophy ＊ learned dinner conversation

trencher-poetry ＊ verses for courses; in common idiom, singing for your supper

tyrophobic ＊ being averse or allergic to cheese

turophily

connoisseurship in matters of cheese-eating

vegetare ＊ to enjoy a diet free from flesh

victitation ＊ the act of taking victuals or food

wistfullness ＊ Anglo-Saxon epicureanism

womb-joy ＊ the gratification of a good appetite

yeastiality ＊ erotic escapades involving bread, dough, or pastry products

CHAPTER 21

Diners: A Glossary of Gourmets and Gourmands

> *"A gourmet who thinks of calories is like a tart who looks at her watch."*
> — **James Beard**

abstinent * a person in the process of fasting

acreophagist * one who consumes a meatless diet; more loosely, a vegetarian

aerophagist * one neurotically compelled to swallow air

ageusic * a person with no sense of taste—clinically and literally speaking

alliaphage * a great garlic-eater

allotriophagist * one with a depraved appetite for the innutritious or indigestible

Amphitryon * a generous dinner host and entertainer at table

amphivore * an animal, including humankind, that partakes of both fauna and flora

anorectic * one suffering from suppressed appetite

anosmic * a person without sense of smell, limiting their ability to appreciate flavour

anthropophaginian * as anthropophagus, anthropophagite, and anthropophagizer—cannibals all

anthropovore * a man-eater, either wicked person or wild predator

Apicius * an eponymous, and possibly legendary, epicure

archimarmitonerastique * a burlesque term for one overly keen on the contents of the cookpot and the comforts of an easy life

architricline * a master of ceremonies at a Roman feast

aristologist * one well versed in the art of fine dining

aristophagist * a blue-blooded vegetarian, for whom the vulgar consumption of slaughter meat is obnoxious to their higher breeding and sensibility

artolater * a bread worshipper; originally a derogatory term for Roman Catholics

artotyrite * a member of a Christian sect that once celebrated the Eucharist with bread and cheese

azymite * an old Orthodox pejorative for any rival Christian who consumed unleavened bread at the Eucharist

banquetant * a feast giver

banquet-beagle * an opportunist glutton, one who can proverbially sniff out a feast

banqueteer * a feast guest

Barathrum * one who eats as though they were a bottomless pit of hunger

Barmecide * one who offers imaginary food, or an illusory feast of abundance

batteler * a college student who obtains victuals on account

battener * a glutton; one who would much rather fasten on a plate of food than fast

beanfeaster * an employee enjoying a slap-up meal at their employer's expense

beefeater * a person of lower social rank said to look rather too well-fed for their station

belly-critic * an epicurean or expert in matters gastronomical

belly-god * one devoted to eating and the enjoyments of the table

belly-kite * one who thrives on a largely unwholesome diet

bestavore * a food snob who deigns to eat only the highest-quality nosh available

bon vivant * one who enjoys the culinary life to the fullest

breadhead * a person knowledgeable and enthusiastic about artisanal bread

breakfaster * one who partakes of a hearty breakfast meal

breatharian * a cultist who claims to obtain all their nutritional requirements from fresh air alone

brephophagist * one who eats babies, for breakfast or otherwise

brocavore * a male hipster foodie

bulimarexic * a person suffering from binge-purge syndrome

bun-duster * an effete male who attends social occasions to scoff tea and dainties with the ladies

buzgut * a grubber of fearsome reputation

cake-fumbler * a parasite, or freeloader at the table

calorie-counter * someone closely attentive to the calorific value of what they eat

canivore * one who enjoys the delights of dog flesh

cannibal * a human who partakes of other human flesh

Carib * archaic for cannibal, as indigenous Caribbeans were once so regarded

carnivore * a dedicated devourer of red meat

cepivore * someone with a great fondness for onions

cerealist * one who advocates or follows a cereal diet; a serial cereal-eater

champer * one given to thoroughly chewing and chomping on their food

cheese-stickler * a judge at a regional English cheese show

chocoholic * one who goes gaga for their cocoa

chowhound * one with a reputation for eating incessantly and immoderately

climatarian * one who only eats food whose production is ascertained not to be natural resource intensive

collationer * one who enjoys light meals

commensal * a dining companion or messmate

companion * literally, one you break and share bread with

concarnivore * one who treats and eats meat as the main component of every meal

connoisseur * a fine judge of flavoursome food and high-quality cooking

convictor * a table companion; one who shares victuals

convivator * a boon companion in feasting or fine dining

cookivore * man as evolved to crave the compounds found in cooked food

coprophagist * a dung-eater, normally indicative of mental disturbance or moral depravity

corn-vorant * an insatiably greedy person, or human cormorant

cosherer * one who sponges dinner with an acknowledged degree of guile

creophagist * a meat-eater or carnivore

cribber * a person with modest appetite

croughton-belly * a person with a reputation for consuming fruit in great abundance

croupier * an assistant to a master banqueter, sitting at the lower end of the table

crumb-catcher * in US ghetto vernacular, a baby just beginning to take solids

crunchy granola * sarcastically, a vegetarian

dando * a greedy sharper who scarpers without paying for their meal

degustator * an expert in matters of culinary taste

deipnodiplomat * one skilled in furthering affairs of state over dinner

deipnosophist * a master of the art of dining, noted for the eloquence of their table-talk

demitarian * one determined to cut their meat consumption by half

demivegetarian * one who restricts their intake of animal flesh to fish and poultry

depastor * simply, one who feeds upon something—don't we all?

devouress * a distaff scoffer

dietarian * one who closely follows the prescriptions of a particular diet

dieter * a person seeking to control their weight by reducing their calorie intake

dietitian * one who sets the dietary prescriptions for the dietarian above

digester * a person blessed with sound digestive capacity

dindoniphile * a turkey-lover—a coinage of the famed epicure Brillat-Savarin

diner-out * one who is accustomed to taking their meals outside of the home

dinner-guest * one invited to partake of a formal meal, be it private or public

discumbent * a guest to meal, notably one who reclines in the act of dining

draffsack * a large paunch; hence, by figurative extension, a lazy glutton

dyspeptic * a person suffering from indigestion

eatnell * a glutton or great scoffer

eatress * a woman who eats well

eggetarian * an ovovegetarian, happy to consume eggs but no other dairy produce

endocannibal * a tribe member who ritually consumes deceased kin

engorger * a glutton, given to stuffing their guts with food

epicure * a hedonist or sophisticate in matters of food and feeding

epulator * a feaster

epulone * a banquet guest

equivore * one fond of horse flesh

eructator * one who belches at meals

Eskimo * a term originally, and erroneously, taken to mean "eater of raw meat"

essayer * one who tests the quality or safety of food through foretasting

esurient * a greedy fellow

esurion * a hungry fellow

exocannibal * one who devours tribal enemies or members of some other social out-group

fish'n'chipocrite

a self-styled vegetarian who is nonetheless happy to eat fish

famisher * one who would deprive others of food or starve them outright

faster * one who voluntarily abstains from food for a set period of time

feast-master * a president at a formal banquet or other festive communal meal

feastress * a female feaster

feeder * one who gorges at another's expense

feinschmecker * a gourmet—literally a "fine-taster"

fermentarian * a celebrant who partakes of leavened bread at the ceremony of the Eucharist

fill-paunch * an inveterate glutton

flap-sauce * a glutton for tasty grub

flesh-fly * one especially greedy for meat

Fletcherite * historically, one who followed a regime of thirty-two bites per mouthful of food; so-called after dietary theorist Horace Fletcher, a.k.a. "The Great Masticator"

flexitarian * a vegetarian happy to consume meat or fish from time to time

flexivore * a committed meat-eater not averse to the occasional vegetarian meal

foodaholic * a person obsessed with quality cooking and cuisine

food-faddist * a scran crank, always following the latest culinary trend or fringe diet

foodiot * one with mere pretensions to a higher sensibility in matters of the palate

foodist * someone knowledgeable about or keenly interested in healthy eating

forager * one who obtains their nutritional needs from the local flora and fauna

freegan * an anti-consumerist consumer of discarded food; an urban forager

fresser * a Yankee glutton, in the Yiddish gloss

friand * an epicure, or one with a highly refined palate

fructivore * a fruit fanatic

frugivore * one who subsists on a diet heavily if not exclusively based on fruit

fruitarian * one who eats fruit primarily, supplemented by berries, nuts, and seeds

full-belly * a bust-a-gut glutton

fungivore * a person who consumes copious quantities of mushrooms

galactophagist * a "milk-eater," one for whom dairy is a dietary staple

galactopoton * a milk-drinker

gannet * a gluttonous sailor

Gargantua * one with a legendary appetite and gut to match

gaster * one hungry to experiment with exotic foods and experience esoteric tastes

Gasterea * putative goddess of gastronomy, gustation, and all things good cooking

gastrocartephilist * a keen collector of menu cards

gastrolater * a belly-worshipper, devoted to gratifying their stomach's every fancy

gastrologer * a learned lover of good food

gastronaut * an adventurous eater

gastronome * a food critic

gastronomer * a diligent student of gourmet cuisine

gastronomist * an epicure or otherwise keen judge of good cooking

gastrophile * one who appreciates a refined dining experience

gastrosexual * a modern male who uses his culinary skills to impress potential romantic partners

gastrosopher * a person well versed in the art of culinary appreciation

geophagist * one who consumes earth or clay as a dietary staple

gillmaw * an obsolete Scots expression denoting a somewhat ill-mannered glutton

gemetta

an Old English table-guest

glosser * a glutton; an arch-swallower

gluten-freegan * a person following a gluten-exclusive regime of vegan fare

gluttoner * one given to eating to ravenous excess

gob-slotch * a person greedy for food, forever stuffing their mouth

golopher * one with an insatiable appetite

gorbelly * a corpulent glutton

gorger * one who devours their food without manners or moderation

gormandizeress * a woman notorious for her gluttonry

gourmand * one over-fond of eating, especially dainties and delicacies

gourmet * one who has earned a reputation as a critic or connoisseur of good food

Grandgousier * one who will greedily swallow anything presented on a plate

Graymite * a vegetarian, specifically one following the reformed dietary regimen advocated by the Reverend Sylvester Graham in the mid-nineteenth century

grazer * one who would rather snack their way through the day than sit down to square meals at set times

greedyguts * your common-or-garden glutton

groak * a hungry child who stares at an adult eating in the hope they too will be fed

grubber * a great feeder

grueller * one who subsists on slops or other unsubstantial or substandard fare

gulchin * a youthful glutton

gulist * one who gluttonously gratifies his appetite

gullet-fancier * an obsolete term for a gourmet; or as we might say today, a foodie

gulper * one who bolts their food greedily and without grace

gundygut * a voracious eater with vulgar table manners

gurgitator * a competitor in eating contests

guster * a professional food taster

gut-hallion * one noted for having a ravenous appetite

gut-monger * one whose stomach comes first and foremost

guzzler * a guttler, guzzle-guts, or insatiable glutton

haematophage * a bloodsucker or vampire

halalcor * in India and Iran, a person who may lawfully consume any and all foods

half-mealer * someone whose stomach regularly goes underfilled

helluo * a glutton or gormandizer of some notoriety

herbivore * jocularly, a vegetarian

heterotroph * an animal or species, such as homo sapiens, which depends on other organisms for food, fulfilling its nutritional requirements by consuming such matter

hippomolgoi * drinkers of mare's milk, as the fearsome Scythian steppe horsemen of old were described in classical texts

hippophagist * a connoisseur of horse meat

hungarian * humorously, a hungry person or a hearty eater

hunger-striker * one who refuses food by way of protest against political or prison authority

hunter-gatherer * a member of a primitive social community who neither grows crops nor rears livestock but rather subsists by hunting, fishing, or foraging

ichthyophagan * a fanciful term for a plain old fish-eater

ichthyophilist * a lover of fish dishes

insectarian * a human bug-eater

Jack-a-Lent * one who fasts from religious observation

jejunator * one who fasts for dietary or health purposes

juicearian * a strict vegan who consumes only fruit or vegetable juices

junketeer * a jolly feaster

kedge-belly * an old dialectal term for a glutton, especially a devourer of meat

killcrop * an insatiable brat who sucks its mother dry

kitchen-artist * an epicure or gastronome

kitchen-haunter * a thoroughly incorrigible glutton

laclabphilist * a hobbyist who collects cheese labels

lactarian * a vegetarian whose diet includes all dairy produce save eggs

lactipotor * one who consumes milk

lactivist * a champion of the cause that "breast is best" for feeding infants

lactovarian * a vegetarian whose diet includes all dairy produce including eggs

Lestrigonian * a rarely encountered literary term for a cannibal

lickdish * one with both a nose for food and an eye for a free meal

linnard * in the old Somerset vernacular, the person last to finish their meal

lithophagus * a person under psychotic compulsion to swallow stones

locavore * someone who as a matter of principle only eats locally sourced food

lotophage * a "lotus-eater" of ancient myth, whose primary food was a narcotic fruit

lurcher * a glutton who moves quickly to get first in line for any share of food going

macerator * one who mortifies the flesh and becomes emaciated through fasting

macrogaster * a swollen-bellied super-swallower

man-eater * either human or animal — cannibal or carnivoran

marasmic * an infant wasting away from chronic caloric deficit

masticator * one who chews their food thoroughly before swallowing

meater * a red meat aficionado

meat-fellow * a dinner companion

meat-nithing * a mean and miserly person with regard to sharing or serving food

messmate * a canteen comrade

misdieter * a person who eats unhealthily or follows adverse dietary advice

monophagian * one who dines alone or eats only one kind of food

moucher * a hearty feeder

mutton-monger * a person with a voracious appetite for lamb or goat meat

mycophagist * an epicure who highly prizes mushrooms foraged in the wild

mycophile * a person fond of eating mushrooms

mycophobe * a person fearful of eating mushrooms

Nebuchadnezzar * Antipodean slang for a vegetarian, from the salad of the same name

necrophage * a starving person driven to cannibalize corpses out of desperation

nosher * a nibbler or snacker; alternatively, one who samples food before purchasing

nutarian * a vegetarian whose diet centres on or is perhaps confined to nut products

nut-fooder * one who is simply nuts about nuts; more derogatively, a vegetarian

nutritarian * a health-conscious consumer who selects food on the basis of its beneficial micronutrient content

nutritionist * a medical specialist in healthy eating

offalist * a person awfully fond of offal or "variety meats"

oligophage * a fusspot eating only a narrow selection of foodstuffs

omnivore * a person who eats all manner of foodstuffs, animal and plant based alike

omophagist * a devourer of raw flesh

onychophagist * a compulsive nail-biter

ophiophagus * one who feeds on snake meat

opportunivore * someone who eats whatever they can find, such as discarded food

opsomaniac * one with morbid cravings for rich and savoury delicacies

opsophagist * one who pampers their appetite with refined fishy delights

orthorexic * a health freak suffering from the effects of a foolish but modish diet

ostreophagist * one with a pronounced predilection for oysters

overeater * one who compulsively eats to excess

ovolactovegetarian * one whose diet excludes meat and fish but embraces dairy products, including eggs

ovovegetarian * a vegetarian whose diet accommodates no dairy produce save eggs

paedophage * a mythic devourer of children

palate-people * "foodies," in seventeenth century parlance

palatician * an epicure; one who cultivates a taste for the choicest food and drink

pamphagite * an unfussy eater with an eclectic palate

panticivore * a sausage-eater; a nonce coinage of the novelist Anthony Burgess

pantophagist * a human omnivore; the proverbial "eat-all"

pecker * one who merely nibbles at their food

pellagrin * a malnourished individual suffering from vitamin B3 deficiency

peptician * one blessed with good digestion

Phaeacian * an archaic epithet for a glutton

phagologist * a dietician

philogastrist * a downright greedy bugger

philopyg * one who is especially fond of ham

Pickwickian * an obese bulimic with attendant cardiorespiratory pathology

pesco-vegetarian

one who desists from red meat and poultry, but does eat fish

picnickian * a participant at an al fresco nosh-up

pinch-belly * a selfish and miserly so-and-so who lets others go hungry

pinch-crust * one who is stingy or stinting in their provision of food

pingler * one who generally has little appetite for food

piscatarian * a fish-eater whose diet is otherwise largely vegetarian

pocillovist * a collector of eggcups

pollo-pescatarian * a semi-vegetarian happy to consume both poultry and seafood

pollo-vegetarian * a vegetarian prepared to supplement their diet with white meat

poltophagist * one who thoroughly chews their food prior to its digestion

polyphagian * a glutton, notably one with bulimic propensities

polyphagist * one whose palate extends appreciatively to a wide variety of fare

porknell * a fat, greedy person who has somewhat come to resemble a stuffed pig

pregustator * a foretaster or forestaller, who approves a meal before it is served

progger * one who forages the American shore for clams, crabs, and suchlike

prognostic * an inventive or epicurean eater

prozymite * a theological epithet depreciatively describing a member of the Greek Orthodox Church who consumes leavened bread at the Eucharist

psomophagist * one who uncouthly bolts their food

pudding-snammer * a cookshop thief, in old street slang

Pythagorizer * a vegetarian who superstitiously shuns the consumption of beans

ravener * a hungry and voracious eater

raw-foodist * a person who avoids food that is heated or processed in any way

repaster * one who partakes of a meal

ruminator * someone who chews their food continually

salad-dodger * derogatory slang for a person held to eat an unhealthy diet

salivator * one who requires sialagogues to assist with eating and swallowing

sarcophagist * any beast, including the human animal, that consumes flesh

savourer * one who takes time and care to taste and enjoy their food

scambler * a Scotsman in the habit of dropping by at mealtime to get free scoff

scatophagian * one who literally eats shit

scoffer * a person who eats immoderately and in haste

semi-vegetarian * a half-hearted herbivore who occasionally accommodates fish or poultry within their diet but draws the line at red meat

shagpoke-gut * a tremendous eater; after the heron, a bird renowned for its appetite

skipitarian * one who raids bins and dumpster trucks for thrown-away food

slimmer * one endeavouring to restrict their food intake in order to lose weight

slotterhodge * a foul and messy eater

slush-bucket * an ill-mannered eater

smellfeast * a freeloader who scents good cooking and comes uninvited to the table

snapsauce * a food thief; alternatively, one who licks their fingers while eating

sneakbill * a gaunt-looking starveling

sooravoolic * another Scots chancer who cadges for food and drink

sopper * one who sups or partakes of supper

sorner * one who sponges for free board and breakfast

soup-kitchener * one who fills their empty belly with charity fare

sproutarian * an uber-vegan who eats only sprouted seeds, fruit, and raw vegetables

starveling * one who is habitually hungry or undernourished

starver * one who visits famine upon others

stiffgut * a person with a reputation for overeating

stodger * a gormandizer; one who regularly fills their face

stuffinger * yet another who eats to excess

suckling * an unweaned infant at the breast

sucrologist * a collector and classifier of sugar packets

supertaster * a person sensitive to even the most subtle variations in food flavour

supper-lover * one who is fond of their food

surfeiter * one who commonly overindulges at the table

swallower * a great eater

sweet-lips * an epicurean or one given to sensuous feasting

sweet-tooth * a person with a weakness for dainties or other sweet delicacies

table-parasite * one who ordinarily eats at another's table—that is, at their expense

tapeador * an intrepid partaker of tapas, tasty Spanish bar snacks

taste-tester * a person employed to sample new food products for flavoursomeness

tenterbelly * a glutton's glutton

theophagite * a god-devourer, in sacramental or otherwise symbolic form

toxiphagus * one who consumes all manner of potions and poisons

trencher-buffoon * one replete with witty repartee at the dinner table

trencher-hero * a hearty feaster

trenchermate * a boon table companion

tricliniarch * one who presides at high table or over a feast

tug-mutton * an old Eton scholar with a reputation for enjoying his food

turophile * a cheese-lover

tyrosemiophile * an avid collector of cheese box labels, especially Camembert

univore * jocularly, a diner who puts away the items on their plate one foodstuff at a time; a serial eater of sorts

vegan * a dietary zealot; consumes no foodstuff of animal origin whatsoever

vindaloonatic

someone crazy for superhot-hot-hot, highly spiced curries

vegangelical * humorously, a crusading, proselytizing vegan

vegetarian * one who consumes animal products such as eggs and milk, but not the flesh of the animal producers themselves

vegivore * someone who craves or has a special fondness for vegetables

wannarexic * a fantasist who falsely claims to suffer from an eating disorder

weight-watcher * one observing a reformed diet with the objective of becoming slim

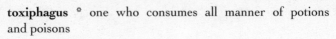
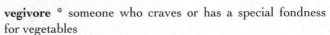

Postscript

And so we conclude our feast of words: time to let our learning digest.

It is the compiler of this dictionary's sincere hope that all readers have been well served with sufficient food for thought throughout the preceding pages of our twenty-one-course lexical blowout. Even those with the most voracious of verbal appetites and the most expensively and extensively educated of palates will surely have discovered many a tasty new word or nugget of nutritional wisdom to expand their knowledge and appreciation of fine food, good cooking, and healthy eating.

Whether the reader chiefly finds profit in using this volume for the primary purposes of reference or research, or is content casually to dip into its pages for the occasional light bite of linguistic delight, he or she will soon have amassed—and mastered—the argot of the aristologist, the cant of the culinarian, and the patois of the palatician.

Let *Eat Your Words* remain your definitive guide to discernment at the dinner table.

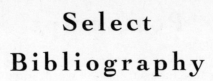

Select
Bibliography

Albala, Ken (ed). *Food Cultures of the World Encyclopedia*. (Westport, CT: Greenwood Press, 2011)

Allen, Gary & Albala, Ken. *The Business of Food: Encyclopedia of the Food & Drink Industries*. (Westport, CT: Greenwood Press, 2007)

Ayto, John. *The Diner's Dictionary*. (Oxford: OUP, 2012)

Davidson, Alan. *The Oxford Companion to Food*. (Oxford: OUP, 1999)

Dictionary of Food Science & Nutrition. (London: A & C Black, 2006)

Dictionary of the Scots Language. www.dsl.ac.uk

English Dialect Dictionary. eddonline-proj.uibk.ac.at/edd/index.jsp

English Vocabulary Word Directory. www.wordinfo.info/words/index/info/

Farmer, John S & Henley, WE. *A Dictionary of Slang & Colloquial English*. (London: George Routledge & Sons, 1921)

Friedland, Josh. *Eatymology: The Dictionary of Modern Gastronomy*. (Naperville, IL: Sourcebooks, 2015)

Goldstein, Darra (ed). *The Oxford Companion to Sugar & Sweets*. (Oxford: OUP, 2015)

Green, Jonathon. *The Cassell Dictionary of Slang*. (London: Cassell, 1998)

Grimes, William. *Eating Your Words*. (NY: OUP Inc, 2004)

Historical Thesaurus of English. historicalthesaurus.arts.gla.ac.uk

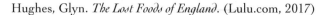

Hughes, Glyn. *The Lost Foods of England*. (Lulu.com, 2017)

Kipfer, Barbara Ann. *The Culinarian: A Kitchen Desk Reference.* (Hoboken, NJ: John Wiley & Sons, 2011)

Morton, Mark. *Cupboard Love: A Dictionary of Culinary Curiosities*. (Insomniac Press, 2004)

Oxford English Dictionary. www.oed.com

Shipley, Joseph T. *Dictionary of Early English*. (Paterson, NJ: Littlefield, Adams & Co, 1963)

Sinclair, Charles. *Dictionary of Food: International Food & Cooking Terms from A to Z*. (London: A & C Black, 2010)

Smith, Andrew F. (ed). *The Oxford Companion to American Food & Drink*. (NY: OUP Inc, 2007)

Thesaurus of Old English. libra.englang.arts.gla.ac.uk/ oethesaurus

Wikipedia. en.wikipedia.org/wiki/Portal:Food

About the Author

Paul Convery is a Glasgow-based wordsmith with over twenty years' experience as a proofreader, copy-editor, and magazine production manager. His earlier academic grounding includes postgraduate language studies and doctoral research in modern European history.

He hopes *Eat Your Words: The Definitive Dictionary for the Discerning Diner*—the fruit of his latest literary and lexicographical labours—will reach a hungry and appreciative reading public.

A lifelong logophile, Paul is also the author of *Drinktionary: The Definitive Dictionary for the Discerning Drinker* (Book Guild, 2017) and *Inkhorn's Erotonomicon: An Advanced Sexual Vocabulary for Verbivores and Vulgarians* (Matador, 2012).

When not working, word-hunting, or writing, Paul can often be found enjoying a quiet curry night out with family or friends. No great culinarian himself, alas, he is nevertheless a passable sous-chef in his domestic goddess's kitchen and a diligent dish-washer-upper.

Mango Publishing, established in 2014, publishes an eclectic list of books by diverse authors—both new and established voices—on topics ranging from business, personal growth, women's empowerment, LGBTQ studies, health, and spirituality to history, popular culture, time management, decluttering, lifestyle, mental wellness, aging, and sustainable living. We were recently named 2019's #1 fastest growing independent publisher by *Publishers Weekly*. Our success is driven by our main goal, which is to publish high quality books that will entertain readers as well as make a positive difference in their lives.

Our readers are our most important resource; we value your input, suggestions, and ideas. We'd love to hear from you—after all, we are publishing books for you.

Please stay in touch with us and follow us at:

Facebook: Mango Publishing

Twitter: @MangoPublishing

Instagram: @MangoPublishing

LinkedIn: Mango Publishing

Pinterest: Mango Publishing

Sign up for our newsletter at www.mango.bz and receive a free book.

Join us on Mango's journey to reinvent publishing, one book at a time.